Jenkins,
The forties

4-78

The FORTIES

★ ALAN JENKINS ★

UNIVERSE BOOKS

Published in the United States of America in 1977
by Universe Books,
381 Park Avenue South, New York, N.Y. 10016

Library of Congress Catalog Card Number: 77-24785
ISBN 0-87663-292-4

This book was designed
and produced by George Rainbird Limited,
36 Park Street, London W1Y 4DE

Picture Researcher: Mary Anne Sanders
Designer: Trevor Vincent
Indexer: Ellen Crampton

The text was set and printed and the book
bound by Jarrold and Sons Limited,
Norwich, Norfolk, England
The color plates and jacket were originated
and printed by Westerham Press Limited,
Westerham, Kent, England

Printed in Great Britain

A village Post Office during rationing (endpaper)

'Shelter Scene. Bunks and Sleepers', 1941, by Henry Moore   p. 1

Detail of 'Queer Vegetation', 1942, by S. Curnow Vosper   p. 2

☆ CONTENTS ☆

List of Color Plates 7

Acknowledgments 8

1. Home Fires Burning 10

2. The Shooting War 26

3. Over Here, Over There 36

4. The King Won't Go 50

5. Soldier From the War Returning 60

6. Blessings of Peace 64

7. Music, Music, Music 72

8. Woman and Beauty 88

9. Hollywood and Pinewood 104

10. World of Sport 120

11. Disunited Nations 131

12. Necessary Journeys 136

13. Loyalties 144

14. Curtain Up and Down 149

15. In the Picture 164

16. Prayers, Boffins and Flying Saucers 178

17. Crime Club 185

18. Prose and Verse 192

19. Read All About It 200

20. Talking to Each Other 206

21. Epilogue 222

Illustration Acknowledgments 225

Index 227

Rainbow Corner, 1944

☆ LIST OF COLOR PLATES ☆

'Shelter Scene: Bunks and Sleepers', 1941, by Henry Moore (reverse of frontispiece)

'Queer Vegetation', 1942, by S. Curnow Vosper (frontispiece)

'A house collapsing on two firemen in Shoe Lane, London EC4',
by Leonard Rosoman   19

'Bringing up a 250-kilo bomb', by Clive Uptton   20

Ralph Richardson as Falstaff in Shakespeare's *Henry IV*,
Old Vic Company at the New Theatre, London, 1945. Costume design by Roger Furse   149

Laurence Olivier as King Lear in Shakespeare's *King Lear*,
New Theatre, October 1946. Costume design by Roger Furse   150

'The Furnaces', from the series of paintings entitled
'Shipbuilding on the Clyde', about 1940, by Stanley Spencer   167

'Somerset Maugham', 1949, by Graham Sutherland   168

Once again, I want to thank a number of people for their help in research and suggestions for this book, particularly John Hadfield of Rainbird and John St John of Heinemann, and my wife for her memories of the Home Front during the War, much of which I spent abroad. (The War, by the way, means World War II unless otherwise stated: I am well aware that to American readers who knew Korea and Vietnam 'the War' can mean either of these two.)

I am grateful to the librarian of Time-Life Inc.'s London office for allowing me to consult their files. I have drawn fairly heavily on my own contributions to various magazines during and after World War II, notably those published by Hulton Press Ltd who were good enough to employ me in these years – *Leader Magazine*, *World Review* and *Picture Post*. For specific information about America, I am indebted to Mrs Bunny North, also to Professors Kenneth N. Stewart and Alfred Grommon, both of Stanford University.

I would also like to thank Mary Anne Sanders once again for her picture research and John Foster White for reading the book in typescript; I am also grateful to Trevor Vincent as designer of the book and to Raymond Mander and Joe Mitchenson for all their help.

Among books consulted were:

Hiroshima (*John Hersey*), THE NEW YORKER, 1946
The Second World War (*Winston S. Churchill*), CASSELL, 1948–54
Hearings Before the Committee on Un-American Activities (*U.S. Government*), 1948
The White House Papers of Harry Hopkins (*ed. Robert E. Sherwood*), EYRE & SPOTTISWOODE, 1949
The Meaning of Treason (*Rebecca West*), MACMILLAN, 1949
The Forties (*Alan Ross*), WEIDENFELD & NICOLSON, 1950
The Flying Saucers Are Real (*Donald Keyhoe*), FAWCETT PUBLICATIONS, 1950
After the Lost Generation (*John W. Aldridge*), VISION PRESS, 1951
Famous Trials, Vols. 4 and 6 (*ed. James H. Hodge*), PENGUIN, 1954–62
Royal Chef (*Gabriel Tschumi and Joan Powe*), WILLIAM KIMBER, 1954
The Unquiet Years (*Herbert Agar*), HART-DAVIS, 1957
King George VI (*Sir J. Wheeler-Bennett*), MACMILLAN, 1958
The Armchair Esquire (*ed. Arnold Gingrich*), HEINEMANN, 1959
Queen Mary (*James Pope-Hennessy*), ALLEN & UNWIN, 1959
The Rise and Fall of the Third Reich (*William Shirer*), SECKER & WARBURG, 1960
Confessions of an Art Addict (*Peggy Guggenheim*), ANDRÉ DEUTSCH, 1960
Age of Austerity (*ed. Michael Sissons and Philip French*), HODDER & STOUGHTON, 1963
The American Establishment (*Richard H. Rovere*), HART DAVIES, 1963
Honest To God (*John A.T. Robinson*), S.C.M. PRESS, 1963
The Evacuees (*ed. B.S. Johnson*), GOLLANCZ, 1968
Musical Comedy (*Raymond Mander and Joe Mitchenson*), PETER DAVIES, 1969
Prime Time: the Life of Edward J. Murrow (*Alexander Kendrick*), DENT, 1970
Sybil Thorndike Casson (*Elizabeth Sprigge*), GOLLANCZ, 1971
How We Lived Then (*Norman Longmate*), HUTCHINSON, 1971
The Penguin Book of Comics (*Alan Aldrige and George Perry*), 1971
London's Burning (*Constantine Fitzgibbon*), MACDONALD, 1971
London War Notes, 1939–45 (*Mollie Panter-Downes*), LONGMAN, 1972
The Biggest Aspidistra in the World (*Peter Black*), B.B.C., 1972
Cole (*ed. Robert Kimball*), MICHAEL JOSEPH, 1972
The World at War (*Mark Arnold-Forster*), COLLINS, 1973
20th Century English Costume (*Mansfield and Cunnington*), FABER, 1973
The ITMA Years (*P.J. Kavanagh*), WOBURN PRESS, 1974
Edward VIII (*Frances Donaldson*), WEIDENFELD & NICOLSON, 1974
Diary of a War Artist (*Edward Ardizzone*), THE BODLEY HEAD, 1974
Queen Mary and Others (*Norman Longmate*), HUTCHINSON, 1971
Austerity Binge (*Bevis Hillier*), STUDIO VISTA, 1975
Freedom at Midnight (*Larry Collins and Dominique Lapierre*), COLLINS, 1975
The Second World War (*A.J.P. Taylor*), PUTNAM, 1975
Keep Smiling Through (The Home Front – 1939–45) (*Susan Briggs*), WEIDENFELD & NICOLSON, 1975
Eclipse (*Alan Moorehead*), HAMISH HAMILTON, 1945
The Linden Tree (*J.B. Priestley*), HEINEMANN, 1948
For Johnny (*John Pudney*), SHEPHEARD-WALWYN, 1957

(*opposite*) **VJ-Day, New York City**

CHAPTER 1

Home Fires Burning

'This . . . is London. This is Trafalgar Square. The noise that you hear at this moment is the sound of the air-raid siren. A searchlight just burst into action, off in the distance, an immense single beam sweeping the sky above me now. People are walking along very quietly. We're just at the entrance of an air-raid shelter here, and I must move the cable over just a bit, so people can walk in.'

It was 11.30 p.m. on Saturday, 24 August 1940. Ed Murrow, European director of Columbia Broadcasting System and its chief reporter, paused to let his microphone record footsteps, the unrehearsed mutter of a man asking another for a light for his cigarette, the approaching din of anti-aircraft gunfire. In New York it was 5.30 p.m., on the Pacific Coast 12.30 p.m.: people had switched on to hear *London After Dark*, a Saturday series which had never so far recorded the sounds of war.

Then a B.B.C. reporter at an anti-aircraft gun post; another C.B.S. man at an air-raid precautions station – you heard a telephone ringing and a switchboard girl saying: 'Stretcher party, one ambulance, one car to 114 High Street, Sector 220. Messenger, don't forget your helmet.' Another C.B.S. man, Eric Sevareid, at the Hammersmith Palais dance hall reported that fifteen thousand people were dancing as usual, soldiers taking off their boots and wearing dancing shoes somehow provided by the management. Vincent Sheean was at a 'hot' microphone in Trafalgar Square; Wilfred Pelletier of Canadian Broadcasting was interviewing a mixture of down-and-outs and raid refugees in the Crypt of St Martin's Church. And Britain's, or rather Yorkshire's J.B. Priestley, in Whitehall near the Cenotaph, ended the programme with the solemn thought that London was 'the centre of the hopes of free men everywhere.'

In earlier broadcasts Murrow had been irritably critical of Britain's apparent apathy about the War.

He wasn't going to die for C.B.S., not he. Now he suddenly seemed to fall in love with the British people. Now he stood suicidally on rooftops during raids, proudly wearing a tin hat, and joined his neighbours in fire watching during the rare periods when he was not broadcasting. He was oddly moved when, in the middle of a raid, a Londoner asked him: 'Do you think we're really brave or just lacking in imagination?' And when London celebrated Christmas in its air-raid shelters, he refused to wish American listeners a merry Christmas. By New Year's Eve he was needling them to come and help: '*You* will have no dawn raids, as we shall probably have if the weather is right. *You* may walk this night in the light. *Your* families are not scattered by the winds of war. *You* may drive your high-powered car as far as time and money will permit . . . .'

We now know that the bombs which formed the background to that broadcast on 24 August were dropped by accident, or rather against Hitler's orders. The real thing – the attempted total destruction of London and other British cities – did not begin until 6 September, when three hundred German bombers, escorted by six hundred fighters, flew over London. This, the British felt, could only be a prelude to invasion, and the code word 'Cromwell' ('invasion imminent') went out all over the country. The ringing of church bells would announce the actual landings from the invasion barges which were known to be concentrated along the coast of France.

In fact Hitler had almost abandoned his invasion plans and was now hoping to end the war by terrorizing the civilian population. The Luftwaffe began with London's Docks and Woolwich Arsenal, which were certainly military targets; but then they concentrated on the East End, Poplar and Stepney and West Ham, where many thousands of workers lived in a honeycomb of slum streets. Fires bigger than any fire

(opposite) Fire Fighting in London during the Blitz

anyone had ever seen broke out – the London Fire Brigade called them '300-pump fires'. And having got them ablaze, the Luftwaffe returned to drop more bombs into them. For many firemen, this was their first fire: they did not sleep for forty hours.

'At Woolwich Arsenal', wrote one of them, 'men fought the flames among boxes of live ammunition and crates of nitro-glycerine.' In the Docks they breathed in burning pepper, burning rubber, burning wheat. Burning barrels of rum exploding. Drums of paint burning with white-hot flames. Tea and sugar ablaze with a weird sickly smell. Schools became rest centres until they too were bombed. Many carefully laid plans were wrecked because two-thirds of all telephones were out of order and messages had to be conveyed by runner. Homeless people streamed out into Epping Forest and slept rough. Leadership appeared from nowhere, meals and medical care were improvised out of almost nothing, and the once-derided Air Raid Precautions Wardens became community heroes.

Another noise was added to the din: the boom of anti-aircraft guns, which seldom hit anything but forced German planes to fly high and were important for civilian morale: you heard a crash, and you said cheerfully: 'That's only our guns.' Like the huge, floppy barrage balloons that floated awkwardly over cities, they were comforting. And on 13 September 1940 Buckingham Palace was bombed: this suddenly healed a slight resentment – 'So *they're* getting it too' – and the swift appearance of George VI and Queen Elizabeth in the ruins of the East End immediately afterwards brought tears to homeless Cockney eyes. A stricken man who had lost his home looked at his monarch in silence and then said: 'You're a good king, sir.'

On 15 September a new kind of courage was recognized when Lieutenant Davies of the Royal Engineers dug out and defused a UXB (unexploded bomb) which had lodged near the southwest tower of St Paul's Cathedral. He was given the George Cross. It was on this day, now celebrated as Battle of Britain Day, that Hitler seems finally to have decided against 'Operation Sealion', the invasion of Britain. The raids went on. People's trousers were blown off them. Buildings were neatly sliced in half so that one saw, as in a doll's house, lavatories perched on the edge, dressing tables with little bottles still on them. (The sort of thing that inspired S.N. Behrman's *New Yorker* story 'The Suspended Drawing Room'.) Unsung men and women did incredibly brave things – in London, in Southampton, in Glasgow, in Hull, in Plymouth, in Swansea. Some enormous bombs came down on parachutes, and were generally called 'land-

St Paul's Cathedral after a bombing raid, photographed from the top of the *Daily Mail* building by Herbert Mason

mines' – there was some trouble about who should deal with the unexploded ones, because the Navy at first were better at it, having learned their job on H.M.S. *Vernon*, the Navy's torpedo and mining school at Portsmouth.

On Sunday, 29 December, with comparatively few bombers but using a great many incendiary bombs, the German Air Force made their most destructive raid on the City – the square mile of business activity containing the greatest concentration of London's old churches, many of them built by Wren. Incendiaries made a noise described by Ed Murrow as *swash-swash-plunk*: other people have said they sounded like hundreds of electric light bulbs shattering. They were more sinister than the moan and crash of high explosives. Twenty-eight incendiaries fell on the greatest of all Wren's churches, St Paul's Cathedral. Some bounced off the double dome. One fell into the Stone Gallery, where it was easily put out. This raid was watched from the roof of the *Daily Mail* building by a photographer named Herbert Mason. 'An artificial wind sprang through the heat caused by the fires, parted the clouds [of smoke], the buildings in the foreground collapsed, and there, revealed in all its majesty, was St Paul's, a hauntingly beautiful picture . . .'

Mason walked up Ludgate Hill, which was 'carpeted in hosepipes; a scampering rat here and there, a reeling bird in the flames. . . . Firemen were fighting a losing battle. Pathetically little water was coming from their hoses. . . .' He went back to the *Daily Mail* roof and took the famous picture that all the world knows.

So ended 1940. The year had begun in what Senator William E. Borah had called the Phoney War. The last words of the great isolationist from Idaho published before he died were: 'We're already *in* the war.' The cover of *Time* magazine carried a portrait of Stalin, 'Man of the Year', the great realist, the only ruler who was likely to profit from the mess the world was in. The Thirties had been the Decade of Distrust: what was the Forties going to be the Decade of? *Time* looked around for signs. It noted that Shirley Temple, aged ten, listened every day to *Gang Busters* and *Lone Ranger* on the radio; that Ruby Keeler and Al Jolson had just divorced; that Heywood Broun's memorial service had revealed that this large newspaperman

had died a Roman Catholic, baptized by Mgr Fulton J. Sheen. Over in Europe the British and French had got themselves involved in a small war. Russia, having signed the Nazi-Soviet pact just before Britain declared war on Germany, had demanded military control of Latvia, Estonia, Lithuania and Finland. Only Finland refused, had been invaded and was hitting back. The League of Nations, having failed to do anything about Germany's invasion of Poland, now indignantly expelled Russia. Britain and France, bored with inaction, reacted emotionally and sent an Anglo-French expeditionary force of a hundred thousand. Even Italy responded to the appeal of 'brave little Finland' and sent warplanes. America, which had always liked Finland because she had been so good at paying her 1914–18 war debt, might have sent troops if the war hadn't been over so soon. Herbert Hoover's 'Help Finland Week' raised $1,600,000.

There was a wave of sympathy for Captain Langsdorff of the *Graf Spee* after the battle of the River Plate, Britain's first big naval victory, as, after scuttling his ship, he took honour's only course and put a bullet through his head. Lacking war news, the papers noted that, at Douglas Fairbanks Sr's funeral, Tom Mix had attended in a black cowboy outfit; that Vincent Astor was wintering at his Bermuda villa 'Ferry Reach' and playing with his private narrow-gauge railway; that there was a new game, said to have been invented by Walter Winchell, called 'Confucius he say' – 'Confucius he say, girl with future should beware man with past' – and many less printable analects. A Youth Congress of 4,500 pro-Russian, anti-Finland pacifists thronged to the White House, demanding a Youth Act, and above all, jobs; they were roughly ticked off by President Roosevelt.

Well-heeled people dashed to Miami Beach, found it cold and wet, wore fur coats over beachwear. U.S. Census officials, asking intimate questions about incomes, mortgages, car ownership, savings, were accused of 'bureaucratic snooping'. As Denmark and Norway were invaded, and a Major Vidkun Quis-

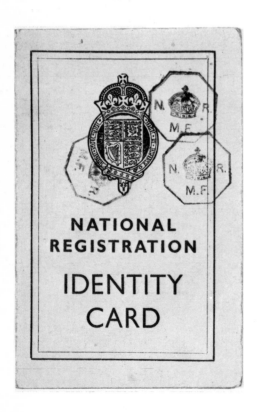

NATIONAL REGISTRATION

IDENTITY CARD

ling gave his name to treachery, *Life* reported from London: 'The British simply aren't interested in war.' What were the British up to? Were they contemplating an alliance with Japan?

It was election year, and Tom Dewey was the Republican favourite to get rid of 'that fellow in the White House'. 'I think it would be marvellous,' gushed a matron in a Helen Hokinson drawing, 'to have a President with a moustache.' As the fall of France drew near, an appeal went out for volunteers to make up the full 250,000 strength of the National Guard. And when France fell *Life* published a long feature about Britain with a double-spread of public school ties, pictures of village pubs and thatched cottages, as if to tell Americans that if they fought, these things would be what they would be defending.

Everywhere in Britain there was silence and, at night, almost total darkness. The blackout had been enforced from sunset on the Friday before Britain was at war; and everyone knew what air-raid sirens sounded like because they had been turned on by accident half an hour after Neville Chamberlain had broadcast his declaration of war on Sunday morning, 3 September 1939. People with cars learned to drive with dim lights at night. Everybody had had a gas-mask since Munich time and knew how to put it on: men with beards, including all Cistercian monks, had to shave them off before they could wear their masks. There were special Mickey Mouse masks for very young children. Masks were comforting, they showed that the Government had actually done something by way of preparation, though there were constant rumours that the Germans had new gases against which the masks would be useless. A special filter was distributed in May 1940, against a gas called arsine. Masks were carried like cameras in neat cases which were used as general handbags for ration books, identity cards and cigarettes.

People learned how to make blackout curtains and cover windows with sticky tape against flying glass. Some went to bed by candlelight, well away from the bedroom windows. Wardens patrolled the streets banging on doors and shouting 'Put that light out!' Pubs had plywood screens and black curtains at their doors so that you could go in and out without showing a light. Everyone carried a tiny torch, dimmed with layers of tissue paper, when they went anywhere at night. Moonlight was feared, though it could make a

(opposite) **A child evacuee**

terrible beauty as it silhouetted ruins – feared because raids came on clear nights. There was some doubt about whether cigarettes could be safely smoked out of doors: a glowing cigarette was a friendly thing in the dark – one wasn't alone. There was, of course, a perpetual shortage of batteries, especially for bicycle lamps.

Traffic lights were reduced to narrow little crosses. Some people got hopelessly lost in the blackout and walked into canals. Around Piccadilly the tarts wore special heels on their shoes that went click-clack like tap-dancing, and they shone their torches on their silken legs.

Preparations for the evacuation from cities of all people, especially mothers and children, who were not actually engaged on war work had been in hand since 1931, when the Committee for Imperial Defence had appointed an Evacuation Sub-Committee. As it was largely voluntary and families had to register in advance, there were widely varying responses in different cities. The national average was 47 per cent in England, and only 38 per cent in Scotland. If you lived in Liverpool, you were probably sent to North Wales; but if you lived in London you might be sent anywhere, and parents would not know exactly where until they got a postcard from the address where their children were billeted. There were tearful scenes at railway termini: 'Your Mummy is crying because she can't come on holiday with you.' Every child wore a label with its name on.

Fleets of buses transported children to stations, and four thousand special trains took them to the country: a rail strike was cancelled to make this possible. Some children took buckets and spades: the buckets were used on the trains, because there were too few, or no, lavatories. Everybody sang 'Run, Rabbit, Run'. The whole mass migration took three days.

In the country, kind people at first competed to be foster-parents, choosing children as they arrived at local schools. Some were horrified to meet the other half for the first time – lice, impetigo, boils and all. They discovered that they were entitled to an 'enuresis allowance' for habitual bed-wetters. Some children had been 'sewn up for the winter' with brown paper. Mothers and children alike sometimes had to have nits removed from their hair with knitting needles. There were constant difficulties about food: the East End seemed to live on fish and chips and

wouldn't touch cabbage. There were children who had never seen an egg and thought you had to bite it like an apple.

Pets were a problem. Some families had them 'put to sleep'. There was a businesslike boarding scheme for dogs (ten shillings a week) and budgies (a penny a day). *The Times* printed advertisements like 'Good home for evacuated pets, 7s. 6d. a week'. The *New Statesman* had one which said: 'Bombed-out cat, orthodox Marxist, seeks good home.' The Zoo was presented with a great many cherished parrots of no great ornithological interest. Following an alarming report that horses were being slaughtered for meat came a reassuring one that 'His Majesty the King has graciously allowed part of the Royal Mews to be set aside for the reception of bombed-out horses.' Most dog-owners went to great trouble to keep and feed their pets: dogs too got used to the raids and, because of their acute hearing, could detect approaching bombers before the sirens wailed. Ownerless dogs prowled over bomb sites, reverting to wolfdom.

It was not easy to get an education during the War. Schools were used as first-aid stations (with separate entrances for 'gas-contaminated' people), rest centres, anything but schools. Public schools such as Dulwich and Tonbridge doubled up in the same buildings. Malvern moved to Blenheim Palace so that their own buildings could be taken over by the B.B.C., and were then thrown out by the Government's new Telecommunications Research Unit which was working on radar, and eventually shared buildings with Harrow. The City of London School went to Marlborough; Cheltenham went to Shrewsbury; Lancing went to Ludlow. Eton College, its top-hats abolished for the duration, accommodated some girls from Wandsworth, who didn't like it and went home. East End State schools amalgamated with village schools, two classes in every room, sharing pens because there weren't enough. At one Berkshire school the floor subsided under the sheer weight of children.

How did the children feel about it? Some hated the country: 'Where's Woolworths? – I miss the sound of the trams.' Others were bewildered by the warmth of their reception: 'We were cosseted and coddled and damn near strangled by the affection of fearsome strangers who had to be called "Auntie" and "Uncle".' Some children had never seen farm animals before and could not tell cows from sheep. A

Evacuation. . . . 'Some were horrified to meet the other half for the first time'

small Jewish girl was transfixed with wonder at seeing a pig being killed. Another Jewish family were so happy that their father, an East End tailor, sent for the measurements of their host and made him a suit, not only free of charge but without coupons.

There were sad cases of children who forgot their parents and did not want to be taken away from Auntie and Uncle. Jonathan Miller, who went to eight different schools between Dunkirk and D-Day, remembers 'special evacuee colds – with a thick jade dribble coming from one nostril.' Alan Sillitoe says being evacuated (from Nottingham to Worksop, only 27 miles away) made him feel *important* for the first time in his life.

Some richer parents sent their children to America, even to Australia: this was thought a little (only a little) unpatriotic, and the practice abated somewhat after the torpedoing of the *City of Benares* and the *Rangitani* with many children on board. There was even a

suggestion that great-hearted America should send ships over to fetch children. Other British parents, knowing nothing of America but what they had seen in Hollywood films, preferred their children to stay and risk death.

There was a lot of discussion, during the Phoney War, about War Aims. If you stood on the Right, you tended to think that we'd better try and win the War first, otherwise aims were irrelevant. If you stood on the Left, you probably thought at this stage that we were 'defending the bad against the worse'. But one of the warning lessons of the First World War had been the danger of not preparing for life after the War. As the Second World War went on gaseous idealism began to take a more concrete shape. The idea of federation was being propounded – 'getting rid of all that frontier-customs-passport nonsense'. Viscount Cecil of Chelwood, after Germany had turned on Russia, making Russia willy-nilly our ally, began to talk about a 'quadrilateral of freedom' composed of the British Empire, the United States, the Soviet Union and the Chinese Republic. Lord Woolton, in 1943, moving over from the Ministry of Food to the new Ministry of Reconstruction, said Britain should aim at 'food, work and homes for all'.

In America Ely Culbertson, after abandoning bridge for four years to research the future, announced a 'Total Peace' plan, involving World Federation, the abolition of all armies, and a force of international police armed with machine guns. Clarence Budington Kelland, the *Saturday Evening Post* author, an isolationist until Pearl Harbor, who had once called Roosevelt's entourage a 'fifth column', in 1943 produced a 'Zones of Safety' plan for the post-war world. Count Coudenhove-Kalergi plodded on with ideas he had been proposing ever since the Treaty of Versailles in *Crusade for Pan-Europe*. Well, somebody has to do the thinking while soldiers fight and statesmen try to steer their way out of confusion and peril.

To troops lying on the Dunkirk beaches with German bombs raining down on them, waiting to be rescued by Royal Navy destroyers, assisted by a motley fleet of pleasure steamers and private yachts, these matters were not, could not be, relevant. In the June sunshine 338,000 troops, 139,000 of them French, were somehow taken off. Among the rescue ships that were sunk was the *Gracie Fields*, described by J.B. Priestley in one of his radio 'Postscripts' as 'the pride of our ferry service to the Isle of Wight'.

In New York somebody at C.B.S. decided that neutrality need no longer preclude the playing of wartime songs, and so radio listeners heard a medley of 'Over There', 'Tipperary', 'Pack up your Troubles', and 'K-K-K-Katie'.

Surely Britain must soon be invaded. There were probably German spies at large, and there would also be parachutists disguised as nuns. Under an emergency regulation known as 18B, more than a thousand refugees, many of them with British passports, together with 763 members of the British Union

Dunkirk, 20 June 1940

(opposite) **'A house collapsing on two firemen in Shoe Lane, London EC4', by Leonard Rosoman**

Leonard Rosoman:

POP cartoon, *Daily Sketch*, 1 April 1941

'West Country Manoeuvres – we are held up by ferocious Home Guards', by Edward Ardizzone

(*opposite*) 'Bringing up a 250–kilo bomb', by Clive Uptton

This old man went for a walk while his wife was preparing Sunday lunch. A bomb came down when he was at the end of the road. After many hours digging Civil Defence workers had to tell him his wife was dead.

of Fascists, were interned. A few weeks before, a call had gone out for a million men, mostly too old for military service, to be Local Defence Volunteers. They wore denim overalls at first, and drilled with sticks instead of rifles. There was some talk about arming them with pikes, which had not been used since Cromwell's time. There were endless jokes about the L.D.V.s, whose initials were given to other words, such as 'Look, Duck and Vanish'. They were trained to do desperate guerrilla things learned in the Spanish Civil War, such as attacking tanks with homemade 'Molotov Cocktails'. Museums were raided for weapons left over from previous wars, until modern rifles arrived from America. Many kind Americans sent over shotguns and sporting rifles. In August Churchill gave the L.D.V.s dignity, status, battle-dress and a new name – did he know he was borrowing it from the American Civil War? – the Home Guard. Gradually they became efficient;

many of them wore decorations from the First World War; but they never quite lost their humility, and when I came home on leave from the Army, they stood me drinks, saying: 'Ah, but you're a *real* soldier!'

Chamberlain went, bewildered, broken. Churchill took over, rhetorical, aggressive. The air-raids began, sometimes ten a day. This was it – the Battle of Britain. In daylight at first. Not yet called up for military service, I sat in a Surrey garden in a deck-chair watching the dog fights overhead; everyone in Southern England claimed that spent cartridge cases had fallen into his garden. In the 'White Hart' at Brasted, Kent, young airmen whose names would one day be famous – Stanford Tuck, Neville Duke, Sailor Malan, Bobby Oxspring – chalked up their daily 'kills'. Dover and Folkestone were shelled from the French coast. Then the night attacks. Still no invasion; but who thought of invasion now? The Blitz brought an utterly new kind of life. A familiar sight after a night raid was police dogs searching ruins for bodies, alive or dead. People went to and from work in trains that suddenly stopped because the lines weren't there. They then walked, found buses, were picked up by cars and trucks. Sometimes they didn't get home in the evening at all, but spent the night in station waiting rooms or buffets.

The shelter life was now normal for thousands of people. In the Tube tunnels bare-breasted mothers suckled their young while laughing at visiting concert parties. The word 'togetherness' had not yet been invented, but this was it. There were two kinds of home shelter: the Anderson (in the garden) and the Morrison (a sort of steel cage for two people). The Anderson, named after a Home Secretary, held six people and could be made reasonably comfortable with tea, food and radio. ('We may as well be blown up in comfort'.) People grew roses and nasturtiums round them. But as the destruction went on, and more

and more people lost their homes, these were inadequate, and bombed-out people never quite trusted the brick shelters which had been hastily put up in streets. Taking refuge in Underground stations was forbidden at first; but it could not be prevented because it was so easy to take a 1½d. ticket and stay there and refuse to move. Passive resistance, in the form of long queues outside stations, won the day, and soon there were twenty-two thousand bunks in tiers of three, with bucket latrines. Clergymen, knowing that this was not the time to preach, organized community singing – of hymns, of the 'Lambeth Walk', of anything cheerful. Variety stars gave free entertainments. By Christmas 1941, thousands of Londoners were leading an astonishingly cheerful troglodyte existence underground, shelters were decorated with paperchains and holly, tea was brewed on oilstoves, the Women's Voluntary Service distributed mince pies, and the B.B.C. broadcast all over the world a programme called *Christmas Under Fire*.

A Morrison shelter

At home everyone learned how to operate a thing called a stirrup-pump for putting out small fires (you had to keep the bath full of water if there was any), and how to remove incendiary bombs with a shovel or a steel helmet (*'never* put it in water, it will *explode'*). Shattered shops displayed notices: 'We are wide open.' Obituary notices of people killed by bombs never referred to raids: the usual phrase was 'died very suddenly'. A newspaper was allowed to print 'A church famed in nursery rhyme was bombed last night' but not to refer to St Clements. 'A famous public school was bombed yesterday' caused all telephone lines to most public schools to be jammed for several hours. On commuter trains normally taciturn people vied with one another like fishermen with raid stories: this was known as bomb-boasting. Kingsley Martin, editor of the *New Statesman*, claimed he was the only man to have been 'bombed off the lavatory while reading Jane Austen'.

Holidays, if any, were spent at home. A series of fine summers made open-air dancing possible, and concerts in parks. You seldom went to the seaside because most of the coast was festooned with barbed wire, betokening a prohibited military area: besides, most piers had been blown up in the middle, as if this could prevent the Germans from landing. Soldiers on leave spent most of their time sleeping and having several baths a day. Girls often spent their holidays on farms helping with the harvest. Dancing, whether in a nightclub or a village hall, stately home or Army hut, barn or police station, was the most popular home-made amusement: dance-halls were always full, became multilingual as Free French and Poles and Dutch intermingled, and foxtrot and waltz yielded to jive when the Americans arrived. Married girls, after the factory shift, took off their wedding rings and went dancing. 'If this is war,' a seventeen-year-old Lancashire girl was quoted as saying, 'why am I enjoying it so much?'

Seeing it all through a nightclub haze, Alan Ross says: 'The sadness and sexuality and alcohol were what everyone was wanting, and war was suddenly real and warm, and this unbearable parting and coming together in the dark, confined places was worth all the suffering and boredom and fear.'

'At home everyone learned how to operate a thing called a stirrup-pump'

(opposite) **Piccadilly Underground station during a raid, 1940**

CHAPTER 2

The Shooting War

At 2.30 p.m. on Sunday, 7 December 1941, an announcer named Milton Cross interrupted a New York Philharmonic concert to break unbelievable news. Pearl Harbor. Most of the U.S. Pacific Fleet destroyed at one blow, with their defending aircraft. ('On the *ground*!' roared Roosevelt, pounding his desk with fury.) The mighty base of which *Fortune* had said, just a year before, 'Pearl Harbor gives us a long jump on the Japanese when and if the great Pacific war of the future breaks out. . . . a strategist must see Oahu as the supporting base for a naval blockade of Japan.' Pearl Harbor: hardly anyone in Britain, and relatively few people in America, knew where it was. Those who did assumed it was impregnable, just as, nine weeks later, Britain seemed unable to grasp why the Japanese were suddenly in Singapore.

America was in the War – by 470 votes to 1 in Congress. No more 'America First'. No more 'measures short of' war. In Hawaii a sailor telegraphed his mother in San Francisco to say he was all right, adding (in Hawaiian pidgin) 'Cool head main t'ing'. On the West Coast America's first blackouts began, and, in a temporary panic, hundreds of Japanese were interned. California's invasion nerves were like Britain's in 1940. In the East the Westchester Cat Club formed a committee to investigate 'what steps should be taken to safeguard the lives of cats in the event of a foreign invasion'. And Helen Hokinson, in the *New Yorker*, drew three dowagers in the Diamond Horseshoe of the Metropolitan Opera, one of them saying: 'Well, there's one thing for sure: we don't have to feel sorry for Madame Butterfly any more.'

'This certainly simplifies things. God be with you.' That was the tailend of a telephone call from Churchill to Roosevelt shortly after Pearl Harbor. Not, as it turned out, the most tactful message; but at that moment neither leader knew the extent of the damage to the U.S. Navy. Churchill then sent a cheer-up

(left) **Pearl Harbor**

message to Chiang Kai-shek in China: 'Always we have been friends. Now we face a common enemy.' Of Pearl Harbor he afterwards wrote: 'To have the United States at our side was to me the greatest joy.'

But was it the same war? Japan was trying to conquer a Pacific empire at lightning speed. America's interest, apart from supplying weapons, was not yet in Europe. The Pacific might have been a separate war but for Hitler's odd, vain decision to declare war on America.

There is war as history organizes it, and there is war as those who took part in it remember it, always from the local viewpoint of a very small sector. I cannot presume to add anything to the mass of war literature, still less can I in one or several chapters comprehend a world conflict, any more than Shakespeare could represent the Hundred Years War within 'this wooden O' of the Globe Theatre. All I can do is to try to point out a few details that by implication sketch in the vastness of operations. Only a commander-in-chief can take a world view of a world war while it is actually happening. Historians chop wars vertically into campaigns: but it is sometimes healthy to remember that on any given day in a world war thousands of things are taking place simultaneously. In the same month of 1942 the Russians are trying to take Kharkov, but are surrounded by the Germans who take a quarter of a million prisoners, while Britain makes her first thousand-bomber raid on Cologne, and in the Pacific huge battles are raging in the Coral Sea and at Midway as America struggles in expensive island warfare, and, in North Africa, Rommel is driving back the Eighth Army towards Sidi Barrani.

We talk about the Phoney War as if nothing happened, for Britain, before Dunkirk, and nothing for America before Pearl Harbor. It had not been a phoney war for the 112 passengers of the *Athenia* (twenty-eight of them American), drowned on the first day of the War. It was not phoney for invaded Poland, Denmark, Norway, Holland, Belgium, and France. It was not phoney for Finland, invaded by Russia to 'protect' her from possible German occupation; or for 299 British merchant sailors, picked up from their sunken ships by the *Altmark*, a German tanker whose task was to supply the battleship *Graf Spee*. The merchant seamen had been hidden in storage space to escape inspection by the Norwegian

Navy. The *Altmark*, bottled up in a fjord by Captain Philip Vian's destroyer *Cossack*, was boarded, and the prisoners rescued: a bit of good old-fashioned derring-do, presumably ordered by Churchill, which, though followed by the German invasion of Norway, did British morale good.

Those merchant seamen, if not among many thousands of 'forgotten' men and women who got little of the glory of war, were insufficiently recognized by history. About 2,500 such ships, carrying vital supplies and exports, were at sea on any one day; they spent the entire War dodging, and sometimes failing to dodge, German submarines. Their crews as civilians were never forced to sign on for another voyage, but they did; they got £2. 5s. od. ($9.00) a week plus danger money; and eleven per cent of them lost their lives. Mark Arnold-Forster compares them with those other almost-forgotten men, Wingate's Chindits in the jungles of Burma, whose rate of casualties was about the same. The worst job was to be in a tanker, whose cargo, in a sinking, was certain to go up in flames. 'We heard some screams for help,' recalls Captain Finch of the *San Emiliano*, 'and rowed over and pulled out of the water a fireman who was terribly burned, so much so that when we pulled him into the boat, the skin from his body and arms came off in our hands.'

Forgotten, too, were the men of Paiforce, who had nothing to do but sit on the oil wells of Persia and Iraq: my own division, sick with malaria and dysentery both at once, spent the winter of 1942 in tents over dugouts in a temperature of thirty degrees below zero.

Still colder were the men on convoys to Russia by the Arctic route; but remembered, if only for disaster. Churchill, after the German invasion of Russia, had promised 'supplies'. Supplies of what? The Russians seemed to need everything. What they got, until 1943, was tanks and aircraft, which sometimes lay about unused on the quayside at Archangel. What they needed, it turned out, was food, medical supplies and trucks, which, however, could be more safely, if more slowly conveyed through the Persian Gulf (in those fraternal days, British factory workers used to paint things like 'A Present for Uncle Joe' on vehicles for Stalin).

The Arctic convoys, avoiding the ice, were within easy range of German airfields in Norway. Convoys were bombed day and night for the last lap of each voyage. The worst-hit convoy was PQ.17, containing thirty-six merchant ships, in July 1942. By an error, it was thought that Germany's last great battleship, *Tirpitz*, was about to attack it. PQ.17, ordered to scatter, was an easy prey for German aircraft, which sank twenty-four ships.

Remembered, for the glamour attaching to the Desert Rats, the gallant comradeship of the wasteland, and the personalities of Rommel and Montgomery, was the war in North Africa. We must suppose because the Suez Canal had to be protected, and there were Italian colonies to the west of Egypt, and we might some day want to enter Italy from the south, that these were sufficient reasons for fighting a highly mobile war, involving Germans, Italians and Americans, on a battlefield 1,600 miles long with dangerously stretched supply lines for either one side or the other, as they shuttled back and forth. We learned a new word, 'logistics', and were told that a soldier who had nothing to do but guard a petrol dump in the middle of nowhere was every bit as good as the Guards in the front line. Rommel, with only forty tanks left, paused exhausted before Alamein. Then, with far more equipment than Rommel, Montgomery attacked on 23 October 1942. A thousand guns bombarding, a week of muddle, then breakthrough (by the 7th Armoured Division and the New Zealanders): Rommel, said the blithe communiqué, was 'motoring westwards in top gear'. As he did so, British and American forces landed in Morocco and Tunisia. All over by Christmas? No, long supply lines again; it took until the following May.

Not until after the War did Britain have any clear idea of the size and bitterness of America's task in the Pacific. Struggling for jungle-covered islands stretching halfway round the earth, with a portable flame-thrower as your primary weapon, is among the worst kinds of warfare. On the same day as Pearl Harbor, Japan attacked Midway Island, Wake Island (a 2½-square-mile atoll about 1,000 miles from Midway), and Guam, another 1,500 miles west of Wake. There were landings in Thailand and Malaysia. During the next five months they had Hong Kong, half of Burma, Singapore (the invasion from Johore by troops on bicycles, the guns that pointed the wrong way, the 'greatest capitulation in British history', the remorse of Churchill, the sacking of Commander-in-Chief

Brooke-Popham, called a 'nincompoop' in the House of Lords); then Djakarta and the Philippines, bombing Port Darwin, in Northern Australia, on the way.

In Burma the Japanese taught the Allies jungle-craft. Bernard Fergusson, commanding a column of the Wingate Expedition, showed how to find your direction in jungle, how to eke out rations by living on the land, how to find water by studying elephant droppings, how to burn leeches off your body with a cigarette end. 'The jungle,' he always maintained, 'is your friend.'

The Burma Road, linking China with India, was thought to be of great strategic importance because the Americans hoped that China would play an important part in defeating Japan: it was for this reason that General ('Vinegar Joe') Stilwell, who spoke Chinese, was given the task of revitalizing Chiang Kai-shek's army.

In all this explosion of energy, attacking in five different directions at once, the Japanese found the Philippines the most difficult target. Again they succeeded in destroying American aircraft on the ground at Clark Field; then they landed in the north of Luzon. The Americans fell back into the Bataan peninsula and then into the fortified island of Corregidor. General MacArthur was certain he could hold the Philippines until reinforcements arrived, but the sickness and starvation of his men were beyond gallantry. Under his successor, General Wainwright, 140,000 men were captured and handed over to a 'death march' and the brutality of General Homma.

The Japanese now stretched their lines too far, and for the first time encountered a reverse. The Solomon Islands and Papua were uncomfortably near Northern Australia – Port Moresby is indeed a mere 350 miles off. In the battle of the Coral Sea, for the first time, aircraft carriers fought each other while the Japanese tried to land at Port Moresby – the American *Lexington* and *Yorktown*, assisted by Australian units, versus the Japanese *Zuikaku*, *Shoho* and *Shokaku*, so far apart (more than 100 miles) that the fleets could not see each other. The *Shoho* was sunk, the *Shokaku* severely damaged, and the landing was prevented. The *Lexington* was also badly damaged, and had to be sunk, but not before pilots and crew had been saved. So orderly was this operation that some of the men filled their helmets with ice-cream from the ship's store and jumped over the side eating it.

In June 1942 came Japan's second reverse at Midway; and this time it could be called, not merely a defeat, but the most decisive battle in the Pacific. Admiral Yamamoto never got anywhere near his objective of finishing off the United States fleet. Yamamoto had eight aircraft carriers, eleven battleships and a hundred and eight other craft, including submarines; Admiral Nimitz had only three carriers, twenty-five other craft – and the priceless asset of the key to the Japanese code, so that the enemy could be surprised and tricked by false signals. With absolutely no idea that the Americans were near, Yamamoto began to bomb Midway. Suddenly American aircraft were there, and in five minutes sank four Japanese carriers with 330 aircraft on board. The Americans lost one carrier, *Yorktown*.

Now began the slow process of winning back islands, terribly expensive in loss of lives, against an enemy to whom surrender was dishonourable, and who sometimes thought they were doing their prisoners a favour by handing them swords to commit suicide with. The Americans were to make about a hundred amphibious attacks on islands before VJ-Day, and they always involved the Marines, Guadalcanal, Papua, Rabaul; nearer and nearer to Japan, so that the new B.29 bombers could attack Tokyo itself. The Gilberts, the Marshalls, Tarawa and Kwajalein and Eniwetok, names people in the Western world had never heard before. Then came a 'Pearl Harbor' operation on the Japanese base at Truk, in the Carolines.

In June 1944 came the 'Great Marianas Turkey Shoot', which crippled Japan's naval air force, clearing the way for the re-occupation of the Philippines after the battle of Leyte Gulf in October – A.J.P. Taylor calls it 'the greatest naval engagement of all time' – which, we now know, practically finished off the Japanese navy. There remained the two heavily fortified islands of Okinawa and Iwo Jima, which between them claimed 18,500 American lives. Then – Hiroshima.

In Italy a very different kind of war, much slower, often in mountains where every gun shot reverberates with a maddening noise, as nerve-wearing as the jungle. The campaign had begun in July 1943 with the invasion of Sicily, the Americans under Patton and Bradley landing in the south and converging on Palermo, then pushing on to Messina to meet Montgomery's Eighth Army which had landed near Syracuse. The Germans managed to get 109,000 of their own and Italian troops to the mainland in good order, equipment and all. Within a fortnight Mussolini, who had promised that no Allied force should ever land in Italy, had been deposed and imprisoned. Sicily was all over in under six weeks, largely because of 'the man who never was' – the corpse of a British officer, found by Spanish fishing boats two months before, whose pockets contained faked letters giving the impression that the Allies were going to land in Greece, not Italy.

The rest of the war in Italy was dictated by the German refusal to give up any inch of Italy without fearful cost. There was some disagreement between British and American commanders (and between General Mark Clark and his colleague General Lucas, by temperament a 'consolidator') about the speed at which they should advance on Rome after the Anzio landing: Clark went right ahead and did it, but at the expense of twice as many casualties as the Germans suffered. The other armies crossed rivers painfully on their way north.

The natural 'winter line' for Field Marshal Kesselring to defend was across the Apennines, the 'Gustav line' whose centre was the famous monastery of Monte Cassino, dating back to the ninth century and before, where the Benedictine Order had begun. The Germans were not actually *in* the monastery, but the Allies were not to know that. Monte Cassino was destroyed by bombing at the request of General Freyberg, who was about to send his crack New Zealand Division into action. But the rubble and the indestructible cellars were more useful to the Germans than the intact building. It took six months to break the line, and there are British, American, Canadian, New Zealand, Indian, French and Polish soldiers who took part in it: the Poles and the French completed the operation.

Alan Moorehead, the Australian war correspondent, much of whose writing concentrated on the demoralization of starving civilians in an occupied country, tried to analyse the nature of fear as he saw it in soldiers who were taking another monastery, Monte Camino, on the way to Cassino:

Exposure. Cold. The overstraining of the body over long periods. Bad food. Lack of sleep. These things did the damage. . . . Fear is not the worst thing. You recover quickly from it. It leaves no scar. . . . A soldier going up to the front line for the first time has to say: 'Now I gamble everything. I put all my life . . . and all that part of everyone I love – I put all this in the way of death!' Then later when you see the man return safely he appears to have gained in stature. . . . There is tide upon tide of happiness as he takes back his life. . . . It is the sort of experience that possibly women have when they voluntarily risk themselves to bear children. . . .

Kesselring retreated to other, weaker defence lines. By September 1944 his army was north of Florence and Rimini. It was about this time that the Allies captured a document which suggests what might have happened if the war in Italy had gone on much longer. Signed personally by Kesselring, who was generally regarded as a friendly, beer-drinking, sixteen-stone good fellow, a *gemütlich* Bavarian, fond of conjuring tricks and playing the piano, it gave orders for the destruction of Italian cities in retreat, every bridge, house, street: 'Demolitions must more than ever be executed *with sadistic imaginativeness.*'

One of the great mysteries of warfare is how it was possible, in 1941, to send millions of German soldiers into Russia to face a winter campaign in a temperature which fell as low as 38 degrees Centigrade below zero, without special winter clothes, and tanks and machine guns without special lubricants for very low temperatures. The only possible explanation is that Hitler, ignoring what had happened to Napoleon before him, really meant it when he said that Russia could be finished off before the winter. As the campaign went on sunburned men were withdrawn from the Afrika Korps and flung, almost unacclimatized, into Russia. Every bit of machinery the Russians captured they could use against the Germans because they had the right oils. One German armoured division reported that it had lost more than five times as many men through frostbite as through enemy action. What did Hitler do? Blame his generals for failing to mop up the sub-human Slavs.

In Leningrad, cut off by the Germans in September 1941 so that it could be supplied in winter only by a road and railway line laid across the frozen Lake Ladoga, a million of its three million people starved to death, ate rats, ate (it is said) each other before being relieved two and a half years later.

Hitler now turned his attention to the Ukraine,

rich in food and industry, and beyond it to the Caucasus and its oil-wells. What he did not know was that several hundred factories had been evacuated from the Ukraine to the east, 600 to 1,000 miles behind Moscow, in the Ural Mountains, with Kuibyshev as temporary capital if Moscow should be evacuated (which, in part, it was in the autumn of 1942). In the Ukraine the Russians followed a policy of destroying everything that could possibly be of use to the enemy – it became known as 'scorched earth'.

Kharkov – a quarter of a million Russians taken prisoner; Voronezh; Kursk; Rostov-on-Don; and Stalingrad, defended to the death by General Chuikov, one of Russia's ablest and most popular commanders, with, as local political commissar, Nikita Khruschev, one day to succeed Stalin. Stalingrad, the struggle for which went on from mid-September 1942 to the end of January 1943, was a worldwide morale booster for anyone who still thought of German military might as invincible. Seventy thousand Germans died there, and ninety-one thousand were taken prisoner, including twenty-four generals and the commander himself, Paulus. The great majority of them were never heard of again. 'Von Paulus should have shot himself,' Hitler commented; and Goebbels ordered three days of national mourning.

Stalin had consistently asked the Allies for a second front in Europe. In Britain both press and politicians, ignorant of the tremendous preparations that were being made, were shouting the slogan, 'Second Front *Now!*'

One afternoon in May 1944 senior officers of Southern Command, England, were called to a top-secret meeting in a Portsmouth theatre where they were addressed by Field Marshal Bernard Montgomery. He began in the usual Monty way: 'I don't approve of coughing or smoking. There will be no smoking. For two minutes you may cough.' He then told them that 'certain brave men' had been in midget submarines to have a look at the German West Wall defences in Normandy and that a plan had been made: D-Day was about to happen.

Three years before, Churchill had dictated the following order:

Piers for Use on Beaches

C.C.O. or Deputy. They must float up and down with the tide. The anchor problem must be mastered. Let me have the best solution worked out. Don't argue the matter. The difficulties will argue for themselves. – W.S.C., 30.5.42.

All round the inlets of the Thames Estuary construction firms, working through air raids, were pouring concrete into caissons 200 feet long, 56 feet wide and 60 feet high. Nobody knew what they were for. Concrete blocks of various sizes, code-named Phoenix, Gooseberry, Bombardon, Whale, were conveyed to Selsey in Sussex, where they were fitted together, ready for D-Day, when they would be towed across the Channel. These were the Mulberry Ports, 15 miles of piers, causeways and breakwaters, weighing three million tons.

By successful deception, such as placing a radio transmitter in Kent and covering Kentish airfields with dummy gliders, the Germans were given the impression that the invasion would come in the Pas de Calais, and that was where most of them (but not the 7th Army) were waiting.

There were other new devices, such as flail tanks for destroying mines, amphibious tanks, tanks which could lay their own 'carpets' so that they would not get stuck in the mud; all these among twelve hundred ships, ten thousand aircraft, more than four thousand landing craft and hundreds of transport ships. The troops also had a new kind of seasickness pill which did not make them sleepy. (Ernest Hemingway, who was in one of the landing craft, says it didn't work.)

At 4 a.m. on 5 June 1944, General Eisenhower studied the weather report for the next twenty-four hours and said: 'O.K., let's go.' He also prepared two communiqués, one for success, the other for failure, taking the whole responsibility himself. D-Day was the most complete, best-planned combined operation the world had ever seen, in which British and American soldiers, sailors and airmen were 'more mixed up' (A.J.P. Taylor's words) than ever before. Mayor La Guardia announced an open-air service in Madison Square Gardens and Maryland's Governor Herbert O'Conor asked all liquor stores to close for the rest of the day after the invasion news.

For two years the invasion of Europe had been planned; for two years the newspapers had been shouting 'Second Front *Now*!' Perhaps the most relieved man was Mr L.S. Dawe, senior English master at St Paul's School, Hammersmith, who augmented his income by compiling crossword puzzles

for *The Daily Telegraph*: he had been grilled by Intelligence because the code words Overlord and Mulberry had by chance appeared in the same puzzle.

The plan was for Utah and Omaha beaches to be captured by General Omar Bradley's 1st U.S. Army; Gold, Juno and Sword to be taken by Canadians and British, under General Dempsey. Two bridges to be captured by the 6th British Airborne Division, plus other objectives. Everything to be done in four hours by night. It took six weeks to get through the 'Bocage', small fields hemmed in by banks of earth and hedges, trying to break out and make for Paris. Should Paris be taken – or just by-passed? Could it be left to the Free French? Allied commanders disagreed; temperaments were beginning to show. General Patton would have liked to have seen the British shoved back into the sea, as at Dunkirk; he thought them so slow. Montgomery, looking for weak spots in the enemy, was foxier and perhaps more careful of human life; difficult to get on with, the Americans found: if only, just for once, he'd light a cigarette, take a drink or use a four-letter word. . . .

After the first anxiety and exhilaration and a curious silence before the first train-loads of wounded were seen in southern England, nerves and tempers in Britain were getting frayed as a new enemy weapon appeared – the V1, 'buzz-bomb', a slow pilotless plane with a load of high explosive whose engine 'cut out' just before it fell, so that there was no time to take cover. There were rumours of a second 'secret weapon', encouraged by German propaganda: would it be a double-sized V1? No – it was a rocket and it gave no warning: just a huge bang, thought at first to be a burst gas main. Since there was no warning, you couldn't worry about it.

Neither weapon was a surprise: both were first suspected by a girl named Constance Babington-Smith, afterwards the biographer of Rose Macaulay, whose job in the R.A.F. was to study air photographs. A photograph of Peenemünde, Germany's Baltic experimental station, had shown a model of a plane and a smudge which looked like a rocket burn. Was there an intelligence leak? As early as January 1944 *Time* magazine had hinted at a 'liquid air rocket bomb' which could be used against targets 70 miles away, and 'an interceptor-fighter plane with a rocket-booster'.

In mid-August there was an American landing at

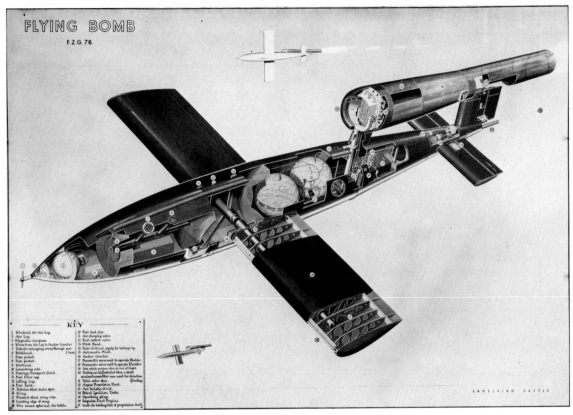

A cutaway drawing of a V1, 'buzz-bomb', by P. Endsleigh Castle

Saint Tropez in the South of France under General Patch: they pushed up the Rhone Valley towards the Vosges mountains. By now it was feared that the Germans would destroy Paris, and that the Resistance there would be too weak to prevent it. Hitler's orders to the military governor, General von Choltitz, were to destroy the city totally if it could not be defended. Von Choltitz ignored the order and surrendered, on 25 August, to the Free French under General Leclerc. De Gaulle followed, proclaiming himself President.

St Paul's Cathedral and Westminster Abbey rang special peals; there was jubilation in the 'York Minster', Soho's French pub, and tricolours flew everywhere. In New York's Rockefeller Plaza, Lily Pons of the Metropolitan Opera, in uniform, sang the *Marseillaise*.

After France, Belgium, Holland and Germany itself. Eisenhower was now supreme commander, sixty per cent of all Allied troops were American, and

Montgomery was forced to play second fiddle. Eisenhower believed in what he called a 'broad front', Montgomery in what he called a 'major blow': they seemed fated to misunderstand each other's use of words. Rivers and canals stood in the way; bridges were now of first importance. At Nijmegen, on the Waal, the British 30th Corps, spearheaded by the Guards Armoured Division, helped by American paratroops, were successful. At Arnhem, on the Rhine, everything went wrong: paratroops landed too far away, and there was furious resistance from two German armoured divisions regrouping nearby.

Just before Christmas came Hitler's last offensive, in the Ardennes, where the Germans had so often been lucky. It became known as 'the Battle of the Bulge'. Here Montgomery was in overall command of American troops, and he was afterwards to claim most of the credit for himself; but it was Patton who brought off the miracle of relieving Bastogne by some-

Conference of leaders of Allied Powers, USSR, USA and Great Britain at Yalta, 1945. Seated left to right: Winston Churchill, F.D. Roosevelt and Stalin

how, in only two days, bringing his whole army away from a general attack in the Saar to a particular task, almost by saying 'left turn'.

The end was near, and yet it was nearly five months away. (I do not want to believe the story that one Wall Street journalist headlined an article MARKET DECLINES ON PEACE SCARE.)

Now the Allies, in their turn, asked the Russians to provide a second front in the east. Stalin responded with unexpected alacrity – there was already some anxiety in both east and west about who should get to Berlin first – but few expected the Russians to move as early as 12 January 1945, advancing 300 miles in blinding snow, visibility nil, in eighteen days, to Küstrin on the Oder, within 40 miles of Berlin, having taken Warsaw on the way. Marshal Zhukov planned to take Berlin 'with a lightning thrust': he would do it

in two days in the middle of February. Suddenly Stalin telephoned from the Crimea (he was in the middle of the Yalta Conference, where he and Churchill and Roosevelt were carving up Germany into Occupation Zones) and said: 'Stay where you are.' Why? No doubt the Russian supply lines were now overstretched, but – only 40 miles! For the Western Allies, Eisenhower took the decision not to risk lives for Berlin – there was much else to do.

The Russians moved against Berlin in April. They had a terrifying rocket weapon called the Katyusha. The first contact between Russian and American troops was made at Torgau, on the Elbe, and the world's press was flooded with pictures of G.I. Joe embracing Ivan Russky, dancing with Russian girl soldiers, the vodka flowing. Hitler appointed Doenitz, whom he could not blame for anything, as his successor, and shot himself. Muddled minor surrenders; then on 4 May Montgomery accepted the surrender of the German troops of the north at Lüneburg Heath, millions of prisoners, including children mobilised at the eleventh hour into the Volkssturm.

On 7 May there had been a thunderstorm in southern England, just as there had been the day before war had been declared. People thronged the streets wearing funny hats and rosettes, had family picnics in the sunshine. Girls wore coloured ribbons round bare ankles. British and American soldiers together climbed the sandbagged statue of Eros in Piccadilly Circus. Barrow boys sold brooches with General Montgomery's head on them. No sirens, no guns: just pealing bells, tugs on the Thames whistling the Morse letter V, while aeroplanes did Victory rolls overhead. Students ran through London's parks banging dustbin lids like cymbals. American sailors and British girls formed a Conga line down Piccadilly. Soldiers tore down hoardings to make bonfires, watched by uninterfering police.

Winston Churchill led members of Parliament to a Thanksgiving Service at St Margaret's Westminster; and as he came out again, a drunken cockney voice yelled from the crowd: 'There's 'is little old lovely bald 'ead!' And when Churchill joined the Royal Family on the balcony at Buckingham Palace, small children watched, not the King or Queen, but the first fully lighted street lamps they had ever seen.

On 6 August a U.S. Army Air Force B.29, called 'Enola Gay' after the pilot's mother, took off from Tinian in the Mariana Archipelago and two hundred thousand citizens of Hiroshima, Japan, were incinerated. The pilot, Colonel Tibbetts, looking down from a height of 33,000 feet two minutes later, afterwards said: 'The surface was nothing but a black boiling, like a barrel of tar where before there had been a city with distinctive houses, buildings . . . now you couldn't see anything except a black boiling debris down below.' Three days later, the second atomic bomb fell on Nagasaki. Why? The Allies were not yet ready to figure that one out. The world had entered the Nuclear Age.

VJ-Day was celebrated, soldiers kissed unknown girls in the street, thanksgiving services were held, and two naked blondes frolicked in a San Francisco lily pond.

Celebrating VJ-Day

CHAPTER 3

Over Here, Over There

Britain had had food rationing since January 1940, beginning with bacon, ham, butter and meat. Lord Beaverbrook, dynamic as Minister of Aircraft Production, who had opposed both rationing and the blackout in his *Daily Express,* now seemed resigned to both. The butter ration was 4 ounces (later 2 ounces) a week; cheese varied from 1 to 2 ounces; eggs one per fortnight if you were lucky (but expectant mothers and children under five got as many as three a week). Two kinds of milk powder, skimmed and National Dried (full cream). Tea 2 ounces a week, but more for

An example of what a family of three could buy with their 96 points in a four-week period in September 1946

An example of what a family of three can buy with their 96 points in a four-week period.

old-age pensioners. Sugar 12 ounces, but more in the jam-making season. There was a 'points' system for canned foods (most of which came from America and the Dominions), cereals and condensed milk. Sweets (2 ounces a week) came on 'personal points'; there was a lot of propaganda about how bad they were for teeth. From America, too, came spam (spiced ham), and dried eggs. From April 1942 there was a National Loaf. No onions. No bananas. No oranges except for children.

Expectant mothers had Green ration books ('eat for one and a bit', boomed the Radio Doctor in his homely way) and orange juice and vitamins A and D. They were not supposed to share their good fortune with the rest of the family, but. . . . They were also allowed to jump the endless, day-long queues at food-shops.

If you were invited to dine or stay at anyone's house you took your rations with you in disgusting little sticky packages. Part of the social revolution of the war was that British housewives, servantless and sharpened by rationing, began to be really good cooks. This began modestly enough by following the government advice on making the best of too little food. The Ministry of Food was headed by an organizational genius, Fred Marquis, Baron Woolton, former managing director of Lewis's department stores in Manchester, Liverpool and Birmingham. He gave friendly little morning radio talks on 'The Kitchen Front', made housewives feel heroic. Propaganda characters appeared – Mr Carrot and Potato Pete. Potato Pete appeared in person at the 1942 Potato Christmas Fair, held in tents in a bombed-out Oxford Street store. It was patriotic to eat more potatoes than bread because most wheat was imported. Carrots, people were told, helped you to see in the blackout – like Cat's-Eyes Cunningham, the R.A.F. pilot who had shot down so many planes at night. (Civilians did

'The Fish Queue', by Evelyn Dunbar, portrays one of the day-long queues at a food shop

not yet know that Cat's-Eyes had radar to help him.) Eat carrot flan. Make a cake out of flour, custard powder and dried egg. Liquid paraffin was available 'for medicinal purposes', but you could also use it as cooking fat. Learn about calories and proteins. Lord Woolton also invented, or at least gave his name to, Woolton Pie, which some people thought delicious, and others thought dangerously costive: it was made of carrots, parsnips, turnips, potatoes, pastry and white sauce. Carrots were also the chief ingredient of 'Wartime Christmas Pudding'.

Sometimes rations were increased or reduced – always headline news; and Woolton generally balanced things so that if there was less jam, there was more cheese. A substitute for bacon, 'macon', appeared. Lemons were so rare that they were auctioned for charity. It was discovered (as I can confirm from a study of Army swill bins) that many of the poor hated 'greens' and did not regard them as food at all. Knowingly or not, people ate horseflesh, hitherto given to dogs: my wife, entertaining an Australian visitor, smothered horseflesh with onions and garlic and moved the man to tears: 'To think that you've spent a whole month's meat ration on me!' Milk – two pints a week, yet in 1942 it came off ration altogether. Some people nevertheless bought backyard goats.

Every scrap of land was used to grow food; parks and squares and rosebeds were dug up – 'Dig for Victory' was the slogan. So was 'Lend a Hand on the Land', responded to by public schoolboys who spent their summer vacations helping farmers. Tomatoes, not geraniums, were grown in window boxes. Thou-

sands of elderly men spent their weekends tending allotments, using soot for manure. Pet rabbits were killed for meat, and if you couldn't bear to eat your own flopsy bunny, you swopped with someone else's. Their skins were used to make gloves.

There were Pig Clubs – one of them in the bombed-out swimming pool of the Ladies' Carlton Club in

Farmer George VI: Pigs lived entirely on kitchen waste at Windsor Castle

Pall Mall. If you had more than twenty hens you were supposed to sell the eggs to the Ministry of Food, but there were dozens of ways of getting round all regulations. There was a surprisingly small Black Market, and a mild racket known as 'under the counter' by which shops kept cigarettes or food for special customers, sometimes at special prices.

The Women's Land Army (£2. 8s. 0d. a week with £1. 5s. 6d. deducted for board and lodging), run by Lady Denman, was one of the toughest assignments on the Home Front. There were stories that, in a succession of hot summers, girls took off their breeches and worked in undies. The most depressed were those girls who had to work on remote Welsh farms where there were no radios, nobody spoke English, and the natives did not regard the War as having anything to do with them.

Eating in restaurants was restricted to one main dish and a maximum charge of five shillings (but the *couvert* charge varied with the fame of the restaurant). How certain famous establishments managed to offer

veal and chicken fricassée nobody knew, but there may be some significance in the fact that guinea pigs for experiments in teaching hospitals were almost unobtainable. There were cafeteria-type restaurants where you could get meat, two vegetables, pudding, bread and butter and tea or coffee, all for a shilling.

Kind friends in America, Canada and Australia sent food parcels, some private, some ('Bundles for Britain') official: the latter were distributed by the Women's Voluntary Service who gave top priority to bombed-out mothers.

It was a thin time for drinkers, who were lucky if they got one (official) bottle of gin or whisky every two months. 'No beer' signs outside pubs meant no beer till the next delivery. All spirits had been made from imported raw material, and this was now forbidden. How, then, was it possible for there to be some nine thousand arrests for drunkenness in 1942, 45 per cent of the 1937 figure? There were considerable stocks in bond, and it was strange how many cases disappeared in transit.

'Land girls going to bed', by Evelyn Dunbar

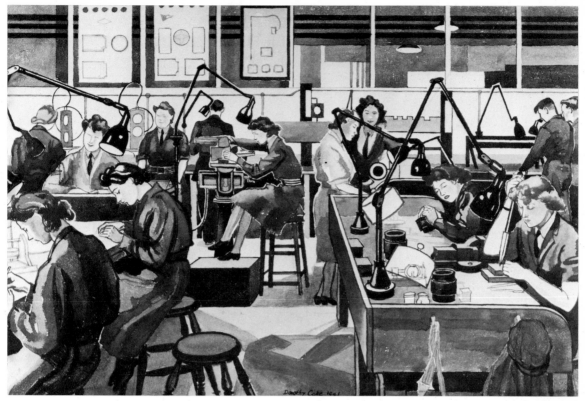

'WAAF instrumental mechanics at work', 1941, Dorothy Coke

In America the Pearl Harbor shock was followed by the restless desire of many citizens to do something to allay their frustration. Blackouts were rehearsed, thousands of people volunteered for Civilian Defense, air-raid wardens and aircraft spotters, equipped with circular cards bearing silhouettes of all known enemy aircraft, proliferated. There were no air-raids, but it was useful to have a civilian force that could help in any sort of emergency. Americans too dug for victory, and called their plots Victory Gardens, bought seed catalogues, read Department of Agriculture leaflets, were known in some places as 'Sunday farmers', discovered the sheer pleasure of eating homegrown food.

From January 1942 there were ration books in the U.S.A., even more complicated and full of gobbledegook than British ones. There were red, blue, brown and green stamps, all worth a certain number of points. As in Britain, there were rackets by which you could buy more than your entitlement, especially of gasoline, officially rationed at three gallons a week, but variable according to the national importance of

one's job. A steak was worth 12 points a pound, a hamburger 7, a can of peaches 18, pineapple juice 22, a pound of cheddar cheese 8. Shopkeepers had to stick the stamps onto sheets of paper and take them to wholesalers, who had to give them to their banks. As America was at no time near starvation, it could be, and was, argued that food rationing was unnecessary. At least it theoretically ensured fair shares.

Soon the shortages appeared, usually of unrationed goods. Shoes – very difficult unless you took a standard size. A newly married girl in Denver, Colorado, where there was a shortage of lavatory paper but enough sugar, sent sugar to her mother 1,700 miles away in New York, where there was plenty of lavatory paper but not enough sugar; her mother, of course, sent back lavatory paper. Nylon stockings went on being mended almost for ever. Before going to work, civilians stood in line for cigarettes, brands never seen before or since, for 'Lucky Strike had gone to war', changing the pack colour to white as it did so.

Suddenly there seemed to be only two brands of

Seated on a Liberty ship, ladies attend a 'school for women welders' at a Los Angeles shipyard in 1943

bourbon whiskey, 'Four Roses' and 'Three Feathers'; Scotch had disappeared to the clip-joints, and to get the bourbon you often had to buy with it some inferior rum.

'Whalemeat', announced the Department of the Interior in 1943, 'will soon reappear on U.S. tables for the first time since World War I. . . . It tastes a good deal like beef.' (It does *not*.) A single whale had as much meat as 125 steers, and 'the tenderest whale steaks come from young California grey whales'. That year, everyone was talking about food: the harvest was expected to be poor, and many people temporarily gave up meat as nationally uneconomic, since a hog needed 7 pounds of corn to produce 1 pound of pork.

If you had servants, you didn't any more: they were away to the war factories, especially women, who were given names like 'Rosie the Riveter'. 'We never go to the movies any more,' said Groucho Marx. 'My wife criticizes the spot welding out loud.' If you needed a new telephone, you were told in apologetic advertisements from Bell that you would have to wait almost indefinitely.

Britain and America, who did not need Irving Berlin's 'My British Buddy' to unite them, were probably closer together than at any time in history. Just as British women of all classes had flocked into aircraft factories ('Precision engineering jobs which a few years ago would have made a skilled turner's hair stand on end are performed with dead accuracy by girls who had no industrial experience', said Deputy Prime Minister Attlee in 1942), so, in the quadrupling of production America achieved between Pearl Harbor and Christmas 1942, three and a half million trousered women were helping to build Liberty ships and bombers in record time. 'Soldiers without guns' was a slogan used on both sides of the Atlantic.

In California vast changes were taking place. This state of seven million people, fruit and movies, not much industrialized, added a million to its population and built aircraft and ships on a scale never seen before. Food, oil, K rations, all came from California. Mass production found its emperor in Henry Kaiser. Detroit turned out bombers, on an assembly line half a mile long, to swell the national target of sixty thousand a year; but could standardized food ships, rolling like tubs, be mass produced? Henry Kaiser might

Donated cooking utensils being sorted for use as possible war materials

not know 'the front end' from 'the back end' of a ship, but he had a talent for simplifying. Why bring steel from the Great Lakes, 2,000 miles away? Let California have its own steel mills. Besides, there were new sources of iron ore in Utah, only 600 miles away. Result: one Liberty ship every day, all welded, just as Groucho said.

Any old cans, old nylons, anything made of metal or rubber or paper? They could all be made into war materials: huge salvage dumps appeared in every town. In Britain housewives had donated aluminium saucepans, with no prospect of getting new ones, to the Government; cavalry swords and historic guns had been sent to the melting pot; park railings were ruthlessly torn up, Victorian and Georgian wrought-iron gates were taken away – were they ever used for anything? (Later it was reported that they had all

been dumped in the sea off Portsmouth.) In the same spirit of sacrifice Mrs Edward T. Stotesbury, celebrated hostess and widow of a J.P. Morgan partner, gave the iron fence (eight feet high and two miles long) round her Whitemarsh Hall estate in Pennsylvania; it was said to contain enough steel for eighteen thousand machine guns.

By now both America and Britain were accustomed to an endless stream of exhortation from their respective governments. 'Careless Talk', 'Buy War Bonds', 'Go To It', 'Lend to Defend the Right to be Free' (Britain's National Savings slogan, which inspired many parodies, such as 'Lend to Defend the Right to be Tight'). The most irritating Government campaign featured a cartoon character called Billy Brown of London Town, who gave unwanted advice, ranging from 'I trust you'll pardon my correction – that stuff is there for your protection' (referring to the sticky tape to protect windows of Underground trains which passengers tore off in order to see the names of stations) to 'Coughs and sneezes spread diseases'. These too, put out by a Ministry of Information run largely by men who had never actually met any ordinary people, lent themselves to parody, some of it obscene.

Just as Britain spoke in new initials – ATS, WAAF, WRNS, for the new women's Army, Air Force and Navy services – so America got used to WACs, WAVES, WASPS (not White Anglo-Saxon Protestants, but Women's Air Service Pilots), and Woman Marines, who did *not* like being called Bams (short for 'Broad-Assed Marines').

'Society,' lamented Lucius Beebe, with nothing left to be arbiter of, 'has vanished in the face of a curious order called Second-Lieutenants on whom gentle birth is bestowed by act of Congress.' No matter: there were more democratic amusements. On leave one didn't go to Harlem so much now, because 'mugging', usually by Negro adolescents, had begun: in certain parts of Brooklyn too, so that 'many will not leave their houses after sundown'. For night-life one went to the Wedgwood Room at the Waldorf-Astoria, to hear a funny pianist called Victor Borge, who had arrived in 1941 speaking no English; or to La Martinique, the Village Barn, and of course the Diamond Horseshoe, which, said *Time*, 'follows its lucrative formula of past-tense fun and imperative-mood sex'.

Be careful what you say + where you say it!

CARELESS TALK COSTS LIVES

At the Stage Door Canteen in Manhattan it was calculated that hostesses danced 2,184,000 miles a year. Marlene Dietrich, Ethel Merman and Gertrude Lawrence went there to dance with soldiers and feed them doughnuts and coffee; Eleanor Roosevelt visited the Canteen, and Irving Berlin left his heart there. It was all organized by the United Services Organization (U.S.O.), whose British counterpart, the NAAFI, never offered anything so good.

If, in Britain, there was a social revolution going on that equalized the risk to all classes, there were two horrible examples of it – one in the West End, the other in the East End. The word panic was never used during the War, but nobody is expected to behave with exemplary coolness in the immediate vicinity of an exploding bomb. The Café de Paris, in London's Coventry Street, was deep under the Rialto Cinema and therefore thought to be safe. You couldn't hear an air-raid in progress at ground level, and anyway, on 8 March 1941, there hadn't been a serious one for six weeks. Young officers and their wives or girls in long dresses came to dance to Ken 'Snake Hips' Johnson's Caribbean band. Because the War was going badly, because many of the officers present were on embarkation leave and would be abroad next week, the Café was full. So was the '400', so was Quaglino's, but they weren't so 'safe'.

Survivors of a direct hit nearly all say that they felt and heard nothing at the moment of impact. No bang: just a low moaning and whimpering: screams came later. One felt something wet, and it was blood: pain came later. A waiter is leaning over your shoulder pouring wine: a split second later the glass is still there but the waiter isn't. Two bombs fell through the Rialto Cinema and into the Café de Paris. The first killed Ken Johnson, another musician, and thirty-two other people, and wounded sixty more. The second was a dud, but burst open and covered everything with yellow high explosive. One or two lights were still burning, and a man using his cigarette-lighter as a torch was quickly shouted down, with so much HE lying around. Some Canadian nurses helped several doctors who were among the guests. Ambulances arrived from Charing Cross Hospital. Table cloths and napkins were ripped into bandages.

A Mrs Blair-Hickman, regaining consciousness, felt someone taking a ring off her finger. There were two men, pretending to help, who were stealing rings and going through handbags. They were members of a gang which, using telephone scouts in the Blitz, were able to be on the spot immediately wherever there would be rich pickings for looters.

Not all the survivors went home. Some, in a kind of fury, went on to a nightclub called the Suivi where girls were seen, in the small hours of the morning after, dancing with blood on their dresses.

Even deeper than the Café de Paris was an uncompleted extension of the central London tube railway from Liverpool Street to Bethnal Green. Here, too, were criminals who deliberately caused false alarms and picked pockets as people rushed for shelter. Nearby, in Victoria Park, the Army was using rocket launchers, which made a whining noise like falling bombs: they were still a secret weapon which had not been explained to the public. Hearing them at about 8.30 p.m. on 3 March 1943, families rushed below. A woman carrying a baby tripped at the bottom of some stairs; the crowd behind, unable to stop, fell on top of her, ten deep, suffocating each other; 173 people died. The death-roll was reported in the press; but that it had been caused solely by panic was not known until after the War.

The invasion which began in Northern Ireland on Monday, 26 January 1942, did not cause panic; indeed it was (most of the time) peaceful. A certain Private First Class Milburn Henke, from Hutchinson, Minnesota, found himself the focus of an elaborate public relations exercise: he was greeted, as he left his troopship, by the Duke of Abercorn (representing the King), a general, an admiral, an air vice-marshal, the chief of police, and the Secretary of State for Air. For Private Henke was thought to be the first American soldier on British soil, the first of millions who were going to drive through to Berlin and Rome. (In fact, a whole battalion had arrived already and were on their way to camp.) Twenty thousand a week arrived in the *Queen Mary* and *Queen Elizabeth*. Back home in Hutchinson, Henke's girlfriend was made president of the 'Always in My Heart Club', a nationwide league of girls who had promised to be faithful to G.I.s overseas.

Never in history had two nations, speaking the same language, discovered how ignorant they were of each other's way of life. From now on the *Daily Express* flew the Stars and Stripes on its roof every 4th of July, and urged the rest of the country to do the same; and for the first time a smattering of American history was taught in British schools. Britain had somehow got used to her European allies: the Free French, Poles, Dutch, Czechoslovakians and the polyglot personnel of the Pioneer Corps. Many Poles, in their pretty uniforms with hats like mortar boards, were stationed in Scotland, and their overwhelming gallantry accounts for the large number of Polish-named families there today. British girls whose menfolk were abroad or otherwise not around were accused of Yank-bashing or Pole-bashing as the case might be.

MINISTRY OF HEALTH SAYS–
COUGHS AND SNEEZES SPREAD DISEASES–
RICE PUDDING
PRUNES
CUSTARD
H.M. BATEMAN
trap the germs in your handkerchief
HELP TO KEEP THE NATION FIGHTING FIT

British and American troops were given little booklets about each other. It was explained to the British that *bum* meant nothing physical, that *rubber* meant contraceptive, that you must never say to an American 'he was my *fag* at school', that *fiddling* (irregularly obtaining some advantage by bending or evading regulations) meant something quite different in America. A notable omission was SNAFU – 'situation normal, all f----d up,' which was learned by word of mouth. Americans were told things like: 'If British civilians look dowdy and badly dressed, it is not because they do not like good clothes. . . . All clothing is rationed. . . . Don't make fun of British speech. You sound just as funny to them.' G.I.s learned 'you've had it', 'browned off', 'pukka gen'; Tommies learned that 'funny money' meant sterling, that 'holy Joe' meant an Army chaplain, that 'Kilroy was here' chalked on a latrine wall meant nothing in particular (though Air Force Sergeant Francis J. Kilroy claims to be the original). It was considered safer never to refer to Dunkirk or Pearl Harbor. What nobody was told was how many Americans were already in Britain even before Pearl Harbor, as volunteers – Marines in Ulster, others in the Canadian Army, three in the Royal Navy, and eighty-four pilots in an all-American R.A.F. unit known as the Eagle Squadron.

In a matter of weeks the Americans took over the West End of London. 'Oversexed, overpaid, over here?' Overpaid, certainly, by British standards – an American private got five times as much as a British private, and an American sergeant got more than a British captain. (The Canadians managed things better: they arranged that their troops drew only part of their pay and saved the rest.) Rainbow Corner, a converted Lyons restaurant at the corner of Shaftesbury Avenue and Windmill Street, was the biggest G.I. club, where Hollywood stars appeared between air raids; it was also reputed to be a focal point of prostitution.

By and large the Americans were well-liked, once you had got used to things like gum-parking in curious places. With gum, as with C-rations, fruit, Luckies, Hershey bars and other luxuries from the cornucopia of the PX, they were generous, especially to hungry children who shouted 'Any gum, chum?' whenever they saw a G.I. In another context, these things were known as 'shack-up material'.

To the British, Franklin Roosevelt was a demigod.

Rainbow Corner, 1944

He was Churchill's friend, his face and voice and smile and confidence added up to a personality they could understand better than any other President they had ever known. They had welcomed his third term with relief. They had welcomed his wife to London around El Alamein time, when bells rang and the Eighth Army was believed to be unstoppable; possibly for the wrong reason ('Roosevelt must think

there won't be any more raids, or he wouldn't have let her come'), but in all sincerity. 'Motherly' was the word for her; and columnists noted that her greatest oath was 'Oh, spinach!'

On the evening of 12 April 1945, I sat playing 'I've got you under my skin' at the battered grand piano in the foyer of Shepheard's Hotel, Cairo. The manager rushed up: 'No music tonight, Captain, please! President Roosevelt is dead.' I walked over to some American pilots who were listening: 'I'm so sorry, I had no idea –'.

'That's O.K., Bud,' one of them said. 'Sure, Roosevelt was a great American; but there are thousands of great Americans dying every day in the Pacific. You just go right on playing.' A Republican? No matter: I drank up and left.

'Like someone in your own family dying. You can't believe it.' Weeping Negroes lined the railroad as Roosevelt's funeral train made its way from Warm Springs, Georgia. In London people seemed stupefied: somebody was heard saying, 'We could almost have spared Churchill better.'

Summing up, A.J.P. Taylor says it was a good war – for Britain; because they had set out to smash National Socialism and they had succeeded; they had lost an empire but gained a welfare state. Was it a good war for America? There are still Americans who believe they could have kept out of it. It was certainly a war of reluctant heroes. The nearest approach to Rupert Brooke, as undisillusioned romantic, or to T.E. Lawrence as a mystic, was Richard Hillary, a young, blond pilot – the word 'handsome' will not do, it has to be 'beautiful' – who had been a sort of anarchist at Oxford and had joined the R.A.F. in a spirit of irresponsibility. The deaths of his friends in the service gave him the kind of religion in which God is never mentioned: he must fight, and he must write. He knew, and his friends somehow knew, he was going to die (it was a common experience this intuition that someone you were talking to was going to die, that this was the last time you would see him). In the Battle of Britain he was horribly burned, the beautiful face mutilated. His book *The Last Enemy* (called *Falling Through Space* in America) seemed a kind of credo: Eric Linklater wrote an essay on him, Arthur Koestler discussed him in *The Yogi and the Commissar*. Just before he was finally killed, aged twenty-three, on a training flight in 1943, he was in a London air-raid. He pulled a bloodstreaked woman clinging to a dead child from under the rubble of a bombed house: she looked at his face, put together again by MacIndoe, the plastic surgeon, and said: 'Thank you, sir. I see they got you too.'

Yes, there were V.C.s and Congressional Medals, Purple Hearts and D.F.C.s, as if courage were a special thing for men in uniform. There was competitive courage, like that of Major Richard Bong, U.S.A.A.F., who brought down twenty-seven enemy planes, and Francis Gabreski who brought down twenty-eight, so Bong brought down three more just to beat him. But Captain Joe Foss, of the U.S. Marines, was admired for the opposite of this: he brought down twenty-six Japanese planes, and then stopped: why should he deprive Eddie Rickenbacker

Lieutenant Audie Murphy

of his First World War record? There was the courage of overcoming fear, like the green young infantryman about to cross the Rhine. An officer fell into step with him, and he realized it was Eisenhower. 'How are you feeling, son?' 'Awful nervous, General. I don't feel good at all.' Patton might have slapped the soldier's face, but not Ike. 'I'm nervous, too,' he said. 'Maybe if we walk along together to the river we'll be good for each other.'

To Lieutenant Audie Murphy, an orphan from Farmersville, Texas, the U.S. Army had been 'father, mother and brother'. In an exposed position, he directed artillery fire by telephone after ordering his company to take cover; then climbed on a burning tank destroyer which was about to explode, and machine-gunned hordes of enemy, some of them only about ten yards away, killing about fifty; then, despite a leg wound, somehow organized a counter-attack. He published a book, went to Hollywood, acted in John Huston's *The Red Badge of Courage*, married and divorced an actress, and eventually gave his twenty-five medals away to children.

There were off-beat heroes not found in any previous war, like Wild Jack Howard, 20th Earl of Suffolk, eccentric and scientist, a kind of mad Francis Chichester, who, after a career of successful bomb disposal at his 10,000-acre Suffolk estate, with a team of ten men and a girl, finally tackled one known in his workshop as Old Faithful, because it was assumed to be a dud. Windows a quarter of a mile away were shattered as it blew up, killing him and eight of his staff. All that was left of him was a sliver of flesh seven inches long. For this he was given a posthumous George Cross.

Would the V1 and V2 casualties have been worse if it had not been for Eddie Chapman? An expert safe-blower, with fourteen years of jail sentences behind him, he came out of prison in Jersey, Channel Isles, then under German occupation in 1941, and, posing as a man with a permanent grievance against Britain, volunteered to spy for Germany in England. Parachuted into Cambridgeshire with the mission of blowing up the De Havilland aircraft factory, he conspired with British Intelligence to give the Germans the impression that the plan had gone off perfectly. Awarded the Iron Cross, he was sent again to England to report on D-Day and the effect of V-weapons. Again he sent back false information, while furnishing the British with information which, he claimed, enabled them to detonate V2s in the air. And the chief instructor at the Middle East school of street-fighting had been a cat-burglar in civilian life. So war absorbs all talents.

But we were speaking of courage. There was a phenomenon in Britain called 'camping it up', prevalent among Guards officers. Displays of courage were vulgar. You met a chap on leave at the Berkeley. 'What are you doing here?' – 'Oh, I just looked in for a manicure after a battle. My dear, I couldn't have been more frightened.' – 'What have you done to your leg?' – 'Fell down the steps to the loo at Claridges.' And, to describe Dunkirk, borrowing a phrase from the First World War, 'Ugh! – the *noise* – and the *people*!'

This was a war in which nobody was shot for cowardice, and anyone behaving strangely was sent to the psychiatrist, who was so respected in the War Office that he was often a Brigadier. True, there was something in the R.A.F. called LMF ('lack of moral fibre') which sometimes cast a slur on an airman who had simply been sent on too many missions and knew he was going to crack on the next.

Richard Hillary was public school, Oxbridge, classicist, oarsman, idealist, middle class, all these unfashionable things. Lovat Dickson, his biographer, wrote that 'what that noble and tragic figure in *The Last Enemy* symbolizes is the best that boyhood and manhood can be'. Are there still, in the English-speaking world, young men like this? In July 1939 he had written to Anne Mackenzie, the girl he was in love with: 'Sometimes now I wish there would be a war – as I feel then that so many things would clarify themselves . . . and there would be no false values and muddled thinking. Life would have a purpose while it lasted.' And again: 'In a fighter plane, I believe, we have found a way to return to war as it ought to be, war which is individual combat between two people, in which one either kills or is killed. . . . Either I shall get killed or I shall get a few pleasant putty medals and enjoy being stared at in a night club.'

He was arguing with a pacifist when he said this. You could say the whole argument was a refusal to think, an evasion of responsibility, a kind of nihilism. But it was said and felt by a young man who loved life. Rupert Brooke would have understood. So would a veteran French pilot and mystic, Antoine de St Exupéry, who disappeared on a reconnaissance mission in North Africa in 1944: 'The dark sense of duty,' he had once written, 'greater than that of love.' Hillary's book was translated into every European language, and it was greatly admired in post-war Germany.

CHAPTER 4

The King Won't Go

February 1942; snowing. I, Local-Acting-Unpaid Lance-Corporal Jenkins, not to be commissioned for another eighteen months, am billeted on a grocer's wife named Mrs Ginger, in the village of Nutfield, Surrey. Six of us sleep on straw palliasses in her front bedroom. Our divisional H.Q. is Sir Robert Mac-Alpine's ugly turreted mansion. The Division has just been inspected by the King, and that means for sure that they are going to send us abroad. We are dismissed; the King is entertained at the Officers' Mess. I walk alone through the empty village in search of a cup of tea. Suddenly I am aware of a silent black Daimler coming towards me, bearing the Royal Standard. A man in a general's uniform leans out, faintly smiling, and salutes me. It is, of course, the King. He does not seem to have any escort. Taken by surprise, I sloppily return his salute. I turn and stare after the retreating car. *He* saluted *me*; me, scruffy, cold, frightened soldier, who in the face of foreign service had five minutes ago been wondering whether I had the courage to desert. I, who fashionably hated the Establishment, now confused with emotion. I had for the first time experienced the mystique of Royalty. *He* saluted *me*.

There had been nothing particularly inspiring about George VI's first speech of the War, at 6 p.m. on 3 September 1939. 'For the sake of all that we ourselves hold dear, and the world's order and peace, it is unthinkable that we should refuse to meet the challenge. . . .' It was in fact quite thinkable, and large numbers of people were thinking it. Then a Churchillian bit: 'To this high purpose, I now call my people at home and my people across the seas.' On New Year's Eve, however, he did something unprecedented. Straining himself to control his stutter, he quoted a poem which nobody knew: 'I said to the man who stood at the gate of the Year, "Give me a light that I may tread safely into the unknown." And

he replied, "Go out into the darkness and put thine hand into the hand of God. That shall be to thee better than light and safer than a known way." ' Was it his own idea? Sir Alan Lascelles'? The Queen's? Was it from the Bible? Celebrities were interviewed: John Masefield, the Poet Laureate, thought it sounded like Chesterton. The King, or someone at Buckingham Palace, had cut it out of a letter to *The Times* just after war had been declared. It had been written in 1908 by a Miss Minnie Haskins to raise funds for a mission. Miss Haskins, now sixty-four, was a retired university lecturer, who seemed bewildered by all the fuss. She did not remember having written it, she had neither seen *The Times* nor heard the King's speech. The poem was reprinted and sold more than forty-two thousand copies; Miss Haskins was invited to contribute a weekly poem to a Sunday newspaper, and before long found herself in *Who's Who*.

As the Battle of Britain approached, and France fell, George VI shared with his subjects the irrational elation of facing Germany and Italy alone; and just as a news vendor in Fleet Street was heard to say, after Dunkirk, 'We've got 'Itler by the froat!', so the King mildly observed in a letter to his mother, 'I feel happier now that we have no Allies to be polite to.'

Well, he had King Haakon of Norway, head of the Free Norwegians in Britain, who knew all about invasion, and thought the Palace air-raid shelter (a housemaids' sitting room in the basement strengthened with timber joists) quite inadequate. He had Queen Wilhelmina of Holland, who did not follow her daughter Juliana and her grandchildren to Canada, but arrived literally on the doorstep of Buckingham Palace on 13 May 1940, as the Germans rolled through Holland. She was afterwards installed in a house at Gerrards Cross, Buckinghamshire. Her son-in-law, Prince Bernhard, served with the R.A.F.

The King and Queen chatting to workmen demolishing buildings after an air raid in London's West End, September 1940

Four houses in different parts of the country had been prepared for the Royal Family in case of invasion (the most likely was Croome Court in Worcestershire), and they would have been taken there by a bodyguard commanded by Colonel J.S. Coats. Crates of provisions had already been sent on ahead. There were rumours that other retreats, in Canada and the Bahamas, of which the Duke of Windsor became Governor in 1940, had been arranged. But the wisdom of a sound royal instinct prevailed. Evacuation, possibly; but not flight. There had been an attempt, eventually stopped by the Government, by rich people – there were said to be eleven thousand of them – to send their wives and families out of the country. The King and Queen, who both practised revolver and rifle shooting in the grounds of Buckingham Palace (to the peril of Lord Halifax, who as Foreign Secretary, had the privilege of walking through them), refused to have any part of this, and

would certainly have died fighting. Asked whether the two young Princesses should not be sent to the safety of Canada, Queen Elizabeth said: 'The children can't go without me. I can't leave the King, and the King won't go.'

The King, irritated because he had never since the Phoney War been allowed to mingle with his troops in the front line (as his brother David had done, as Prince of Wales in World War I), hearing that Churchill intended to land in France with the invasion troops, demanded that he should go too. Which of them overruled the other is uncertain, but in the end neither of them went.

This was perhaps a pity, for George VI badly wanted to expose himself to danger, and to be seen doing so: it would not have been the first time, for he had served in the Royal Navy as a sub-lieutenant at the battle of Jutland in 1916. However, the Royal Family had danger enough at home. The Queen, since a queen must be a queen ('Ain't she bloody lovely!'), continued to wear dresses of lilac and pink, even when visiting bombed areas immediately after raids. There were stories of her rescuing a dog from the rubble; holding a baby while the distraught mother, whose home had been destroyed, tried to dress it; and drinking endless cups of strong tea out of chipped mugs in canteens. And when, in September 1941, the Luftwaffe made a determined effort to score a direct hit on the Palace and succeeded in placing a stick of bombs right in the forecourt, just missing the main building, but destroying the Chapel: 'Now at last,' she said, 'I can look the East End in the face!'

The question of whether the King should be allowed to fly over enemy territory to visit his forces arose continually. His brother the Duke of Kent was killed in an R.A.F. bomber crash in Scotland (but not by enemy action). The death of Leslie Howard, in a neutral passenger aircraft over the sea in June 1943, had shown that no unescorted plane was safe. When, therefore, the King a week later wanted to see his victorious armies in North Africa, he was flown out in Churchill's luxurious York transport plane under the name of 'General Lyon'.

At last he momentarily had the illusion of being with his troops; but what of that other army, the millions of factory workers who supplied them? If he could not take a job in an aircraft factory, he could at least find out how it felt. So, two nights a week, at 6 p.m., he put on overalls and worked at a bench for three hours making parts for R.A.F. guns.

It seems probable that the Royal Family shared the wartime discomforts of their people, not least because of the lack of central heating in Buckingham Palace and other royal residences. Visiting them in October 1942, Eleanor Roosevelt found the King and Queen sniffling with heavy colds, wearing old clothes for warmth; noted the bomb fragments that had shattered the single glazing of the windows and lodged in the King's wardrobe; and wrote in her diary – 'We were served on gold and silver plates, but our bread was the same kind of war bread every other family had to eat. Except for game that occasionally appeared, nothing was served that was not served in any war canteen.' She also observed that the royal servants wore, not scarlet livery, but blue battle-dresses designed by the King: one page had resigned in protest.

Princess Elizabeth celebrated her seventeenth birthday with a dance at Windsor Castle to which young British and American army officers were invited. Those who were there remember the occasion as rather stiff, with question-and-answer conversations. The Princess had met very few young men who were not her cousins; had been educated largely by her governess Marion Crawford (Crawfie) and by Mr C.H.K. Marten of Eton, whose history textbooks were to be found in every school library; and, although she had broadcast, in a tense little voice, to evacuated children in 1940, she had never actually (in her Uncle David's phrase) 'met the people'. She made her first solo public appearance, at a meeting of the Governors of the Queen Elizabeth Hospital for Children, in the summer of 1944. At Christmas there was a Royal Pantomime in the Waterloo Chamber of Windsor Castle, *Old Mother Red Riding Boots*, 'devised by Princess Elizabeth, Princess Margaret and Hubert Tannar', at which music was provided by the Salon Orchestra of the Royal Horse Guards.

Her first brush with parental authority seems to have been early in 1945, when, against their wishes, she insisted on training as a driver in the Auxiliary Territorial Service. The end of the war in Europe curtailed her army career, and the next stage was her coming-of-age. The Royal Family's public relations were then less fluent than they are today, and to get any information from the Palace one had to go through Captain L.A. Ritchie, R.N. (retd.), who wrote thrilling sea stories under the pseudonym 'Bartimeus'. His press handouts, which bore the marks of much interference from other hands, were short on interesting facts, and said a great deal about the Princess's wholesome character. The Royal children were fond of picnics, pantomimes and charades. The only anecdote was about her childhood: asked what she wanted to be when she grew up, she had replied: 'A horse.' Her escorts at this time were eminently suitable: the Duke of Rutland and the Earl of Euston, both educated at Eton and Cambridge and both officers in the Grenadier Guards, of which she herself was Colonel.

As early as January 1941 Sir Henry (Chips) Channon had met young Prince Philip of Greece in Athens and gossipped into his diary: 'He is to be our Prince Consort.' If so much were preordained, appearances of a genuine royal romance were remarkably convincing. Christmas cards had been exchanged since 1940; Philip had been a guest at Royal Lodge, where the Princesses had lived for most of the war, on Christmas Eve 1943: his photograph was on her mantlepiece; the King had written to Queen Mary: 'We both think she is too young – she has never met any young men of her own age.' King George of Greece seemed to think it a good idea. Prince Philip, serving in H.M.S. *Whelp* in the Pacific just after the War, was away long enough for hearts to be looked into. Besides, there was Philip's constitutional position about the Greek throne to be cleared up: he could not be both King of Greece and Consort to the Queen of England – or could he? It was a fascinating idea to play with.

In February 1947 the entire Royal Family sailed in the *Vanguard* to South Africa. It was known that the Nationalist Party wished ultimately to secede from the British Commonwealth, but General Smuts thought that this might be counteracted by a royal visit. It was a crowded, rather boring tour, much of it in a special gilt-edged White Train of fourteen coaches, nearly 600 yards long, enlivened by the sight of Victoria Falls, a vast rally of mounted Basutos, a 'salute of hooded cobras' arranged by a snake charmer at Port Elizabeth, and a visit to Cecil Rhodes's grave.

At home in Britain frozen sheep and cattle were dying in the snow, in the coldest winter for fifty-three years, and the country's power and fuel installations failed. The King cabled to Prime Minister Attlee, asking whether the Royal Family should return: there had been a few nasty comments in the press about the luxury of the Royal Tour in the sunshine of South Africa. Attlee replied: no, it would only make people think things were even worse than they were.

The engagement of Elizabeth and Philip was announced seven weeks after their return in May, and the wedding was fixed for 20 November. Prince Philip, confusingly, became naturalized as Lieutenant Philip Mountbatten, and on the eve of his wedding became also Duke of Edinburgh with an earldom and a barony as well; so that for some time nobody was certain what to call him.

For a description of the wedding let us turn to the American press. Mrs Cobina Wright, described as 'Noted American Society Woman and Authoress' in the normally anti-British *Journal-American*, said she was 'breathless' with wonder, and went on describing the wedding for days. As 'a personal guest of the bridegroom', she had a good seat in Westminster Abbey, which, although the wedding was 'like any well-arranged ceremony in an American small town', was 'more imposing than cathedrals along Main Street'. She 'really felt a lump in her throat' when she 'noticed Queen Mary putting her handkerchief to her eyes'. She saw a bust in the Abbey of Henry Wadsworth Longfellow – 'it gave me a thrill to realize this American poet is enshrined in this hallowed spot.'

At a Buckingham Palace reception before the wedding Mrs Wright was so 'overwhelmed by the size and beauty of the jewels worn' that she almost forgot to notice the dresses; nevertheless, she noted that the Queen wore 'oyster-white satin with a very bouffant skirt with paillettes', and Miss Sharman Douglas, daughter of the American Ambassador, wore 'deep green velvet with an off-shoulder neckline and a bouffant skirt'. The New Look had obviously struck the Palace hard. It was understood that Princess Elizabeth was entitled to a hundred clothing coupons, her bridesmaids twenty-three each and the pages ten.

Miss Nancy Randolph of the New York *Daily News* reported that the bridal bed had pink silk crêpe-de-chine sheets and pillow-cases appliquéd with satin leaves; and that a Scotland Yard detective would be sleeping in an attic immediately above. On both sides of the Atlantic other couples who were getting married on the same day were interviewed. By this time the royal couple were being referred to as Liz and Phil. It was noted that in Britain there were brides who did not have enough coupons for a wedding dress. The New York *Daily Worker* pushed the story back to page 3, reserving page 1 for the people who really mattered: '18 Couples Wed Quietly at City Hall: Non-Royal Lovers United in Simple Rites.' And in Westminster Abbey a little page-boy was world news for a day when he tripped over Princess Elizabeth's train.

Six reigning monarchs, and an assortment of Royalty and ex-Royalty, were present. Somehow it cheered the hungry British up, and seems to have had an illogical public relations effect too, for one of the American guests said afterwards: 'A country which can throw such a party as that will never go under.'

To his daughter on her honeymoon the King wrote: 'I was so proud of you and thrilled at having

you so close to me on our long walk in Westminster Abbey, but when I handed your hand to the Archbishop I felt that I had lost something very precious. . . . Our family, us four, the "Royal Family" must remain together, with additions, of course, at suitable moments!! I have watched you grow up all these years with pride under the skilful direction of Mummy, who as you know is the most marvellous person in the World in my eyes. . . .'

The fourth member of 'us four', who now dropped the 'Rose' and was known simply as Princess Margaret, began to strike out in a direction of her own. When the possibility of the throne is so remote, there is no need to be quite so Royal. Fifteen when the war ended, she was quick to claim independence and friends of her own: the 'Princess Margaret set' reflected her own enthusiasms – for popular music (Ian Stewart, leader of one of the Savoy Hotel bands, gave her jazz piano lessons), for show business (Danny Kaye was a frequent guest), for Americans generally. Was there a touch of Uncle David in her? Her best friend was twenty-year-old Sharman Douglas, daughter of Ambassador Lewis Douglas, whose one eye was a tribute to his love of trout-fishing (the other had been hooked while casting on the bank of the Kennet). Her older friend and instructor in artistic matters was Judy Montagu. She was seen about a lot with 'Sonny', Marquis of Blandford, son of the Duke of Marlborough, who was four years older; but in 1948 it seemed, to judge from nightclub gossip, that Sonny was more often escorting Sharman. Would there be another Anglo-American marriage, like Kathleen Kennedy and the Marquess of Hartington? No, there would not.

With a mixture of raised eyebrows and envy, newspaper readers noted that Princess Margaret, only eighteen, frequently 'came home with the milk' – letters to the Editor asked whether this wasn't a bad example, undermining parental authority and all that? The Princess Margaret set drank pink champagne, which irrespective of vintage, began to outsell the conventional golden stuff. The Palace press handouts began to unbend a little: two more anecdotes – she had sometimes put tapioca in her sister's bath and salt in her tea; and, aged six, hearing of her uncle's abdication, had asked: 'Are they going to cut off his head?'

To offset the delicious frivolity, Princess Margaret was frequently to be seen watching the processes of democracy in the House of Commons, where, from the narrow gallery reserved for Mrs Clifton-Brown ('Mrs Speaker') and her friends, she had a back view of the Government (Labour) and a front view of the Opposition (Tory). She also visited Scotland Yard, East London Juvenile Court and Battersea Power Station.

For a long time Princess Margaret had wanted a holiday abroad by herself. In 1949 a 'tour of emancipation' in France and Italy was arranged for her, taking in Naples, Capri, Rome, Florence, Venice and Paris. In Rome she had an audience with the Pope and attended the International Horse Show. To her dismay she found that she was on a Royal Tour with full entourage. She was already beginning her long hate-affair with press photographers. She must not dance the rumba in Paris nightclubs because hip-waving was undignified. In Paris she called on three couturiers, Jean Dessès (recommended by her knowledgeable Aunt Marina), Dior and Molyneux. To a dancing partner she was reported as saying: 'Look into my eyes – they're the most beautiful eyes in England – surely you believe what you read in the papers?' In Italy she delighted people by not leaving a Florence nightclub until dawn; and it was felt uneasily at the Palace that Margaret in Italy was outshining her big sister at home. The Princess Margaret set were said to talk to each other in 'clang-slang' – 'Abyssinia' for 'I'll be seeing you', and 'in a while, crocodile' as the inevitable reply to 'See you later, alligator.'

Her cousin, Lord Harewood, described as 'the first cultured musician of Royal blood for over a century', was music critic of the *New Statesman*, editor of *Opera*, friend of Benjamin Britten and patron of the new, extremely fashionable Aldeburgh Festival in Suffolk. It was learned with pleasure that he planned to marry Miss Marion Stein, a Viennese pianist.

It was not considered necessary for the Home Secretary, Mr Chuter Ede, to be present at the birth of Princess Elizabeth's first child on 14 November 1948, there being no longer any serious fear of a substitute being conveyed to the Palace in a warming pan (or bed pan, as we used to say at school). Inexplicably, the birth was at first announced in America as 'a girl baby'. No name was given. Long-range cameras trained on the grounds of Buckingham

(*opposite*) **Princess Margaret dancing with Billy Wallace at a 'Thank-you-Nurse' Ball in December 1948**

The Royal Family after the christening of Charles Philip Arthur George, 15 December 1948

Palace registered no appearance of a pram. Was there something wrong with the child? Not until his christening a month later was his name announced: Charles Philip Arthur George. 'Now,' Princess Margaret said, 'I'm Charley's Aunt.' The christening took place in a silver-gilt lily font made for Queen Victoria's first child, in the white-and-gold Music Room. Offical photographs were taken by Baron (who had an assistant named Armstrong-Jones) and Beaton. Later in the day Prince Charles was shown to the press at whom he bawled suitably until given a Georgian silver rattle. His nursery at the Palace was simply the Princesses' old schoolroom with desks moved out and a cot moved in. On 5 January he made his first public appearance as he was driven by his father to Sandringham. A strait between Elephant and Cornwallis Islands in the Antarctic was named after him. On 4 March he was inspected by his grandfather's Privy Councillors. In May he was photographed again, this time in the act of grabbing his mother's pearl necklace. His nurse at the Palace had been Miss Rowe, and at his parents' house, Windlesham Moor, near Ascot, Miss Lightbody.

Queen Mary, plagued with sciatica, now spent a good deal of time in her wheel chair at Marlborough House. Her old chef Tschumi, who had left her in 1932, was back again, frustrated by national austerity and the old lady's penny-watching economy. 'It is a great bore getting old,' she said on her eightieth birthday in May 1947. She had spent the War at Badminton House as the guest of a rather embarrassed Duke of Beaufort, whose wife was her niece. To accommodate her and her fifty-five servants, the Beauforts had to squeeze into two bedrooms and a sitting-room. Queen Mary, who neither rode nor cared for dogs and knew nothing about farming, seemed perplexed by life in the country where she remained for six years. 'So *that's* what hay looks like!' she exclaimed in wonder. She, who knew so little about ordinary people, was able to observe evacuees from Birmingham. During the Phoney War she popped up to London every week by the 8.28 a.m. train from Chippenham. But when the bombs began to fall, she had to stay at Badminton. She had a company of soldiers to defend her in case of invasion, and four despatch riders for her personal use.

How was she to occupy her time? She would 'improve' the Duke of Beaufort's estate. She set the Badminton staff to work tearing down ivy from trees. She had more trees lopped, and others cut down: she wanted to cut down an ancient oak outside the drawing-room window 'because it excluded light', but the Duke objected because Lord Raglan (of the Crimean War) had played in it as a boy. Hearing that there was a salvage campaign, and imagining that any equipment left out in all weathers was useless, she sometimes deprived farmers of their field harrows. She was allowed to inspect an unexploded bomb. She took to wearing the Gloucestershire Regiment badge in her hat. She went to Windsor for the christening of Prince Michael of Kent and the confirmation of Princess Elizabeth. After her son the Duke of Kent was killed, she spent more time with Princess Marina and her children. Like everyone else she ate Woolton Pie for lunch, and saved little bits of soap. Although scrupulous about petrol rationing, which prevented many a trip to the antique shops in Bath, she now travelled mostly by car, and frequently gave lifts to soldiers and airmen, questioning them closely: she was especially pleased to meet an American parachutist and an R.A.F. observer who had been in the disastrous Dieppe raid. She knitted a great deal, and never failed to listen to the B.B.C. 9 o'clock news, and to Hitler's speeches, which she criticized for his 'abominable German'.

And when victory came, she wept to leave Badminton: 'Now I shall have to be Queen Mary all over again!' She busied herself redecorating Marlborough House; and she had the Duke of Windsor to stay (without Wallis).

The outbreak of war had found the Windsors at Château La Croë, Cap d'Antibes. They motored overland to Cherbourg where they were collected by Lord Louis Mountbatten in H.M.S. *Kelly* and conveyed to Portsmouth. The King received his brother briefly on 14 September: they had been on distant terms ever since the refusal to address Wallis as 'Her Royal Highness'. The Duke was offered the choice of two war jobs, Deputy Regional Commissioner in Wales, or Liaison Officer with the British Military Mission to General Gamelin. He chose the former; the offer was dropped, and instead he was told to report to the British Military Mission at Vincennes. The Duchess wanted to give La Croë to the Army as a convalescent home for British officers. There was some difficulty about the Duke's rank: as ex-King he was a Field Marshal, but the job he was offered carried only the rank of Major General. He is said to have written one or two useful reports, and (according to his faithful A.D.C., Major 'Fruity' Metcalfe) to have warmed up the French with talk and laughter at what might otherwise have been sticky luncheon parties. He was never allowed to exercise his gift for 'talking to the men'.

As the Germans advanced on Paris, the Windsors with difficulty made their way into Spain. There was thought to be some danger either of his being kidnapped in Spain by the Germans or otherwise persuaded to be the puppet ruler of a conquered Britain. He was offered, and finally accepted, the Governorship of the Bahamas.

On arrival in Nassau he found Government House uninhabitable and was with difficulty dissuaded from spending the rest of the summer at his ranch in Canada while it was being refurbished. Having at last settled down, he seemed to make the best of it: the Duchess, thought extravagant in many American press reports, seemed to regard Nassau as a place of exile. 'Their presence,' says Frances Donaldson, 'gave an enormous fillip to the tourist trade on which the island economy depended.' The Duke chaired an Economic Committee and founded an Infant Welfare Clinic. The Duchess was local President of the Red Cross and ran a canteen for American soldiers and sailors. The Duke sometimes gave offence by refusing to attend events such as concerts and art exhibitions. He quarrelled with powerful people. He seemed not to understand race relations. He intervened in the notorious Harry Oakes murder trial, calling in a police officer from Miami whose investigation was unsatisfactory. And yet, the general verdict of both Americans and British who saw them during this time was that the Windsors did a reasonably good job in the Bahamas.

The Duke's cousin, Earl Mountbatten, did understand race relations, as he understood leadership, discipline, technology – and people. Autocrat he might be; insensitive never. On New Year's Day 1947, in the middle of Britain's most dismal post-war winter, he was sent for by Clement Attlee, Prime Minister of the Labour Government, and invited to replace his friend Field Marshal Lord Wavell as Viceroy of India. He did not want the job, and at once proposed conditions that, he hoped, would frighten Attlee into offering it to someone else. He demanded plenipotentiary powers – a blank cheque to do as he thought fit, at breakneck speed if necessary. 'How can I possibly negotiate,' he said bluntly, 'with the Cabinet constantly breathing down my neck?' Attlee gave way, and in February the Government announced that political power would be transferred to Indian hands by June 1948. In March, Mountbatten flew to Delhi, expecting to be assassinated. Nobody, at that moment, knew whether independent India was going to be a loose federation of states or a partition into Pakistan and Hindustan. Partition, he knew, would never work: he would only allow it if it seemed the only way to avoid bloodshed.

But there was already bloodshed. In the delta of the Ganges and the Brahmaputra, at a village called Srirampur, Mahatma Gandhi, now seventy-seven,

lay sick in body and heart. Non-violence, his lifelong creed, had failed: all around him Hindus and Muslims were killing, raping, looting and burning.

Louis and Edwina Mountbatten behaved as no Vice-regal couple, indeed few British people before them, had ever behaved in India. They did not ride among the Indians: they *walked*, showing themselves, smiling, without guards. The Viceroy *walked* to Nehru's house to visit him. 'We've finally got a human being for a Viceroy,' Nehru said, 'not a stuffed shirt.' Mountbatten was careful to have three *Indian* officers as his A.D.C.s, and to see that British and Indian guests were invited in equal numbers to dinner parties; and Edwina ordered Indian vegetarian dishes for them, with towels and finger bowls so that they could eat without cutlery in their accustomed way: nothing must be allowed to embarrass anyone.

Edwina had had an excellent training for the job. She had led the St John Ambulance Brigade during the War, she had toured Japanese prison camps. She could be moved to compassion, but never to revulsion. She could, say the authors of *Freedom at Midnight,* preside at a banquet in evening dress and tiara, 'and, the following morning, in a simple uniform, walk through the mud . . . to cradle in her lap the head of a child dying of cholera.' She went swimming with Nehru; she greeted Gandhi with a kiss, and offered him her shoulder to lean on.

Perhaps Mountbatten was not quite the ideal Viceroy of Gandhi's imagination, in an ideal India whose life would be based on rice and cows, with no machine other than the spinning wheel: a bungalow-dwelling Viceroy with no servants who grew his own food and cleaned out his own toilet-box; but God, or the King-Emperor, had sent him a man he could love and respect.

On the afternoon of 18 July 1947 in London three Bills received the Royal Assent in the House of Commons: their prosaic order gave no special importance to the last – the South Metropolitan Gas Bill, the Felixstowe Pier Bill, and the Indian Independence Bill. The partition was on. Mountbatten had been asked by both Mr Jinnah, leader of the Muslim league and future governor of Pakistan, and Nehru, who was to be first prime minister of the republic of India, to stay on as Governor-General. The transfer of power would take place on Friday, 15 August. In fixing the date, Mountbatten made a pardonable

(*left*) Lord and Lady Mountbatten with Earl Listowel, Secretary of State for India, 19 May 1947

mistake: he had omitted to consult astrologers, who were unanimous that this day would be disastrous.

It would have been disastrous anyway. Everyone knew there would be trouble, but nobody had guessed how much. How do you organize mass migrations over hundreds of miles so that 6½ million Muslims somehow get to Pakistan from India, and 5½ million non-Muslims get to India from Pakistan? It looked as if Mountbatten had allowed only nine weeks for all this, and reorganizing civil service and armies too. In September Nehru and Patel, his deputy, whose partnership was by no means easy, in desperation asked Mountbatten to take over the running of the country. People were burning their possessions because they could not carry them. In the daily deluge of the monsoon, the only water supply, they crowded on to railway stations, hung on to the roofs and running boards of crammed trains, crushed each other to death, beat off looters. Refugee columns left their dead to the *pai*-dogs and vultures.

Mountbatten, Supremo once again, formed an Emergency Committee of experts to direct railways, radio, aviation, medical services, everything. Security guards on trains were to open fire on attackers, on pain of court martial and death. But how do you organize the saving of life, when the caste system forbids a Brahmin to carry the sick body of an Untouchable? Failing to get help from a driver to load a dead body into a truck, Edwina Mountbatten lifted it herself.

Gandhi made a last effort to exert his mystical power: he would 'fast unto death'. Both Hindus and Muslims, knowing how weak he was, begged him not to. At Birla House, New Delhi, in January 1948, Gandhi asked his woman doctor, Sushila Nayar, to sing him to sleep with 'When I Survey the Wondrous Cross'. She knew, from a urine sample, that he could not stand any more fasting. Outside, demonstrators, for whom the world had moved far beyond non-violence, shouted: 'Let Gandhi die!' The Mountbattens visited him: Edwina wept. Somehow his friends at last persuaded him that peace was possible, and he agreed to take a little orange juice and glucose. His spirit revived: he would visit Pakistan, he could still make India, in spite of partition, a land with equal rights for all. A little goat's milk: he grew stronger: soon he could resume his daily prayer meetings in the garden of Birla House.

In Bombay, a Brahmin named Nathuram Godse, thirty-seven, editor of *Hindu Nation*, a Mahratti daily newspaper in Poona, booked a flight to Delhi. He had once been a follower of Gandhi; but now he belonged to the R.S.S.S., a fascist movement which had already planned to assassinate Jinnah and Mountbatten, and might plot against any leader who advocated partition. He was now convinced that Gandhi had not only failed to prevent the creation of Pakistan, he was actually responsible for it. The R.S.S.S. flag was orange, and bore a swastika, symbol of Aryan superiority. Godse, chaste as a monk, a sufferer from migraine headaches, was said to hate the sight of blood; yet he seldom missed a war or a gangster film, and was addicted to the works of Erle Stanley Gardner. He was reading a Perry Mason story before he slept on the night of 29 January 1948.

He had experimented clumsily with pistols and hand grenades, and on 20 January had managed to let off a bomb at one of the prayer meetings, which Gandhi had dismissed as 'only the Army practising'. Godse and his fellow conspirators were known to the police: he must, he said, get Gandhi before the police got him.

At 5.20 p.m. on 30 January, as Gandhi walked through the garden to the place of prayer, Godse bowed low before him, as if about to kiss his feet, and shot him three times. Mountbatten rushed to Birla House to find Nehru and Patel embracing over Gandhi's body. It was of first importance that the world should know that he had been killed by a Hindu, not a Muslim, otherwise there would be a further bloodbath. Mountbatten wanted to have Gandhi's body embalmed and carried through India on a funeral train; but it was known that Gandhi had wanted to be cremated like any other Hindu. Godse and another conspirator, Apte, were hanged in 1949; five more were jailed. The Mountbattens left India according to plan in June 1948. The great-grandson of Queen Victoria, the first Empress of India, had been the instrument of India's freedom. He returned to the Royal Navy as a mere Rear Admiral. He had never wanted to be Viceroy of India; and he had to wait another seven years for the job he had always wanted – First Sea Lord, with power to give the Navy up-to-date nuclear weapons, about which he is credited with the observation: 'If it works, it's obsolete.'

CHAPTER 5

Soldier From the War Returning

'Enjoy the War,' says an old saw, believed to date back to Germany in 1914–18, 'for the Peace will be terrible.' Reversing Clausewitz, we were to find that politics was the continuance of war by other means. You cannot, I was recently told, write a book about the Forties; they don't exist, they are neatly chopped into five years of war and five of peace. Not so. We learned in the Forties, as Orwell's Newspeak said, that war is peace and peace is war, and there are no such things as opposites. We no longer had any external enemy to hate; so we began to hate a race of people called 'Them', sometimes identified as the Government, which seemed to control everything, to occupy every building that might offer us a home.

To my shipload of returning soldiers, sailors and airmen, as we came down the Southampton gang-plank in thick fog in February 1946, it seemed that we were entering a defeated country. A grey limbo of ruins, rubble, exhausted faces. The smell of corruption, the bribe, something called 'key money', often several hundred pounds, that had to be slipped to an estate agent or a private landlord before one could enter a flat. The rudeness of estate agents, indeed the rudeness of everybody, was noticed by returning veterans in America as in Britain.

Civilians did not seem overly glad to see our sun-burned, well-fed faces. They kept talking about bombs and food; they were not in the least interested

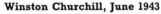

Winston Churchill, June 1943

in what had been happening to us in faraway countries. There were moments when soldiers and civilians stared uncomprehendingly at one another, each seeming to say: 'You don't know anything about war.'

We wandered from one kind of Government office to another, getting ration cards and clothing coupons, meeting a new kind of 'Them', dreadful little men and women, always officious and sometimes venal, known as Temporary Civil Servants. We looked for a room to live in: reading that an atom scientist named Nunn May had been arrested for betraying secrets to Russia, I dashed round to his lodging to try to get his room: I found a queue ahead of me. I went back to my office and found, sitting at my old desk, a man I knew had been a conscientious objector. Well, he had had the courage to say No; I hadn't.

In Britain in May 1945 a mainly Tory caretaker government succeeded the 'National' coalition. Both Labour and Conservative election manifestoes promised social security in different forms. Several explanations have been offered for the overwhelming Labour victory in the July General Election, Aneurin Bevan's 'bloodless revolution'. There was a vague feeling that 'the Tories won't be able to handle the peace', reinforced by memories of the Twenties and Thirties. The dominating fear was of an acute housing shortage; and the Left, promising reconstruction plus nationalization, seemed more likely to get results. Churchill and Beaverbrook alienated many voters by talking about a socialist Gestapo in the making. There was some delay due to the Forces vote (for the first time, ten million servicemen, thousands of miles away, influenced affairs); and there was no doubt which way most of them voted. They voted Labour because, quite irrationally, they thought Labour would get them out of uniform more quickly. The few motorists who had any petrol volunteered to run a 'get you home' service for soldiers, sailors and airmen at railway stations. Withal, demobilization (on the basis of 'first in, first out') took nearly two years to complete.

The worlds which British and American servicemen found on their return had much in common. Both came home to children they had never seen, occasionally fathered by other men. America, less exhausted, with no rubble, was just as mad keen to get the boys out of the forces. The day before Britain's general election, and twelve days before the A-bomb fell on Hiroshima, Senator Wiley (Republican, Wisconsin) made an astonishing speech asking why the Russians didn't enter the Pacific War, or better still, attack the Japanese in Manchuria? Using sentimental .terms such as are only heard in English-speaking democracies, he said: 'In millions of homes, mothers, fathers and sweethearts are waiting anxiously for news of Russia's intentions.' As Herbert Agar observed, 'the Marxian text book . . . has no chapter on innocence.' The Russians, who had killed more Germans per day than all the other Allies put together (though we did not yet know the figures) lost $7\frac{1}{2}$ million military personnel and an estimated thirteen million civilians. They didn't trust anybody, and were still afraid the Allies would make a separate, lenient peace with Germany. Nobody in Russia was ever allowed to make a speech or write an article about 'getting the boys home'.

In the optimism of 1945, with the collapse of Germany and the imminent defeat of Japan, General Eisenhower visited Moscow and came back saying: 'Nothing guides Russian policy so much as a desire for friendship with the United States.' One of Roosevelt's last speeches had hailed 'this new year of

Lord Beaverbrook

1945' which could be 'the greatest year of achievement in human history' which 'must see the substantial beginning of the organization of world peace.' And Harry Hopkins, with Roosevelt at the Yalta Conference, was certain that America and Britain could learn to live with the Russians: 'We really believed in our hearts that this was the dawn of the new day we had all been praying for.'

Only Churchill confessed to 'forebodings'. He knew that the peace would be terrible. Four days after victory over Germany, he sent the famous telegram to Truman: 'What is to happen about Russia? . . . what will be the position in a year or two when we may have a handful of divisions, mostly French, and when Russia may choose to keep two or three hundred on active service? . . . An *iron curtain* is drawn down upon their front. We do not know what is going on behind.' He was to use the phrase again in March 1946 at Fulton, Missouri, in an isolationist setting, when America was reducing her armed forces from eleven million to one million: 'From Stettin in the Baltic to Trieste in the Adriatic, an iron curtain has descended.' Was Churchill trying to get an alliance with America? No matter: others were now in power, prepared to introduce National Service in Britain, but set against standing armies. Demobilization could not be too quick, certainly not for the soldiers. All the talk about war aims meant nothing to men whose first war aim was to go home.

There was a lot of theorizing about 'readjustment'. One had known men in the Army who, separated from their wives for five years, were afraid of impotence. The most mentally scarred soldier I ever met had never recovered from the sight of Belsen. Men who had been in Japanese prison camps were a special case: many of them would be physically ill for years afterwards. We who had suffered so much less felt guilty about them. A medical officer told me that the ones most likely to make out in civilian life were those who had had a balanced diet in childhood, and (much more important) a good education, for they had mental and spiritual resources – men like Laurens van der Post, who had run a prison university in Sumatra.

In Britain the Army Education Corps had provided schools (one of them at the Marquess of Salisbury's Hatfield House) where you could learn a trade, carpentry, accountancy, practically anything to help you get a job in Civvy Street. In America there was the G.I. Bill of Rights, by which the Government would pay at least $500 a year for a college training, with a living allowance ($90 a month if you were married). The principle was 'subsidized self-help'. The government would guarantee 50 per cent of a loan up to $4,000 (£800) provided it was used to buy a home, farm or business. This was the fruit of a 1944 election speech by Roosevelt which had called for an eight-point economic 'bill of rights' entitling everyone to a job, food, clothes, recreation; better conditions for farmers, freedom from unfair competition for businessmen, care for the old, sickness and unemployment benefits. Vague generosity had become practical help.

In Britain there was no codification of benefits into a separate 'bill of rights' for soldiers. Social security was about to go beyond this. The law said unequivocally that a man must be given back his old job. Training for professions and trades was under the care of the Ministry of Labour. Whether you wanted to be a bricklayer or a university professor, the procedure was the same: you had to state your case to a committee and show how your training had been interrupted by the war. If you had been a self-employed businessman who had given up because of the war, you could borrow from the Government to start up again – if they approved of the sort of business you were contemplating.

There were reasons why demobilized troops, on both sides of the Atlantic, sometimes felt betrayed. They had been promised some kind of Utopia, and veterans, accustomed to see immediate results from barked orders, expected it immediately. Look what a godawful mess civilian life was! General Motors on strike, the threat of a nationwide railroad strike, Harry Truman asking Congress for a law which would allow him to draft strikers into the armed forces! Almost everybody was mad at somebody about something. And there were all these G.I.s bringing back wives from Europe. 'G.I. Brides' left Britain in a series of shiploads. Some of them, poor girls, having nothing but the movies to go by, expected swimming pools with everything, found one room in a tenement, and came home on the next boat.

'Two million seven hundred thousand new houses by 1948' was the Truman target. Okay, but where the hell do we live in the meantime? Some ex-soldiers converted old barns into makeshift apartments, others lived in improvised communes (and this may have been the beginning of the Beat Generation). Some cities bought caravans for married couples. There was a government campaign urging people to let rooms to returning servicemen.

This was not easy for Britain to understand. Britain, many of whose cities were in ruins, had the worst housing shortage of any Allied country. As the bombing stopped, people streamed back to the cities from the country, and property prices shot up. If you wanted to do anything to help yourself, you found there was a Government restriction against it. If your house was bomb-damaged, you were not allowed to spend more than £10 on repairs. London was still full of Poles and Czechs and Dutch who had fought with us but had not yet been repatriated; and of Jewish refugees who would never go back. It was easy for the homeless ex-soldier to resent them; and soon Sir Oswald Mosley, out of prison since 1943, would be appealing with his new Union Party to their frustration. Some new enterprises were at pains to point out that they employed no foreigners. In London a bunch of ex-soldiers started and advertised an 'All-British Window Cleaning Co.'

In 1944 an architect named Edric Neel had persuaded a group of building companies to put up money for research into new kinds of structures which would be temporary and quick to assemble. They were eventually known as 'prefabricated houses' or 'prefabs', and the Ministry of Works spent £61 million on them. They were meant to last ten years; but in a housing shortage that became permanent many of them lasted much longer. They were unbeautiful, despite the roses round the door and the homely cabbage patches in front, but, being of concrete and steel, they were tough, and filled bombed sites and wasteland until it could be used for something else. Somehow it took three years to build forty-three thousand of them.

In the summer of 1946 it was possible for a family to find itself 4,000th on the local council's waiting list for a house. Some were ex-servicemen with young children who could not even find lodgings because the landlord had a 'no children' rule. 'Living with in-laws' in unbearable propinquity stretched nerves to breaking point.

Agitators took over, organizing mass meetings in Leicester Square, and 'Vigilantes' went about cities looking for apparently vacant buildings, even if they had 'Sold' notices outside, including blocks marked 'requisitioned', presumably for Government offices in an ever-increasing bureaucracy. An empty Nissen hut at an airport could house two families, so if there was no one looking, you moved in. Landlords might cut off the water, gas, electricity; but in desperation you could use candles and spirit stoves.

This was called 'squatting', a word borrowed from American pioneers of the early 1800s; and the climax was reached in the 'Great Sunday Squat' of September 1946 at Duchess of Bedford House, an empty block of flats in Kensington. Like so much Communist organization, it was orderly, efficient and quiet. Elsewhere in the country, squatters occupied abandoned Army camps. They were not evicted, because the Government suddenly realized that this was really rather a good idea which they ought to have thought of themselves. All the squatters had done was to by-pass a lot of form filling and delay by plodding temporary civil servants.

There was perhaps one kind of ex-serviceman who never succeeded in readjusting to civilian life. He had left school to join the R.A.F. He had done magnificently in the Battle of Britain or wherever he had flown. He had risen, perhaps, as high as Wing Commander, commanded his unit well, was popular with his men. Demobilized, he was nothing. He perhaps sold not-very-good insurance policies on commission. He spent his gratuity. He borrowed. He drank too much. He had vague ideas of emigrating, probably to somewhere where there were still native servants. Sometimes he was on the fringe of crime; sometimes he shot himself. I knew him; you probably knew him; Terence Rattigan certainly knew him, for there he is in *The Deep Blue Sea*, Freddie Page, boring people to death with anecdotes of the great days of 1940.

CHAPTER 6

Blessings of Peace

On 12 April 1945, Harry S. Truman was in the office of Sam Rayburn, Speaker of the House of Representatives, when a telephone call came through, summoning him to the White House. This did not surprise him: he assumed that Roosevelt was in Washington to attend the funeral of Bishop Atwood, and it was natural that the President should send for him. On arrival at the White House he was taken, to his surprise, to Mrs Roosevelt's study. She told him that her husband had died suddenly in Georgia, and that he, Harry Truman, was now President. Truman was speechless for a moment; then, seeing Eleanor's distress, asked: 'Is there anything I can do for you?' 'Is there anything *we* can do for *you*?' Eleanor smiled. '*You*'re the one in trouble now!'

He took the oath, saying to the newspapermen: 'Pray for me!' He was totally unprepared for the job, and he knew it. An hour later he was holding his first Cabinet meeting; and after it, Henry L. Stimson, Secretary of War, took him aside and told him about the atom bomb. The scientists were confident that it would work, but Admiral Leahy, Chief of Staff to the President, thought it 'the biggest fool thing we've done . . . it will never go off.'

'A haberdasher out of his depth' he might be, yet Truman was at ease with all kinds of people in his forthright Midwest way. He would show them that 'the White House is no place for children.' Two weeks later he was addressing the San Francisco conference on international organization, calling for one that would make 'future peace not only possible but certain'. Arthur Vandenberg, Roosevelt's chosen delegate, the Republican Senator from Michigan who had opposed Lend-Lease and (until Pearl Harbor) American participation in the War, was ailing and out of his element: there were many Poles in Michigan, and Vandenberg was horrified by Russian treatment, not only of Poland, but of all the fringe countries which would soon be called 'satellites'. Other diplomats were for handling Russia gingerly, lest she fail to implement her secret undertaking at Yalta to enter the war against Japan after the defeat of Germany. It looked as if Molotov, Russia's foreign commissar, distrusted as the author of the Russo-German Pact six years before, was trying to sabotage Roosevelt's idea of a United Nations organization. Truman tackled him roughly. 'I've never been spoken to like this in my life!' Molotov spluttered. 'Carry out your agreements, and you won't be!' said Truman.

'Lively and pert to the point of bumptiousness,' writes Herbert Agar of Truman, 'more widely read in history than any President since John Quincy Adams, more wilful than any President since James K. Polk, more incompetent in dividing the good from the bad among his own friends at home than any President since Warren Harding. . . .' Well, he had entered politics through the corrupt political machine of Tom Pendergast in Kansas City, but no mud seemed to have stuck on his Baptist-Masonic-American Legion image. He *did* read books, too, and if he lent you one, he would make sure you returned it by writing on the endpaper: 'Harry S. Truman. Bought and paid for.' Asked by journalist John Hersey what ten books he would choose to prepare a man for life in the Atomic Age, he said: 'Nothing but the lives of great men. There's nothing new in human nature; only our names for things change.'

How would the little man make out? Would he get on with Churchill, for example? After Hiroshima and Nagasaki they certainly agreed on one thing: the terrible weapon was 'a merciful abridgement of the slaughter' which had probably saved a million American lives and half a million British by making the invasion of Japan unnecessary, since, although some members of the Japanese government had

The principals at the Potsdam Conference. Seated, left to right: Clement Attlee, Harry S. Truman and Stalin. Standing, left to right: Admiral William Leahy, Ernest Bevin, James F. Byrnes and Vyacheslav Molotov

wanted to talk peace four days before Hiroshima, the generals were determined to fight on to the last man.

All through the War the Allies had been guessing what Europe would be like afterwards. At Moscow in 1943, that year of conferences, the outline of the United Nations had been sketched, and decisions had been taken to impose democratic regimes on Italy and Austria, and to stage the trial and punishment of war criminals. In August 1944, at Dumbarton Oaks, Washington D.C., world security, it was agreed, must be based on some kind of United Nations organization: true, the League of Nations had not succeeded, and there was always the fear that, as before, America would back out of the thing she had started; but it had

to be tried. A month later, at Quebec, among many other things, Roosevelt and Churchill had discussed a strange idea of Henry Morgenthau Jr, Secretary of the Treasury, for the 'pastoralization' of Germany. Not only Germany's capacity for war production, but *all* German industry would be destroyed, leaving it a land of sheep and cattle, crops and cottage industries. Thinking better of it when he got home, Roosevelt decided against all speculation about Germany's future. We just had to wait and see what was left when the War was over. Anyway, it was election year, and in his manifesto before his fourth term Roosevelt spoke generally of 'human rights'. At Yalta in February 1945, there was no more talk of pastoralization': there was to be 'elimination or control' of German war plants; and Allied occupation zones were defined.

In Eastern Europe the Russians had defined their own zones, and so, between the rivers Oder and Neisse, had the Poles. At the Potsdam Conference, which ended a few days before Hiroshima, the Allies were faced with *faits accomplis*. Only minor matters were agreed upon, yet there was still hope of 'getting along with Russia'. Stalin looked curiously at the new Labour Prime Minister, Clement Attlee: he had been used to dealing with Churchill, and was puzzled by a British Prime Minister who did not seem to have a world outlook. Writing home to his aged mother, Harry Truman said: 'You never saw such pig-headed people as are the Russians. I hope I never have to hold another conference with them – but of course I will.' Before they parted, Truman and Stalin drank to a future meeting in Washington. Stalin added: 'God willing.' It never happened.

The Cold War had begun, an atmosphere of chess-playing diplomacy, espionage, propaganda, Clausewitz-in-reverse; and with it, a new vocabulary – shooting war (the opposite of Cold War), war of nerves, hot line, sphere of influence, graduated deterrence, total war, clean bomb, containment (George C. Kennan's policy of encircling Russia). We were well on the way to the Newspeak and Doublethink of *1984*.

The derelict centre of Europe across which East and West now narrowly regarded each other was full of refugees – about ten million of them. Some were physically or mentally ill; most were malnourished; some who were either unwilling or unable (usually through political changes) to go home stayed where they were, stole to feed their children, were too spiritually exhausted to have any clear idea of their future beyond survival. Many of them had become 'stateless'. Some were war criminals in hiding. They were called Displaced Persons. This had been foreseen as early as 1943, and there was an organization ready to deal with it – the United Nations Rehabilitation and Relief Administration (U.N.R.R.A.), which eventually handed over its task to three other organizations, the International Refugee Organization, the United Nations International Children's Emergency Fund and the World Health Organization. Somehow, by the end of 1945 nearly seven million refugees

had returned home. More than a million and a half, some of them Jews who had been back to their own country and found relatives dead, possessions gone, anti-semitism still raging, some of them Jews trying to get to Palestine, remained in refugee camps in Germany, Austria and Italy. America eventually took 395,000 of them.

There were also, somewhere, many thousands of deserters from various armies. Some were arrested in Paris cabarets; in derelict coaches on railroad sidings, where they had been living by train robbing; in remote woods where they had been living rough on trapped rabbits and stolen vegetables; on farms where they had been living respectably as labourers. In January 1947 the British Government announced, not an amnesty, but an offer of leniency to all deserters who gave themselves up by 31 March. Only 837 responded.

Others were never found at all. Nineteen thousand of them – the 'Lost Division' – were Americans. By 1948, Pentagon records showed that nine thousand had been found. A new standard of leniency, encouraged by psychiatrists, made a difference between long-term desertion and temporary absence without leave. But many absentees were still afraid of being shot if they returned to their units. One of the most memorable cases on the Pentagon files was that of a forty-one-year-old soldier with a good record who fell in love with a woman of sixty in the South of France. She was a great-grandmother, and he was in a state of shock over the death of his wife. He settled down to help her on her farm. When he was eventually arrested and tried, the court martial solemnly brought in a verdict of 'Desertion due to an overwhelming Oedipus-complex'.

Cold war, cold winter. In Britain the winter of 1946–7 was the coldest for fifty-three years. Sixteen degrees of frost, unremarkable if you happen to live in north-east Saskatchewan, were recorded in London. Icebergs were observed off the coast of Norfolk. In Lancashire a man borrowed a pneumatic drill to dig up his parsnips. There were 14-foot snowdrifts. Vehicles were abandoned and became frozen for months. The stoker of an early-morning steam train from Huddersfield to Bradford, unable to see signals through an ice-encrusted window, put his head out of the cab and was seriously injured by a huge icicle hanging from a bridge. There were railway accidents everywhere, until the transport finally stopped and just froze. Thousands of cattle and sheep were lost. There was no heat anywhere, because power stations had run out of coal, and gasworks needed coal too, and there wasn't much coal anyway, and what there was couldn't be got to the sources of power because there was no transport. Any light there was, was provided by candles. People, having nothing else to do in the cold and the dark, went to bed and begot children (how else can we explain the higher-than-normal number of births nine months later?). One way of getting warm was to go and sit in the Savoy Hotel, which made its own electricity. It was forbidden to use home electric fires during factory hours. In February 1947 industry in the south, the Midlands and the north-west had electricity cut altogether. Unemployment shot up to 2½ million; exports fell to nothing, losing £600 million of foreign currency.

During all this, the British, as if the war were on again, were detestably cheerful. The Conservatives had a sour slogan directed against the Ministers of Food and Fuel and Power: 'Starve with Strachey, shiver with Shinwell.' Why were there now three times as many civil servants as miners? Because the Labour Government was bent on nationalization instead of efficiency. On New Year's Day 1947 every British coalmine had a notice on the gate: 'This colliery is now managed by the National Coal Board on behalf of the People.' Some miners were bewildered: 'We thought the Board was going to be run by our

'In Britain the winter of 1946–7 was the coldest for fifty-three years'

mates, not by a lot of retired Generals on Area Boards.'

The British still went on being cheerful when, in the middle of March, after three months of ice, the thaw came suddenly, with floods of a size never seen before. Forty miles of the River Severn overflowed, the Thames near Windsor was suddenly three miles wide, crops were ruined, livestock was drowned: the enduring picture in one's memory is of a mountain of dead sheep being burned in Wales. For a few days part of London had no drinking water. The following spring and summer were glorious, and of course there was a drought, and no one had a refrigerator because they were generally imported and needed electricity or gas. You couldn't escape to another country because holidays abroad were banned. (Well, officially, anyway. There were, as we shall see, ways and means.)

The Government lurched from one crisis to another, or perhaps crisis had become permanent. 'We're Up Against It!' wailed official posters. 'We Work or Want.' Lease-lend had ended abruptly in August 1945, and the British suddenly found themselves on even shorter rations than during the war. The 1945 harvest was bad. There was a world wheat shortage. German prisoners, helping East Anglian farmers and broadcasting every week to their relatives in a programme which began with *In der Heimat*, were rumoured to be getting more to eat than British families. And for the first time in history bread was rationed: you had cards of little squares called bread units (B.U.s). Bakers angrily complained that the quality of flour given to them was only fit for cattle. Housewives began to hoard food: 'Everyone carried a shopping bag,' recalls Muriel Spark in *The Girls of Slender Means*, 'in case they should be lucky enough to pass a shop that had a sudden stock of something off the rations.'

Maynard Keynes had negotiated an American loan of £937½ million to replace lease-lend. By the end of February 1947 more than a quarter of it had been spent, and by June three-quarters of it had gone. On what? It was supposed to be used for re-equipping British industry, wasn't it? Well, about £5 million had been spent on machinery. But £55 million had bought American tobacco, and £43 million had gone on American dairy produce, and £18 million on American movies and – in these sweetless, hungry times – chewing gum.

In America, food rationing had been ended by an announcement the day after VJ-Day, that ration books would cease in July 1946: no new ones would be issued, and stamps would be used up by then. This was a great relief to mothers whose small children delighted in sticking the pretty coloured stamps on the nursery wall.

Harry Truman was a Democratic President.with a largely Republican Congress (this is one of the things in the American system that baffles the British observer), and the Republicans were campaigning with a new slogan: 'Had enough?' Enough of what? It was said that Truman had no foreign policy, he listened too much to generals. He would either get tough with Russia (which had just seized Czechoslovakia) or turn his back on Europe.

In February 1947 Britain warned America that she could no longer continue her economic aid to Greece, which was being defended against full-scale Communist guerrilla warfare, believed to be supported from the three Communist-controlled countries on her northern frontier, and Turkey, which was resisting pressure from her hereditary enemy to give Russia bases on Turkish territory. If Truman had not had a foreign policy before, he had it now, even if it was something of a volte-face. Greece and the Eastern Mediterranean had been a British 'sphere of influence'. Truman now asked Congress for $400 million economic aid to Greece and Turkey. Americans might not like the regimes in those countries, but that was not the point. It could be shown that the Balkans and the whole of the Middle East were in danger of turning Communist. In what became known as the Truman Doctrine, he said: 'I believe that it must be the policy of the United States to support free peoples who are resisting attempted subjugation by armed minorities or by outside pressures.'

It used to be Britain that talked about white man's burdens; now it was America. In May 1947 Winston Churchill described Europe dramatically as 'a breeding ground of pestilence and hate' which could collapse at any moment into economic ruin (and of course, by implication, Communism). A month later the American Secretary of State, General Marshall, offered aid to any Government willing to help in the task of recovery. This included Russia and her satellites, who, however, rejected it as 'dollar imperialism' (and indeed it could be seen at the time as a step towards a Common Market with the eventual removal of customs and a common currency, if not as a potential Western military alliance). The Marshall Plan, conceived by backroom boys in the State Department and pushed hard by Dean Acheson, which was going to cost $17,000 million over four years, was warmly praised by the London *Economist* as 'the fullest expression so far of that American idealism on which all the hopes of the West depend'; and by Foreign Secretary Ernest Bevin as 'generosity – beyond our belief. . . . We grabbed it with both hands.'

Not that Britain noticed much difference for some time. Her 'dollar deficit' was about £475 million. In Chancellor of the Exchequer Dr Hugh Dalton's autumn budget the price of cigarettes jumped from 2s. 4d. (47 cents) to 3s. 4d. (67 cents) for twenty. 'Smoke your cigarettes to the butts – it may even be good for your health!' he intoned, in his actor-manager's voice. (He was a doctor of economics, not of medicine.) Dalton resigned, towards the end of 1947, after an indiscreet, Stock Exchange-ruffling statement to the lobby correspondent of the London evening *Star* just before his Budget speech.

He was succeeded by Sir Stafford Cripps, a saintly intellectual, scientist and Christian Marxist whose face and economics stamped the word 'austerity' on the whole decade. He might have been Prime Minister, but entirely lacked the common touch: Churchill said of him: 'There, but for the grace of God, goes God.' In two years' time Cripps would do what he had practically promised not to do – devalue the pound sterling from $4.03 to $2.80, arguing that a country could not both export and enjoy a high standard of living. It was typical of his episcopal style that his devaluation press conference was held at Church House, Westminster.

The shock of devaluation was, at the time, stunning. Was this the end of sterling? The end of the City of London as a financial centre? Would Britain be in hock to America for ever? Yet the ill wind blew good to some: to authors, for example, who if they sold a story to the *Saturday Evening Post* for $1,000 now received £330 instead of £250; and I knew a girl reporter in the London office of *Newsweek* whose salary shot up from £1,500 to £2,000 a year overnight.

The British were hungry. John Strachey, Minister of Food, whose lunchtime restaurant was the Écu de France in Jermyn Street, tried to make them like whalemeat and an insultingly-named fish called snoek from South Africa, which, being in the sterling area, could supply food without causing Britain to spend dollars. Ten million tons of snoek were imported to replace the tasty Portuguese sardines which were a normal part of British diet. Radio comedians soon discovered that the name was enough to raise an instant guffaw. Had it been called barracuda, which it nearly resembled, people might have got used to it: they seemed to like the barracuda which was sent from Australia. The Ministry of Food gave a snoek-tasting party and issued snoek recipe leaflets. All in vain. Whalemeat was just about acceptable, and it was claimed that Lyons Corner House, in September 1947, was selling six hundred whale steaks a day; but snoek – one never actually met anyone who had tasted it, and there was a rumour that it was eventually sold as cat food.

Since whalemeat was oily, it was thought to help the deficiency of fat in the diet of an almost meatless and butterless nation. Strachey, an intellectual whose buoyant enthusiasms had ranged from Sir Oswald Mosley to the Communist Party and the Left Book Club, looked at the world shortage of fats at that time, and decided that vegetable fat would be better for people anyway. So began the great Groundnuts Scheme, officially known as the Overseas Food Corporation. It was going to grow food for a rationed nation, it was going to provide work and civilized living for thousands of Africans in what was then Tanganyika; and it would cost £24 million over six years. Fuel oil would be brought by 127 miles of pipeline from Mtwara on the east coast into the heart of what was jocularly called 'Nutland' at Mikindani; food for the workers would come from Mtwara by a railway which hadn't been built yet, and much of that food would be canned, expensive and imported from Britain, which hadn't enough to feed itself, and anyway there wasn't enough shipping space after so many merchant vessels had been sunk during the War.

Bureaucrats, deeply experienced in bureaucracy, ran the Overseas Food Corporation. The target was 1½ million tons per annum, and it was thought that 600,000 tons could be reached in three years. It was to be a triumph of scientific farming. Thousands of acres of trees were bulldozed: they were supposed to be used to make houses for the workers, and houses could be built at the rate of five a day. Shops, schools, banks, hospitals, sports clubs, tsetse-fly control – they had thought of everything at Noli, the village that was going to become a town, the centre of the scheme. Just one little area of doubt: the survey had not been completed. When it was, it turned out that the soil wasn't really suitable for groundnuts. So G.H.Q. was removed to Nachingwea, 32 miles away. But here the transport difficulties seemed insuperable: there were not enough spares, and the nearest depot might be hundreds of miles away, so that for want of a spring a jeep could be immobilized for weeks. The weather, which had not been studied very much, could turn nasty, and the 1949 crop was ruined by drought. Critics in industry said that there should have been a hydro-electric dam before anything else, for irrigation, drinking water and cheap electricity, that food should have been grown on the spot instead of being imported, that roads should have been built first. . . . In charge of the whole thing was Sir Leslie Plummer, a pushy director of Beaverbrook Newspapers, whose main qualification for the job, apart from owning a small farm in Essex, was that he was a good Labour man who had been converted to socialism by 'the wastefulness of capitalism'. 'Peanuts Plummer' was quickly forgotten, and the Groundnuts Scheme, a tragicomedy of blunders and bad luck, if it achieved nothing else, was good for race relations. At the end of the working day it was heart-warming to see mixed teams of British and Africans playing football together. They did try a British versus Africans match, but the Africans won 6–0.

The British knew little about their African Commonwealth, or about coloured people generally. There were only two large concentrations of black people in Britain – about seven thousand in Cardiff and eight thousand in Liverpool. When, in October 1945, delegates from many parts of Africa and the United States met in Manchester for the Pan-African Conference, the few people who paid any attention were alarmed to hear talk of freedom from white domination, of an all-black Africa, and of force being used to gain these ends if necessary. Africans had learned, from World War II, that it was wrong for one nation to dominate another. They had also seen white savages killing each other on an unimaginable scale. Mr Joe Appiah, representing the West African Students Union, shouted, 'The only language the Englishman understands is force.' (He afterwards married Peggy, daughter of Sir Stafford Cripps.) One of the political secretaries of the Conference was an unknown law student at the London School of Economics named Kwame Nkrumah. He was assisted by a farm labourer from Sussex who would one day become President of Kenya, Jomo Kenyatta, described in *Picture Post* as 'the Abyssinian delegate'. From America came seventy-three-year-old Dr W.E.B. Du Bois, head of the American Negro Association. Four years later South Africa was to announce a policy of *apartheid*, and a young Oxford-educated chieftain called Seretse Khama, who wished to take a white London typist to be Queen of Bechuanaland, was refused recognition by the British Government.

All this still seemed far away. What was important was to settle things in Europe and Japan and China first. In Germany, the Allies had staged the Nuremberg trial of Nazi leaders for (some said) having lost the war: twelve were sentenced to hanging, three to life imprisonment; and there was a strange moment of levity, incomprehensible to the accused, when Sir David Maxwell-Fyfe, in his deadly demolition of Goering's defence, quoted P.G. Wodehouse: Goering, he said, was like an acquaintance of Bertie Wooster's who 'had not actually been *seen* pulling the wings off flies'.

The Allied Control Commission in Occupied Germany and Austria, split into American, British, French and Russian Zones and policed by four armies, gave a number of people their first, and perhaps last, idea of what colonialism was like. In a starving country where girls sold themselves for chocolate or soap, and cigarettes for some time were currency, many were involved in rackets and corruption. Some, drawing fat allowances, got used to a lifestyle never known before or since; others, particularly the young National Servicemen, conscripted from 1947 onwards, were bored and depressed. There was a dodge for smart operators by which you signed on for three years and then bought yourself out for £20. 'Reluctant conscripts' were at least better off than the 'Bevin boys' who had been sent down the mines; and theorists of the day said that two years' military service was helping to keep juvenile crime down.

For two years the conscripts were lonely and sex starved. Fraternization was officially barred. In the spring of 1949 troops were allowed to walk arm in arm down the street with German girls, provided they had one arm free for saluting officers. This privilege had been won slightly faster by the Americans than by the British. General Montgomery had permitted his troops to talk only to 'little children under the age of eight'. General McNarney had specifically banned 'hugging, kissing, petting, walking with the arm around the body and holding hands in the street' but did not seem to mind what went on indoors. The Russians worked out a 'pay-as-you-frat' system of fines for their troops. In July 1945 three British privates got fifty-six days' detention for letting a German civilian invite them for a drink, and another got 112 days' for kissing a German girl. By October, nature was beginning to take its course, and you could marry a German girl if you had the Zone Commander's approval, which you were unlikely to get. By September 1946 it was permissible to invite German girls to Army cinemas. By June 1947 a high-level directive was urging 'cultural fraternization' to encourage the democratic way of life. A year later Anglo-German and Americo-German weddings were almost daily occurrences. A lone voice in the wilderness was that of a staff major at Herford who told the press: 'What we need here is cricket bats, not Fraüleins.'

In Japan, as in Germany, it was thought dangerous to destroy too much industry, especially when it became clear that China was going Communist. General MacArthur, Supreme Commander for the Allied Powers, was the chosen instrument for demilitarizing and democratizing Japan. A number of things happened very fast. On 1 January 1946, the Emperor calmly announced that he was no longer divine. In June, Japanese women voted in an election for the first time. Among the new democratic privileges was a legalized Communist party, trade unions, and, in February 1947, a general strike which hoped to overthrow the Government but was quickly proclaimed illegal. The Japanese accepted these things inscrutably. Their new constitution held them to perpetual peace, which the shock of Hiroshima and Nagasaki made desirable. The younger generation, especially girls, seemed fascinated by the freedom of American life, had facial operations to make their eyes larger and less oriental, and ate American food. Nutritionists studied them carefully, and one came to the conclusion that the Japanese, who for centuries had been small and excitable because they ate so much fish, would henceforth, by dint of breakfast cereals and more dairy produce, become large and calm, and possibly even scrutable.

CHAPTER 7

Music Music Music

The Forties began with the tune that was to be so rudely interrupted by the Café de Paris bomb: for it was 'Oh Johnny!' that America was singing on New Year's Eve 1939; 'Oh Johnny!' that an overflowing Paramount Dance Hall crowd contorted itself to in the first All-England Jitterbug Championship in January 1940. It was one of several revivals during the decade. Written in 1917, it had been found in a pile of old music by Orrin Tucker, the Chicago band leader, who gave it to his vocalist Bonnie Baker; and so, by way of radio, it went out to the world again. If there was any particular corny tune that ended the Forties, it was probably 'Music! Music! Music!' ('. . . Put another nickel in . . . In the nickelodeon') which resorted to the ancient device of inserting eight bars of Liszt's second Hungarian Rhapsody in the middle.

The Big Band era, prolonged by the dancing mania of wartime, was safe for a few years in the hands of Ellington, Goodman, Basie, the Dorseys, Glenn Miller and Woody Herman. 'Jazz is tenderness and violence', said Gertrude Stein, listening to Miller's orchestra shortly after the master's death in an aircraft that disappeared into the English Channel. Herman, astonished at the demand for his music (he was at one time giving five shows a day on Broadway), afterwards said: 'Hell, we weren't *that* good.' Most band leaders joined the Forces and formed their own bands within them: in Britain the new names of Billy Ternent and George Melachrino (and, just after the War, Ted Heath) came up to join the established ones of Ambrose, Lew Stone and Billy Cotton; and the shortage of manpower brought forth all-girl bands, led by Blanche Coleman, Gloria Faye and Ivy Benson.

Something which would have happened in wartime anyway, but has remained in popular music ever since, was that the singer became as important as the band. In the late 1950s the band would shrink and become merely the 'backing' to the voice.

Did America have a Forces' Sweetheart in the same way that Britain had Vera Lynn? There was Frances Langford, of course, who toured field hospitals singing to wounded soldiers who said: 'She makes you think of your wife, not of her;' but sometimes the disembodied radio voice is preferable to the real thing. I lay in a field hospital in Persia, having malaria and dysentery both at once, and Vera Lynn on short-waves made me no more than homesick; but John Steinbeck tells a story of Frances Langford standing by the bed of a G.I. with a head wound and singing 'As Time Goes By'. The boy began to weep uncontrollably, and Frances left in a hurry. Bob Hope was sent to try and cheer the ward up with jokes about powdered eggs, only to discover that you mustn't make wounded men laugh too much because it hurts them. Frances Langford was no luckier in Kairouan, North Africa: singing 'Embraceable You' to a wounded pilot, she saw him turn away when she got to 'I want my arms about you': he had no arms.

The progress of Vera Lynn from East End workingmen's clubs when she was only thirteen (7s. 6d. for three songs) through the bands of Joe Loss, Maurice Winnick and Ambrose, with 'The Little Boy that Santa Claus Forgot' as her biggest pre-war hit, belongs to folk history. In the autumn of 1941 she sang 'Yours' in her first West End show, *Apple Sauce*, and this led to all the others – 'We'll Meet Again', 'When they Sound the Last All-Clear', 'The White Cliffs of Dover'. Not sexy; not maternal; nasal, tear-jerking, especially with that contrived catch in her voice . . . what was her appeal? 'Boadicea plus Gracie Fields,' as one critic said? She herself says it was because she sang clear English, and all other band vocalists were singing American. 'I'm the girl in the street singing to the man in the street,' she said, at a time when her records were selling equally well in America; adding demurely: 'I sing in tune – and on the beat.' She sang

(*opposite*) **Glenn Miller during a recording session**

Bobbysoxers waiting to see Frank Sinatra at the Paramount Theatre, New York, November 1945. *Song Hits* magazine offered anti-swoon mints to the queue

with Glenn Miller and did duets with Bing Crosby at Rainbow Corner. Her only serious rival was plump, blonde Anne Shelton, who was considered more socially significant, maybe because she sang 'Yiddish Momma'.

In Hollywood, in the fall of 1942, Dinah Shore appeared – 'an incendiary voice,' people said, 'as if she's singing to you alone'; and patrons of the Savoy-Plaza Café Lounge in New York noted the 'shyly sultry' Lena Horne, 'like a bashful volcano with magnificent teeth,' who sang with Charlie Barnet's band. 'I haven't got any voice,' she murmured. 'I don't know anything about music.' Nobody agreed with her. Peggy Lee, all breath and desire, was singing with Benny Goodman, and Doris Day with Les Brown's 'Band of Renown': her 'Sentimental Journey' placed her among stars like Ella Fitzgerald and Judy Garland.

Malnutrition might have been one's first impression of Frank Sinatra in October 1944, when he was rising twenty-nine and looked about seventeen. It was known that he had a punctured ear-drum and so was unfit for military service. But was he doing the war effort any good, with 3,500 bobbysoxers at New York's Paramount Theatre, some fainting, and all squealing? No other singer had provoked quite this reaction. The King of Swoon (yes, he had a good press agent) had first attracted attention as one of the Pied Pipers (Jo Stafford was another), a group which had sung with Tommy Dorsey in 1940. There was a bit of a fuss at the Hollywood Bowl, normally dedicated to classical music, but the Bowl got used to the squealing too. The London *Times*, always a little slow on the uptake, said 'Mr Sinatra is unknown in this country and likely to remain so.'

Mr Sinatra sang 'I'll Never Smile Again', 'Embraceable You', 'I Only Have Eyes for You' and, quite unfashionably, a song about his wife, 'Nancy'. He temporarily ousted Bing Crosby, but only temporarily; got himself some bad publicity through having been seen in Havana with Lucky Luciano; used his fists too frequently; and had throat trouble. When the decade closed, it was not thought that he would make a come-back.

As for Jo Stafford, who, like Tommy Dorsey on the trombone, could manage long phrases without breathing, she was sharing with Dinah Shore the top place for girl singers by 1946, first at La Martinique in

Manhattan, then with Perry Como on the radio in the 'Chesterfield Supper Club'. Her record of 'Symphony' sold half a million.

In the wake of Sinatra, after the War, came 'the sepia Sinatra', Billy Eckstine. He had run an unsuccessful Bop group, but suddenly his 'Fool That I Am' sold 200,000 records, he had a fan club, and he went on to sell over a million records of his version of Ellington's 'Caravan'. Nat King Cole was coming up to an enormous popularity, Eddie Fisher, Vic Damone, and, so different, the superbly relaxed Perry Como (an ex-euphonium player who was labelled 'the cool balladeer'), and Frankie Laine, born Frank Lo Vecchio, who made matrons cry, and Johnny Ray, who cried himself.

In Britain, Al Bowlly, Denny Dennis and Sam Browne, well established, carried on through the raids. Al Bowlly, said to be a Syrian born in Mozambique, he of the wobbling Adam's apple, who seemed to believe every word he sang, was killed by a bomb in Jermyn Street in London.

(left) Vera Lynn, 1944 (below) Peggy Lee, 1947

(*above*) **Jo Stafford, 1946** (*below*) **Lena Horne, 1944**

Nat King Cole

With a few exceptions, wartime songs lacked style. In war we all play roles, believe things we know to be untrue, behave like Pavlov's dogs, reacting to stock stimuli: we needs must love the lowest, for it is assumed that this is what the masses want. There were few songs so deeply charged with emotion as those of World War I: 'We Don't Want to Lose You', 'Keep the Home Fires Burning', 'If you Were the Only Girl in the World'. We marched to a cheerful tune called 'I've Got Sixpence'. There were vainglorious songs like 'There'll Always Be an England' (highly offensive to Scots, Welsh and Ulstermen), which had been written *before* the War because it was

noted that 'God Bless America' was top of the pops in the States and Britain had nothing like it except 'Land of Hope and Glory'. 'We're Gonna Hang Out our Washing on the Siegfried Line' was hastily dropped after the German invasion of France, and inspired a jeering German parody with words, it is said, by Goebbels himself. 'Der Fuehrer's Face' and 'What a Surprise for the Duce' – well, they cheered people up at the time. No aggression or hatred, and Noël Coward's 'Don't Let's Be Beastly to the Germans' was the first wartime song to use the word 'Hun'. The B.B.C. was doubtful about it: they seemed to think Coward really meant it when he wrote:

'Let's help the dirty swine again
To occupy the Rhine again.'

Certainly nobody meant to invite the Japanese back to Pearl Harbor. Frank Loesser's 'Praise the Lord and Pass the Ammunition' was inspired by an army padre's advice to his men as the Fleet went down ('The sky pilot said it/And you gotta give him credit').

We all had our troopship songs. As the rolling *Duchess of Atholl*, famous before the War for luxury cruises, but now a troopship with 'other ranks' (enlisted men) in tiers of bunks eight deep, zigzagged for seven vomiting, U-boat-dodging weeks from Liverpool to the Cape of Good Hope, we sang 'Slow Boat to China', 'She'll be Comin' Round the Mountain', 'Deep in the Heart of Texas' (you clapped at the end of every four bars), and, because we had a battalion of Geordies on board, 'Blaydon Races'. Dirty songs, too, like 'The Quartermaster's Stores', and a certain parody of the Egyptian national anthem: the American counterparts were possibly 'Dirty Gertie of Bizerta' and '4F Charlie'.

There were songs of yearning and separation – Vera Lynn's 'Yours' and 'No Love' (where love clearly meant sex, and the words were parodied to make sure it did), 'The White Cliffs of Dover' (invested with improbable bluebirds) and 'Don't Get Around Much Any More'. Songs became riskier, and Britain's B.B.C. had sleepless nights over 'Why Don't We Do This More Often?', 'It Can't Be Wrong' and 'That Lovely Weekend'. It was banned on all American radio networks because the lyric didn't actually state that the couple were married. Even Eric Maschwitz's 'Room 504' lyric sounded sinful, since it was probably in one of those hotels where they didn't mind how you signed the register. And what couldn't you read into a lyric like 'Baby, It's Cold Outside' (1949)?

Into the romantic category came 'As Time Goes By', Ivor Novello's 'We'll Gather Lilacs', 'Deep Purple' and 'A Nightingale Sang in Berkeley Square'. The 'Nightingale', first sung by Judy Campbell in a revue called *New Faces* in 1940, had a special magic for officer-class Londoners: she wore a misty white dress with lots of lace, and danced in floating ecstasy as her husky voice breathed the absurd words: '. . . angels dancing at the Ritz.' Who today would dare to write a lyric that even mentioned the Ritz?

" *I'm going to get lit up*
When the lights go up in London,
I'm going to get lit up
As I've never been before;
You will find me on the tiles,
You will find me wreathed in smiles,
I'm going to get so lit up
I'll be visible for miles"

Zoë Gail singing 'I'm Gonna Get Lit Up When the Lights Go Up in London' in *Strike a New Note*,
Prince of Wales Theatre, 1943

Some songs could never have existed outside blacked-out wartime Britain: Gracie Fields' 'They Can't Black Out the Moon', and Zoë Gail's 'I'm Gonna Get Lit Up When the Lights Go Up in London'. This also caused trouble at the B.B.C., for 'lit up' had come to mean 'drunk': Miss Gail was clearly encouraging people (with their ration of one bottle of gin per eight weeks) to intemperance. A joyous girl, who died too young, she was invited to switch on *all* London's lights – in 1949, for dim lighting continued until then – but, on VE-Day, celebrated with champagne on a balcony high above Piccadilly Circus.

The silly song returned in December 1943 with 'Mairzy Doats' ('Mares Eat Oats . . . and little lambs eat Ivy'). Played by Spike Jones's City Slickers, a comedy band sometimes called the 'Kings of Corn' which had already given 'Der Fuehrer's Face' to the world (and would make Christmas 1948 memorable for 'All I Want for Christmas is My Two Front Teeth'), it was reckoned the biggest freak hit since 'The Music Goes Round'. 'It annoys people,' said the gleeful publisher after selling 350,000 copies of sheet music, 'so they buy it.' Never mind: it saved a man's reason. In 1948 Alexander Dolgun, working at the United States Embassy in Moscow, was arrested, tortured, and thrown into an all-black windowless cell, next door to the wind tunnel of an aeronautical research institute which made a deafening noise. Dolgun resisted it by singing 'Mairzy Doats' at the top of his voice: 'The effect on me was fantastic. . . . I had discovered an instrument for my survival.'

Oh, yes – that 'White Christmas' song; well, if you insist – it came from the film *Holiday Inn* (1942). Irving Berlin wrote it; Bing Crosby sang it; it sold twenty million copies (six hundred thousand in the first ten weeks). Soldiers cried when they heard it. Bing was singing it in the Queensberry Club, London, a Forces canteen, when a bomb fell. Everyone dived to the floor except Bing, who carried on regardless.

There is the strange case of Cole Porter's 'Don't Fence Me In', sometimes quoted as an example of Porter 'going commercial' and topical in wartime. By no means: he had written it as long ago as 1934, and it had once been intended as the theme song for a musical biography of Will Rogers. It was eventually used in *Hollywood Canteen*, sung by another Rogers (Roy), the Andrews Sisters and Bing Crosby.

In January 1945 the columnist Sidney Skolsky pronounced it 'the most instantaneous song hit Cole Porter ever had. It's first on the Hit Parade, first in sheet music, and it's the first-selling record.' Singer Kate Smith, not suspecting that the song was a send-up, thought that it 'breathes the yearning of free men'.

There were two curious sequels. A man called Ira B. Arnstein, whose hobby was suing song-writers for plagiarism, brought a million-dollar action against Porter and lost it; and army psychiatrists everywhere said the song's popularity was due to 'service reaction against wartime discipline'. It also became the symbol of Britain's post-war claustrophobia and austerity, and was sung to Sir Stafford Cripps, Chancellor of the Exchequer, by a deputation of the Housewives' League, who for good measure added another song of those years, 'Open the Door, Richard!'

Lili Marlene. Was she really a golden-hearted whore (the composer denied it) as she waited under that lamp outside the barracks? Norbert Schultz, friend and drinking companion of Weill and Brecht in pre-Hitler Berlin, had written the tune in twenty minutes in 1938; later it had been recorded by Lale Anderson, a little-known Swedish singer. Schultz had had much more success with 'Bombs Over England'. 'Lili Marlene', originally called 'Song of the Young Sentry', had been forgotten. In 1941 Nazi broadcasters, taking over Belgrade Radio, found they had only three records to play to their troops in the Balkans. One was 'Lili Marlene'. It was played twice nightly for five hundred nights, picked up on short waves by U-boats in mid-Atlantic, by Rommel's troops in North Africa – and by the British Eighth Army. Goering's wife, Emmy, sang it at a charity concert in the Kroll Opera House, Berlin. The Norwegians wrote a parody of it in which the lamp-post was used to hang Hitler. Goebbels hated it because he thought it made soldiers homesick. An English lyric-writer, Tommy O'Connor, gave 'Lili Marlene' more sentimental words for British consumption. Poor Lale Anderson was sent to a concentration camp for saying, 'All I want is to get out of this horrible country.' And Schultz lived to be clapped on the shoulder and congratulated by Field Marshal Montgomery at an Alamein reunion.

After the War popular music began to change. Ellington, Herman, Lunceford, Harry James – big bands were still in demand, but other things were happening. A revival of 'trad', starting in the early

Dizzy Gillespie and his band

years of the decade, began to reach Britain towards the end. In 1943 Bunk Johnson, teacher of Louis Armstrong, got himself a new set of teeth and gave a New Orleans-style recital at the Geary Theatre, San Francisco: he had found Kid Ory, presumed dead, alive and running a chicken farm near Los Angeles. Johnson died six years later, but he had started something. In Manhattan's Town Hall, Eddie Condon was keeping Chicago-style alive in so-called Jive Concerts: late in 1945 he started his own nightclub in Greenwich Village with Bud Freeman and Wild Bill Davison as resident players, but any visiting fireman could join in. No nonsense about orchestrations or music stands, which Condon considered 'organized slop'.

Duke Ellington, nostalgic for the old romantic Harlem that no longer existed, had 'gone classical'. His forty-five-minute *Black, Brown and Beige,* first heard at a Carnegie Hall concert in aid of Russian War Relief, contained 'bits of waltzes and Stravinsky' and seemed to be breaking out of the jazz mould. More in character was *Harlem Air Shaft,* about the city sounds and smells he remembered from the ventilation tunnels in New York tenements.

What had been called 'Swing' in the Thirties was dying. Perhaps jazz itself was dying, we used to think. 'Progressive' jazz was for listening, not dancing to, said Stan Kenton, when he gave a concert at New York's Paramount Theatre. There was something called Bop, or was it Be-bop? It was played by smaller, less expensive groups or 'combos'. Trumpets squeaked an octave above what was thought to be technically possible, new cross-rhythms were tried, new dissonances, and everybody seemed to be playing faster and cramming more notes into every bar. Charlie Parker, Dizzy Gillespie, his cheeks blown out like a football, and Miles Davis were the new names, Thelonius Monk the new pianist. The Royal Chicken Roost, on Broadway, now called itself the Metropolitan Bopera.

In Britain the initiated now knew the names of Tito Burns and Ronnie Scott, who seemed to be influenced by Bop. Bop had its own vocabulary: what was 'hot' in the Swing era became 'cool' in the Bop era. All previous jazz was 'square'. If you liked a player, you said he was a 'real bitch'. Bop was 'head music'. Bop enthusiasts affected beards, berets and dark glasses. Some of them became Muslims. Bop was, above all, *loud*: Benny Goodman couldn't understand it – 'they just play too damn *loud*.' He would have been at home with the new 'trad' bands that were coming up in England – Humphrey Lyttelton, George Webb's Dixielanders, and a very young Chris Barber, nineteen, who in 1949 had just formed his first amateur band 'to play like King Oliver'.

In America there had always been some jazz musicians who took marijuana: it was said to be good for improvisation. By 1943 it was reckoned that twenty per cent of players were smoking 'hay', 'loco weed', 'grass', 'reefers' (many were the words for it), and Gene Krupa, the great drummer, was jailed in California for possessing it.

No 'weed' was needed by Oscar Peterson, the new Art Tatum, who had the advantage (which the Boppers would have despised) of a classical training. Born to two West Indians in Canada, he had given up the trumpet because of weak lungs and had concentrated on the piano. Runs, rhythm, gorgeous harmonies, he was an eclectic rifler of all previous jazz pianists; his 1949 debut in New York caused critics to couple his name with Mozart's.

All this sophistication needed antidotes. For some years John Lomax and his son Alan, with guitars at the ready, had been collecting and recording American folksongs, ballads, cowboy songs, blues and those curious outbursts known as 'hollers'. Now these songs began to reach the general public, with Burl Ives singing 'Blue-Tailed Fly' and Josh White's 'One Meat Ball'. A fruitful source of Negro songs was a man known as Leadbelly, who had done time for murder.

From the West Indies came a sound new to people who had never been there: the calypso, accompanied by 'steel bands', instruments made out of junk like old gasoline cans. The words were largely improvised,

topical, satirical, and the singers gave themselves names like Lord Beginner. The calypso of 1945 was 'Rum and Coca-Cola', banned on many radio networks because it was 'free advertising', but selling thirty-seven thousand copies a day. Written by Rupert Grant ('Lord Invader') to an adapted creole lullaby, it was a satire on the American occupation of Trinidad, alleging general prostitution:

'Both the mothers and the daughters
Working for the Yankee dollars.'

At a calypso festival it was possible to blackmail prominent citizens by threatening to sing scandalous words about them. If you had been there in 1946, you would have heard 'China Never Had a VJ-Day', and a cheerful social comment, 'Three Cheers for the Government VD Campaign', besides the ever-popular account of the Abdication:

'It was love and love alone
That caused King Edward to leave the throne.'

The insatiable demand for music during and after the War was expressed in the disc boom, with labels new and old proliferating in America – Capitol, Hit, Asch, Beacon, Blue Note. In America, but not yet in Britain, there was confusion about the new extended and long-playing records: R.C.A. Victor was producing 45 r.p.m., Columbia $33\frac{1}{3}$ r.p.m. and Capitol was offering both. Decca sat tight at 78 r.p.m. The miracle of having a whole symphony on two sides took some getting used to; so did the mechanics – many people bought $33\frac{1}{3}$ turntables and plugged them into old 78 r.p.m. machines (which from now on would be known, not as gramophones or phonographs, but as record players).

There was a hunger for classical music. At Bloomingdale's department store, under the supervision of Mr Ira A. Hirschmann, Manhattan's 'New Friends of Music' were giving weekly quartets and making chamber music pay. In Britain, God knows, it was hard; when St George's Hall, next door to the B.B.C., got a direct hit from a bomb, an orchestra which had been unwise enough to leave its instruments there overnight, lost them all; but Dame Myra Hess organized lunchtime concerts at the National Gallery, denuded of pictures during the Blitz, and famous musicians turned up in uniform on short leave from their units to play. There were concerts in the

Dancing to a Wurlitzer juke-box, 1941

Royal Exchange, the Hallé and London Symphony orchestras toured factories under the aegis of the Council for the Encouragement of Music and the Arts (C.E.M.A.), and Sir John Barbirolli found that workers actually *liked* Debussy. Barbirolli, quitting the New York Philharmonic in 1943 to heal the sick Hallé, then reduced to twenty-three players, expanded it to 110, trained it, and, loving Manchester more than London, turned down the $40,000 (£5,000) a year (twice his Hallé salary) offered him to take over the B.B.C. Symphony Orchestra. It was difficult to say who loved him more, Ralph Vaughan Williams (who called him Glorious John) or Manchester teenagers.

Orchestras, cheerfully mucking in with Glen Miller or the Squadronnaires, gave camp concerts for the troops. Britain and America exchanged conductors: Malcolm Sargent conducted the N.B.C. Symphony in a concert of contemporary British music. Sir Thomas Beecham, faithless to his old flame Lady Cunard, married Betty Humby the pianist: he visited America, never failing to be rude to his hosts. Sir Henry Wood, in his own phrase, 'ran on regardless' with his Promenade Concerts as best he could, though the destruction of the Queen's Hall meant that they would have to transfer to the Royal Albert Hall. Death took him in 1944.

One night in 1943 Bruno Walter, due to conduct the New York Philharmonic, fell ill, and his place was taken, at a moment's notice, by a young man of twenty-five named Leonard Bernstein, who did everything, including jazz. Rodzinski, though hating jazz, which he thought was causing family life to degenerate while fathers were abroad in the Army, had appointed Bernstein his Assistant Conductor. Bernstein, who had also performed Ravel's Piano Concerto as soloist and was writing a rollicking musical, *On The Town*, found himself conductor of the New York City Symphony Orchestra in 1945. Four years later his 'Symphony No 2 for Piano and Orchestra', inspired by W.H. Auden's *The Age of Anxiety* and described as 'a baroque eclogue in a 3rd Avenue bar', was conducted in Boston by his old teacher Koussevitzky. Puzzling in form, it was said to have 'twenty-five themes growing out of each other'.

To the Establishment of Toscanini, Fürtwangler, Stokowski, were added new names. Herbert von Karajan had spent the War at the Berlin State Opera, and was about to commute between the Berlin and Vienna Philharmonics: Salzburg and Bayreuth would follow. Van Beinum building the Concertgebouw in Amsterdam; de Sabata with his odd bursts of speed, as if trying to catch the last train home; Rafael Kubelik, refugee from the claustrophobia of post-war Prague, on his way to the Chicago Symphony Orchestra. And in Boston, Koussevitzky, retiring after twenty-five years to cries of 'Goodbye, Koussy!' was succeeded by the more tense, more impatient, Charles Munch from Strasbourg.

Few composers were yet ready to express the War in music; but in 1942 Shostakovich's 7th (Leningrad) Symphony was conducted by Stokowski with the Los Angeles Philharmonic, its full eighty minutes being cut for soldier audiences. His 9th Symphony (only thirty-three minutes) had its United States première at Tanglewood Music Shed in the Berkshires, conducted by Koussevitzky, who thought it 'Haydn-ish': the composer himself said it was 'a merry little piece – musicians will love to play it and critics will delight in blasting it.'

Is there some special relationship between opera and war, or the aftermath of war? Opera was on its

Richard Lewis as Grimes in *Peter Grimes*, Covent Garden, 1947

way to becoming a people's art-form, coming down closer to earth. Benjamin Britten's *Peter Grimes*, produced in London in 1945, was hailed by an American critic as 'the first first-rate popular opera since *Der Rosenkavalier*'. It had been commissioned, in memory of his late wife, by Koussevitzky, who gave it three performances in the Berkshires. The librettist, Montagu Slater, had somehow achieved, in popular terms, 'a psychopathic case-history of sadistic fishermen' – in Britten's native Suffolk. Peter Pears, tenor, was admired for his 'coloratura-like soarings'.

Peter Grimes was followed by Britten's *The Rape of Lucretia* (1946) and *Albert Herring* (1947), with sets by John Piper: both were given at the Glyndebourne Festival in 1947, under the direction of Carl Ebert, who had spent the War as musical adviser to the Turkish government. There was also a new production of Gluck's *Orfeo* with a young Lancashire contralto, Kathleen Ferrier, one of the great voices of the century, singing Orpheus, originally scored for a *castrato*. Kathleen Ferrier, who had never had a singing lesson until 1940, went to New York in 1948 to sing Mahler's *Song of the Earth* with the New York Philharmonic under Bruno Walter.

Neither J.B. Priestley, as librettist, nor Arthur Bliss, as composer, had ever written an opera before. In 1945 Priestley sketched out a story of the Gods who, because mortals no longer believe in them, roam the world as strolling players, becoming divine every Midsummer's Day, when they are able to smooth out human predicaments. It took Bliss and Priestley four years to reduce their material to a practical length, and *The Olympians* was produced in 1949 at Covent Garden by Peter Brook and conducted by Karl Rankl.

Covent Garden, having been a dance hall for part of the War, had reopened in 1947 with the Sadler's Wells Ballet in residence. Frederick Ashton's *Cinderella* (to Prokofiev's music), Helpmann's *Miracle in the Gorbals* (the first English ballet with a working-class setting) and Massine's *Clock Symphony* led a brilliant revival (helped by striking sets designed by contemporary artists) after a war in which Ashton had served as an R.A.F. officer and several male dancers had been used as physical training instructors.

In 1949 Sadler's Wells made their triumphant American tour; and even though Margot Fonteyn was prima ballerina, New Yorkers remembered above all twenty-two-year-old Moira Shearer as 'the pin-up girl of British ballet', echoing the London critic who had marvelled at her 'deer-like littleness and midsummer colouring'.

Pursuing Covent Garden's new policy of lavish productions, with scenes by contemporary artists who might not ever have attempted stage decor before, Peter Brook's erotico-fantastical production of Richard Strauss's *Salome* followed just over a month later, with decor by Salvador Dali, who was asked to 'avoid surrealism'. The result was described as an 'interesting disaster'. What would Strauss have thought of it? We do not know. He had been cross with the American soldiers who, overrunning Bavaria in the

Robert Helpmann in *Miracle in the Gorbals*, Covent Garden, 1946 spring of 1945, had interrupted him as he was composing *Capriccio* and ordered him to clear out of his house at Garmisch-Partenkirchen because it was wanted for military purposes. But he had been pleased by the warmth of his reception at the London Strauss Festival in 1947, a year before his 'denazification'. On 9 September 1949, he died aged eighty-five. He had fared better than Franz Lehár, who was under house arrest for refusing to leave his 'non-Aryan' wife, Sophie. His house was ransacked by Russian soldiers who destroyed his manuscripts because he was a 'capitalist'. He died in November 1948.

Neither would have cared for the new kind of opera which Gian Carlo Menotti was writing. He called them 'chamber operas', wrote his own libretti with a great sense of theatre, and gave them prosaic titles like *The Telephone* and *The Medium*. They were of the Forties and Fifties, replete with pain, offering no escape. But the satire, and the sight of people singing into telephones, made them box-office hits in New York, though they were less successful in London.

In Europe many opera houses lay in ruins. After Mussolini had been strung upside down at a Milan garage, a mob demonstrated outside La Scala shouting: 'Toscanini must open the new opera season!' The maestro, now seventy-eight, had refused to conduct in Italy since the early Thirties. Now he returned to give a series of concerts in aid of rebuilding La Scala. The Vienna Staatsoper, whose 1944 season had ended appropriately with *Götterdämmerung*, had been hit by five American bombs in March 1945; but it was the Russians who first entered that part of the city in April, and in the ruins of the opera house they found German deserters, attempting to disguise themselves in the costumes of Wagner and Verdi operas. A Russian major, acting on orders from Marshal Tolbukhin, ordered Josef Krips, the conductor, and as many singers as he could find, to put on an opera for Labour Day, 1 May. Vienna at this time had no gas, telephone, water or electricity, and the streets were still strewn with dead bodies. Nobody had eaten for days. The only available theatre was the smaller Volksoper, and the Staatsoper scenery had to be cut to fit it. Rehearsals were held in the back room of a bar, and somehow *The Marriage of Figaro* was given on May Day to tumultuous applause from an audience composed largely of Allied soldiers.

A year later the first full-size Salzburg Festival since the War was held. Salzburg, said to be crawling with unidentified Nazis, was still largely populated by American troops, who were none too pleased when the Festspielhaus, known to them as the Roxy Cinema, was requisitioned for Hans Hotter in *Don Giovanni*.

The Metropolitan Opera, New York, was in the red for $233,000 when it sent to Glyndebourne for Rudolf Bing in 1949. It was a controversial choice of Director, since there were those in America who thought United States talent should be given a chance: the names of Melchior, even of Billy Rose, were suggested.

There had been no ban on Wagner in Britain, as in World War I; and Wagner was among the first composers to return to Covent Garden after 1945. Kirsten Flagstad, now over fifty, suspect at first because of her husband's association with Vidkun Quisling, the Norwegian fascist, sang Isolde and Brunnhilde gloriously: 'a born Valkyrie'. And as Covent Garden struggled to establish a young company, it was possible to predict a wonderful future for Geraint Evans, first heard as the Night Watchman in *Die Meistersinger* in 1948.

Silent was Sir Arnold Bax, Master of the King's Musick in 1942, composing almost nothing after his 7th Symphony. Silent, too, was Sibelius, to whom New York musicians sent eighty-three boxes of cigars for his eighty-third birthday in 1948; he had eight years and ten months to smoke them in. Noisy was George Antheil, 'No. 1 bad boy of U.S. musical dadaism'. His 4th Symphony, broadcast by Stokowski and the N.B.C. Symphony Orchestra, was thought 'martial, soulful, vulgar, sentimental and loud'.

Innocent were the Trapp Family Singers, in dirndl and lederhosen, giving coast-to-coast recitals of church music and folk songs from the Austria they had left in 1938: they could not know that they would return to Europe in *The Sound of Music*. New and disturbing was a voice from the Paris slums, somehow produced by a frail body, calling itself Piaf, which could be heard at the Versailles nightclub in Manhattan.

And plangent were the sounds of Anton Karas's zither, in the 'Harry Lime Theme' from *The Third Man*, which closed the decade.

CHAPTER 8

Woman and Beauty

'Make Do and Mend', said the British Government slogan, and a cosy publicity lady called 'Mrs Sew-and-Sew' explained how to do it. So you turned two dish cloths into a sort of jersey, men's old overcoats into tweed coats and skirts, patchworked old pieces of knitting and unravelled woollens into warm waist-coats, turned old cotton dresses into aprons, old curtains into skirts, wore your husband's old gardening jacket around the house; and dressmakers, with no materials to spare, advertised: 'Last season's dresses, coats, etc. made to look new.' Wool was precious because it cost more coupons than rayon or even silk, and because, in a bombed and often fuelless world, it was warm. Knitting was something you could do in an air-raid shelter when there wasn't enough light to read by, or on a bus, or anywhere. A popular design was the Victory Jumper, with V-neck, V-motif, V-everything.

'A Knitting Party', by Evelyn Dunbar

(opposite) **'W.V.S. Clothing Exchange', by Evelyn Gibbs**

Clothes rationing, introduced in Britain in June 1941, and long outlasting the War, meant sixty-six coupons a year per person; by a weird piece of planning ingenuity, surplus margarine coupons could be spent on clothes instead if you liked. Women were better off than men, theoretically, because women's clothes needed slightly fewer coupons. A man's overcoat required sixteen, a shirt eight, underpants four. There was soon a lively, illegal trade in buying and selling clothing coupons: housewives bought them from their charwomen (if they were so lucky) at a minimum price of 2s. 6d. (about 60 cents at 1941 exchange rate) each. Hugh Dalton, President of the Board of Trade, always one for overdoing things, advised men not in uniform to go collarless, tieless, sockless to save material, and swore that he himself would not buy a new suit for the duration. It was patriotic to sleep without pyjamas or nightdress, but warmer, especially if you were married and your husband was away, to buy thick Viyella pyjamas and wear them about the house in daytime too.

Lucky the girl who had a G.I. boyfriend and could get nylon stockings; but everyone knew who you were going out with. Nylons, first sold in Wilmington, Delaware, would, it was claimed, 'halve stocking bills without loss of glamour': why, the average silk stocking only lasted 130 hours! If you had no stockings at all, you painted your legs with suntan lotion, drawing a seam with eyebrow pencil. Lucky, too, the girl who knew someone in a parachute regiment: it was a crime punishable by imprisonment, but a length of parachute silk could be made into sets of undies: you could tell who was wearing them because she rustled as she danced. It even helped to know an undertaker, because muslin was used for coffin linings.

Women's shoes simply disappeared. Unlucky the girl who didn't have average feet. Shoe queues were sometimes so bad that one had to queue for a ticket to get into the queue. There were not many styles to choose from, all were heavy, 'sensible', with wedge heels and peep toes; they were worn (on special occasions) with silk stockings, or (for every day) with leg make-up. And when peace came again ankle-strap shoes with platform soles, or outdoor wedges in French straw for summer, were thought glamorous.

In 1942 'Utility' clothes appeared, in standard patterns designed to save cloth, buttons, everything: they all carried the Utility mark, two crescents and a

Even pyjamas imitated uniforms

The Utility mark

Winston Churchill wearing a zip-up siren suit

pean fashions began to come together. Clothes restrictions had long-term advantages: they made British women more quality conscious, and they made America create her own fashion industry. Suddenly, in 1940, New York was cut off from Paris, had to think for herself. The fact that a few French designers (such as Mainbocher at 57th Street) had set up shop in New York did not seem to help much. With hindsight, we can now see what happened. Fashion went from peace to war to peace again, first influenced by military styles, then reacting violently against them.

Blouses and hats imitated uniforms: the 'battle-dress top' or 'Eisenhower windcheater', Tank Corps berets, peaked caps with a splodge of glitter. Thus did American girls who were not in uniform make believe that they were. In England, men got used to the sight of girls in the new uniform of zip-up boiler suit (with wide trousers) and gas-mask case slung over one shoulder (shoulder-bags, sometimes carrying the owner's initials, date from this time). 'Englishwomen have never looked prettier,' Mollie Panter-Downes told *New Yorker* readers in her London letter, 'than they do these days when they are dressing more

A fashion of 1942 encouraged because it required few coupons

number, had been invented by a committee, and were sold at controlled prices. If Englishwomen wanted, yearningly, to follow fashion, they had to do it vicariously by looking at American fashions in *Vogue* or film magazines like *Silver Screen*. A small number of girls still changed into long dresses for evening dates: a 1939 debutante who had gone to work in an aircraft factory immediately after the declaration of war somehow managed to change out of her overalls into a long dress, dance all night at the '400', and be back at her lathe, in overalls, by eight o'clock in the morning. For the record, the Government's advice that 'period pains must not hold up the war effort' was considerably helped by the fact that at no time was there a serious shortage of either pain-killers or sanitary towels.

America had Regulation L.85: clothes were not rationed, but the stuff they were made of was rigidly controlled. Circumference of skirt – six feet, not more; belts two inches wide, hems two inches. From Pearl Harbor onwards, British zip-up siren suits (modelled by Churchill) notwithstanding, American and Euro-

**Georgia Carroll wearing the latest in fashion in
America in 1941**

sight lest it be caught in a machine. Hats came slowly back in the late 1940s with (in 1948 and 1949) a kind of short bob cut, including the ugly-smart 'urchin cut'.

After the War, hair-styling became an industry, thriving on constant invention. For one thing, it had to fight the new 'home perms'. It might be the Greer Garson look, remembering *Mrs Miniver*, or the 'bubble cut', remembering Ingrid Bergman in *For Whom the Bell Tolls*. The year 1949 saw something called the 'tulip cut', almost indistinguishable from a pudding basin; and a 'terribly amusing' blonde bun on a brunette head.

Evening dresses, despite rationing of material, somehow managed to use lots of stuff, with padded 'military' or 'baseball' shoulders; when shoulders went bare around 1946 there was the new strapless bra, with wire frame, to hold you up, and a fad for beauty spots and patches, moons and stars, stuck near the eyes, mouth or shoulders: they were excellent conversation-starters.

Girls of the Forties fall into two main categories: pin-ups and fashion-leaders, fashion meaning style of girl as much as style of dress; and some girls were

The new strapless bra

simply, often going hatless, and working so hard that sleep comes easy at night, bombers or no bombers.' (Tell that to the Land Army girls in their leaking Wellington boots, their faces black from the smoke of the coal-fed traction engines that still drove threshing machines.) Mouths were painted vivid red, an effect which was sometimes achieved in Britain, where few girls had more than two lipsticks to last the War, by such devices as beetroot juice.

Hatlessness had the advantage that it showed off your hair, and hair was plentiful: chignons, bunches of curls, tied with ribbons, more curls framing the face, the big 'Victory Roll' in front. The 'Veronica Lake' style had a side parting so that a great hank of shoulder-length (preferably blonde) hair hung over one cheek: may I refer you to a song, sung by Paulette Goddard, Dorothy Lamour and Veronica Lake herself in Paramount's *Star-Spangled Rhythm* – 'A sweater, a sarong and a peek-a-boo bang'. While hair was long, tinselly snoods were worn.

But not if you worked in a factory, where there was a strict rule that hair should be short and tucked out of

(*above*) Jean Kent modelling a travel coat of
whipcord, designed by Joy Ricardo, November 1946
(*left*) A dinner gown in black satin, designed by
Simmone, October 1946
(*opposite*) Betty Grable

both. The appeal of Betty Grable, a mature twenty-
nine by the end of the War, was understood mainly by
soldiers: the famous picture of her, which was spread
double-life-size over the entrance of the London
Pavilion Cinema in Piccadilly Circus, showed her
looking back over her shoulder in a tight white
swimsuit which encased the world's neatest bottom.
Wholesome, suggesting sex-without-sin, she earned
$300,000 a year for spreading, and feeling, enjoy-
ment: 'I just feel *good* singing.'

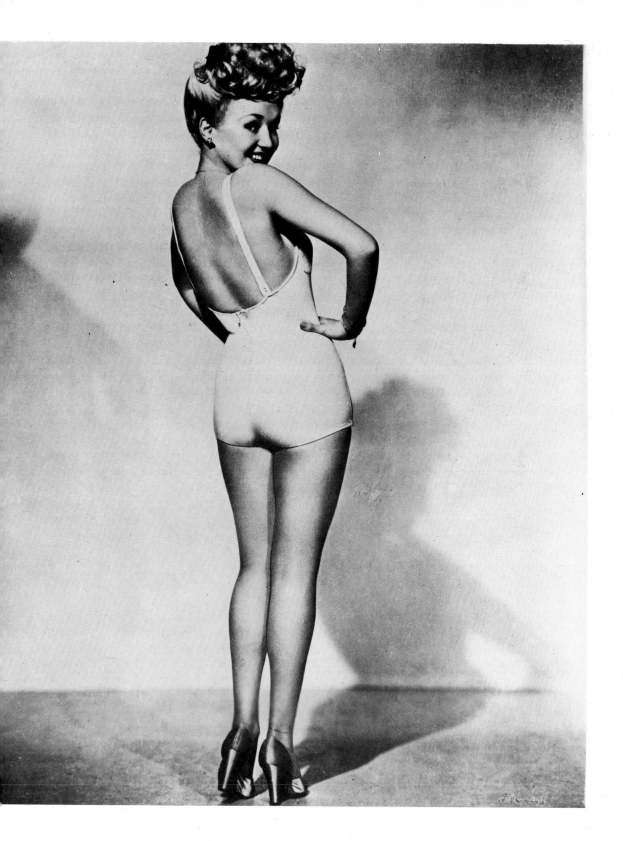

Britain had no precise equivalent to Grable, indeed borrowed her for the duration. Britain's 'Forties Girls' too were mostly drawn from the cinema, and after the War from the Rank 'Charm School', an adjunct of Mr Rank's bid for equality with Hollywood. Diana Dors, born Diana Fluck, who had won her first bathing-beauty contest at thirteen in 1945, was too late for the War; but never mind – at fifteen she was a Rank starlet, equipped with a new name, labelled 'the sultry blonde bombshell with the wiggle', and ready for her celebrated appearance in a gondola at the Venice Film Festival wearing a diamond-studded mink bikini. Margaret Lockwood – too ladylike for the Sergeants' Mess; Patricia Roc – ah, now you're talking; but we didn't know her until about 1945. Phyllis Calvert, Ann Todd, Deborah

Ava Gardner

(*opposite*) **Diana Dors**
(*below*) **Patricia Roc, July 1947**

Kerr, Glynis Johns – officers' wives, coolly British with the promise of inner flames. Virginia Mayo, elected by *Stars and Stripes* 'Miss Cheesecake 1948'. Ava Gardner, all ready to replace Lana Turner. But all made way in 1949 for a girl of seventeen who looked like becoming the most beautiful woman of the century. 'A perfect type of the Black Irish.' 'Hasn't got a bad angle.' 'Most beautiful woman we've ever photographed.' She had returned to the States with her art-dealer father and actress mother just before the War, became a child star in *National Velvet*, was engaged to the son of a former Ambassador to Brazil, and was about to star with Montgomery Clift in *A Place in the Sun*: Elizabeth Taylor.

97

Until late in 1943 magazine covers (especially *Time* and *Life*) tended to feature generals and statesmen, glaring righteously out of the page; but soon cover girls returned, no doubt to the great relief of circulation managers – girls such as Frances Vorne, 'pin-up girl of 1944', sometimes called 'The Shape', and Anita Colby, who was not only in a film called *Cover Girl* but held the appointment of 'feminine director of Selznick Studios'. Leggy Jinx Falkenburg, sister of tennis-player Bob, was no mere pin-up – her picture was *riveted* to planes at an American Army flight school.

Models, formerly called mannequins, were international news: one knew their names, escorts, diets. Barbara Goalen, austerity-thin with big Bambi eyes and tiny feet; 33-18-31, $7\frac{1}{2}$ stone, she first appeared in *Vogue* and *Harpers' Bazaar* in 1947. A young widow

Rita Hayworth, 1942

with two small children, she needed the money, which was five guineas an hour for top models. 'Bettina', who modelled Rita Hayworth's wedding dress for her marriage to Aly Khan, and 'Sophie', who would marry film director Anatole Litvak – both of Jacques Fath; and Jean Dawnay, a blonde ex-air hostess, daughter of a general, who modelled for Dior for six months, a rare honour for an English girl.

'Debbery' did not return to Britain until 1947; it did so in a very much simplified form – no more feathers; and the girls, different from the girls of 1939, were said by one observer to show 'a tired maturity of behaviour'. Never again would there be the pre-war ballyhoo that had pursued Margaret Whigham. One of the few London debs who really made the news was Sharman Douglas, daughter of the American ambassador, a friend of Princess Margaret who was impeccably squired by Lords Blandford and Westmorland. In America debbery had struggled along through the War, becoming more decentralized. In America's last year of peace, 1940, eighteen-year-old Patricia Plunkett was voted Deb of the Year, taking over from Brenda Frazier, and it was already a foregone conclusion that Gloria Vanderbilt, fifteen, would succeed her. But attention was deflected to Dallas, Texas, to Camilla Davis, whose father, it was stressed, was *not* an oil man, but a banker who had been at Yale, so there! For Camilla, Elsa Maxwell organized a fancy dress party at which guests put on their masks and costumes *after* they had arrived. At the War's end, the Deb of the Year was Anne Lincoln.

Paris, freed in August 1944, did not wait for muddling generals and politicians to end the war. Within weeks Maggy Rouff, Lelong and Schiaparelli were showing 'liberation fashions'. Schiaparelli designed a dress with a bustle *in front*; Lelong had a lot of accessories, such as charm bracelets of tiny Jeeps. Madame Lanvin, now seventy, had an evening dress called 'Liberty', backless and almost frontless too, and a rather tatty pink frock called 'Free France'. Well, it was a brave gesture, but the prices were too high, the materials inferior (no wool and not much lace), and the sales disappointing. Some of their best old customers were still in prison: they had been Vichy supporters.

Not for another two years did the greatest fashion revolution since 1918 happen. At 10.30 a.m. on 12 February 1947, at Christian Dior's salon at 30

(opposite) **Elizabeth Taylor in** *National Velvet*

Avenue Montaigne, Paris, the world's fashion editors sat, not with any great expectation, for the Paris collections had so far been dull. Perhaps the Liberation excesses had exhausted everyone; perhaps, after all, fashion leadership had gone, during the past two years, to London and New York. Carmel Snow of *Harpers' Bazaar*, *doyenne* of fashion writers, was heard to say crossly: 'This had better be good.'

Suddenly, an unfamiliar gooseflesh-sound – forgotten since 1939 – the swish of *petticoats*. The model girls strode in, reported Ernestine Carter of British *Harpers' Bazaar*, 'arrogantly swinging their vast skirts (one had eighty yards of fabric), the soft shoulders, the tight bodices, the wasp-waists, the tiny hats bound on by veils under the chin. . . . [They] swirled on, contemptuously bowling over the ashtray stands like ninepins. . . . This new softness and soundness was positively voluptuous.' Cheers broke out, and some of the spectators wept. Janey Ironside, afterwards Professor of Fashion Design at the Royal College of Art, said: 'It was like a new love affair, the first sight of Venice, a new chance, in fact a new look at life.'

It can be argued, as London's Victor Stiebel did, that the New Look would have come anyway; but Dior, who had worked for Lucien Lelong, was a new name, backed by Marcel Boussac, the textile king. Noting the padded hips and bosoms, *Harpers' Bazaar* headlined it 'Paris Rounds Every Line'. 'The new stance is a hippy one . . . a new way of walking.' The prices – and you needed a whole new wardrobe too – were terrifying: up to £250. In London the press did not seem to know what to say. It was *Life* magazine in New York that invented the name, and not until Dior's second collection in the summer of 1947 – the New Look. Jacques Fath's collection that year made it clear that Dior was a vulgar upstart; Fath went to the other extreme and produced hobble skirts. Dior gave another show at London's Savoy Hotel in the autumn, and a private show for the Royal Family. Princess Margaret wore a New Look dress for her parents' silver wedding, and Princess Elizabeth ordered calf-length skirts for her own wedding trousseau.

For the rationed British it was sheer cruelty: not for two more years would there be enough material for New Lookery. Radical *Picture Post*'s Marjorie Beckett observed primly: 'We are back to the days when fashion was the prerogative of the leisured wealthy woman.' For girls with short legs and big bottoms it was hopeless, but they still yearned for the romantic luxury of Dior. By 1948 Fenwick's of Bond Street had found it possible to offer the 'new fashion look', calling it a 'ballerina suit', for £5. 12s. 6d. and eighteen coupons. You could make up for this extravagance by 'wearing almost nothing underneath it'. At the Labour Party Conference at Southport, Mrs Bessie Braddock, M.P., was indignant: the voluminous skirt was 'the ridiculous whim of idle people'. In the Rue Lepic, Paris, women tore the dress from a model's back, screaming 'forty thousand francs for a dress, and our kids have no milk!' In Dallas, Texas, women formed a Little Below the Knee Club to resist it. Sometime in 1949, America dropped the 'New', and called it just 'the Look'.

James Laver, the fashion historian, not often silly, wrote: 'After a war . . . men will feel oppressed and frightened by excessive femininity.' Wrong: British men were absolutely sick of girls in tin hats and siren suits and starveling skimpiness; those billowing skirts somehow convinced one that underneath them were nyloned legs and ankles of incomparable slenderness.

During the War in America, and just after it in Britain, the cult of the Teenager began. Britain would have to wait until the Fifties and Sixties for anything like *Seventeen* magazine (1944), which was part of a general recognition of teenagers as first-class citizens with spending power who needed special clothes, make-up and records. (Not yet the rat-tail hair, the black jeans, the blackboard jungle, the Ban-the-Bomb marches. These Forties kids were not much concerned with the aftermath of war.) Acne, shyness, dating, dieting, doing whatever the gang did; jeans rolled up to just below the knee, odd socks, shirt tails left outside, and (in America) milk bars with juke boxes and a weird social function (for girls only, all wearing pyjamas), the Slumber Party with pillow fights.

Men have no legitimate place in this chapter; yet they too had fashions of a sort. In Britain they came out of the Forces with standardized free clothes, presented by a grateful Government, called Demob Suits (with pullover, but no waistcoat, and – curiously – *two* buttonholes, one in each lapel), and an allowance of clothing coupons. Service greatcoats were converted to civilian overcoats, leaving the pip-holes in your epaulettes to show you had been at least a first-lieu-

Princess Elizabeth wearing the 'New Look', 1948

tenant. Government Surplus shops sold quantities of Navy dufflecoats, many of which were bought by chilly civilians. A 'utility' suit could be had for as little as four pounds, and heaven help you if you were not a standard size and shape.

The great male fashion influence of these times was John Taylor, editor of the *Tailor and Cutter*, who publicly reprimanded the Duke of Edinburgh for failing to provide a fashion lead as the Prince of Wales had done before the War. The Duke lacked flair and originality, didn't press his pants often enough, stuffed his pockets too full, went bareheaded in spite of the hat trade's publicity slogan 'If you want to get ahead, get a hat'. John Taylor was perhaps the only man in London, in 1949, to wear a tweed Norfolk jacket with single vent almost up to his shoulder blades.

There were two odd trends in the late Forties, both doomed quickly to become *déclassé*. The Edwardian look, with narrow 'drainpipe' trousers and jacket (with deep cuffs) buttoning high, sometimes worn with a fancy vest, either new or inherited from Grandpa, was taken up by young thugs known as Teddy Boys. One of their insignia was the 'bootlace tie'. The Drape Shape, as if made for a much larger man than its wearer, so baggy as to conceal a bad figure but with ample room for a holster under the armpit, was associated with American gangsters, and a version of it known as the Zoot Suit had been worn by Danny Kaye and Frank Sinatra for a short time. Underworld and Show Business had combined to popularize it, though it was on its way out by mid-1949. It was said to be attractive to the kind of woman who likes gorillas. Some American States considered banning it by law. It was, surely, an American fashion? No. John Taylor showed that it had been invented by a Savile Row tailor named F.P. Scholte at the close of the nineteenth century, and Scholte had adapted it from Guards officers' greatcoats.

In London the Zoot Suit was worn mainly by street traders known as 'spivs' or 'wide boys' who lurked at street corners to offer you nylons and other goods in short supply. It was usually worn with a smashed-looking hat and a glaring fish-tail tie.

Such a tie would have displeased Mrs Malcolm D. Whitman, born Lucilla Mara de Vescovi in Rome in 1893. She was not a Countess, though her mother had been a Baroness and she claimed descent from Tintoretto. Mrs Whitman, under the name of Countess Mara, ran a 'Men's Shop' on Park Avenue, at 51st Street, New York City, which specialized entirely in pictorial ties, some of them hand-painted. Around 1948 Countess Mara ties became a kind of secret link between men who could afford to pay up to $20 for a cravat. Strangers, seeing that each was wearing an instantly recognizable tie with 'CM' and a crown on it, got into conversation and discussed ties, sometimes establishing fruitful new friendships. Sports, animals, mermaids, Roman heads, Aesop's fables, key rings, torn love letters, 'artistic nudes' (masquerading as Adam and Eve or Leda and the Swan) – rarely could one meet another Mara-wearer and say 'snap!'.

It had all begun back in 1930, when Mr Whitman had come proudly down to breakfast in a new tie he had bought himself. What did his wife think of it? 'It's – quite nice. But it's like all your other ties.' Could his wife design a better one? You bet she could. Soon she was selling her designs to Abercrombie and Fitch, Marshall Field in Chicago and – the mark of total arrival – Neiman-Marcus in Dallas, Texas. For the 1948 Presidential Election, after a good deal of research ('if I can't sleep, I count ties, not sheep'), she designed Republican and Democratic ties, with motifs of donkeys and elephants. Stuffy old Britain, which hadn't even got around to flowered ties yet, considered Countess Mara ties vulgar.

In Britain stockbrokers and advertising men were perking up old business suits by wearing carnations in button holes. The Royal Air Force 'handle-bars' moustache survived for a few years, notably on the ample face of Jimmy Edwards the comedian; but it somehow connoted fast-talking unreliability, perhaps because it was identified with a wartime comic-strip by Jak (enormously popular in Middle East service newspapers) called 'The Two Types'. There were fewer cigarette cases and no more silver matchboxes as smokers went over to petrol (but not yet gas) lighters. And, from April 1949, there were more clothes; for on that date Mr Harold Wilson, President of the Board of Trade, announced the end of clothes rationing, publicly tearing up his own ration book as he did so. Now Austerity was over; journalists wrote heady articles about 'bonfires of restrictions'; and people who had grumbled ceaselessly about clothes rationing felt a strange let-down; for now there was no longer any excuse for being shabby; nothing to blame any more.

Women's page editors had to think again, too. Throughout the War and for four years after it ended, they had relied heavily on 'Why Nottery?' I quote an example from the *Sunday Pictorial*: 'Why not turn that old bedsock into a snazzy little hat?' I quote it sadly, for if you are under forty you won't believe it.

(*opposite*) **The Zoot Suit, 1942. The accompanying chain was often swung round and round while dancing**

Scene from *Mrs Miniver*, 1942

Hollywood and Pinewood

The war had begun with a panic closing of cinemas and theatres in London and other British cities: joke notices appeared outside – 'Nearest open theatre, Aberystwyth, 212 miles'. They reopened with Charles Laughton in *Jamaica Inn*; Robert Donat and Greer Garson in *Goodbye, Mr Chips*, assisted by large numbers of boys from Repton School; knockabout comedies starring Will Hay in his mad schoolmaster role and George Formby singing to his ukulele; *The Wizard of Oz* and *Gone With the Wind*. It was customary, if the air-raid siren sounded, either to project a slide or for the manager to announce it from the stage. The audience generally stayed put.

In Hollywood there was trouble with the Dies Committee, represented by cartoonists such as Fitzpatrick in the *St Louis Post-Dispatch* as an ugly sleuth in a deerstalker examining girls' garters with a magnifying glass to see if they were red. A former Los Angeles house painter called John Lewis Leech, who had become a Communist organizer in Portland, Oregon, was naming Hollywood actors as sympathizers – Fredric March, Francis Lederer, Humphrey Bogart, James Cagney: all angrily denied it. Director Frank Tuttle and his wife Tanya, playwright Clifford Odets, actor Franchot Tone, author Budd Schulberg – there was to be much naming of names in the next few years. The Hollywood of these years was recorded by Schulberg in his two best novels, *What Makes Sammy Run?* and *The Disenchanted*, based on the last days of Scott Fitzgerald; and by Fitzgerald himself in *The Last Tycoon*.

Slowly Hollywood began tooling up for war production. There were to be a few excellent films, and many bad ones. For what do you do to entertain people in a highly emotional time, before your own country is involved and has the simplicity of a definite enemy to hate? You give them escape, with music and laughter, and black-and-white patriotism, and richly costumed history (this too is escape but it can conceal propaganda to keep spirits up in war). You go back to well-loved classics like *Jane Eyre*. You can call your hero an 'anti-fascist' but not a socialist, and your villain a reactionary but not actually a Nazi until you gather, from Roosevelt's speeches, that war is inevitable; or until something happens at Pearl Harbor.

During America's Phoney War, which was much longer than Britain's, there was a desire to make a powerful picture about Britain's war situation as seen by America, in such a way as not to frighten Americans too much; to do it with American stars, but in a British way – using the understatement which was then Britain's greatest contribution to the cinema, seen in documentaries which Britain was so good at. The result was *Mrs Miniver* (1942) with Greer Garson and Walter Pidgeon, about the sufferings of a middle-class family with servants in a country village. It was not the view that Britain had of herself, but it worked: American tears were shed, 'Bundles for Britain' flowed faster.

By contrast, America's first war films were full of heroic bragging. (We shall see how Hollywood gradually learned the power of understatement.) Erich von Stroheim as General Rommel, shown as brutal and rather stupid; a succession of villainous Japs; Lana Turner as a poor little rich girl making out in the Women's Army Corps; and just as one day Errol Flynn would reconquer Burma almost single-handed, so it was necessary to have an American hero in *A Yank in the R.A.F.* (which, incidentally, was well liked when it came to Britain in 1942). Britain also made mistakes in early war films: Korda's *The Lion Has Wings* (with Ralph Richardson and Merle Oberon), about the R.A.F., showed the Germans as cowards. Much better ones followed as documentary and fiction-feature came closer together. *Target for Tonight* (1941) showed the real-life crew of a

Leslie Howard and Eric Portman in *49th Parallel*, 1941

Wellington bomber – they were all afterwards killed – and Crown Film Unit's *Coastal Command* (1942) was praised for its 'astonishing realism'. *Desert Victory* (1943), opening with the tremendous artillery barrage at El Alamein, hardly put a foot wrong: its commentary was factual, the pictures spoke for themselves, there was never a boastful word. *Western Approaches* (1945) came a little late for its subject – the Atlantic convoys.

They turn up today occasionally on television, and I am embarrassed by the terribly-terribly-Britishness of the language, the frightful decency of everyone, the brave little platitudes people spoke to each other, the remoteness from the world of the Seventies; until I remember that in war everyone is acting a role, pretending to be brave, pretending to be a soldier, or a mother whom no amount of bombing can break, pretending that it's all going to be all right and it

can't happen to us. . . . We *did* talk like that.

Terribly-terribly-British was Leslie Howard, always in the Pimpernel role of the reluctant hero striving to avoid conflict but brilliantly effective with minimal last-minute effort when forced to fight. In *First of the Few* (1942) he temporarily abandoned this role to play R.J. Mitchell, designer of the eight-gun Spitfire which won the Battle of Britain. In *Pimpernel Smith* he had been a quiet English travéller saving people from Germans; in *49th Parallel* (1941) he was a seeming coward up against a German U-boat crew, hiding among Hutterites in Canada while trying to escape to the United States, with Eric Portman as a swinish Nazi officer mouthing phrases like 'our glorious Fuehrer'. British Pimpernelism, which always had to be explained to overtly aggressive foreigners, perhaps ended with Leslie Howard's death in a shot-down airliner in 1943.

One of Our Aircraft is Missing, in which a crashed aircrew escape from France helped by the Resistance; *We Dive At Dawn* (submarines); the brilliantly scripted *Next of Kin* (a sermon on security); *Millions Like Us* (women in factories, snooty socialites and working-class girls getting to know each other) – fictionalized documentaries were improving all the time. Perhaps *The Way Ahead* (1944), with David Niven, showing a fighting unit being pulled together without class-consciousness, was the best of the Army pictures; and there was a dear little film about the ATS called *The Gentle Sex* (1943) in which girl soldiers sang 'Hi-yi-yippy-yippy-hi' (She'll be wearing khaki bloomers when she comes').

Just too late (June 1945, a month after VE-Day) came the best of all pictures of wartime Britain, *The Way to the Stars*, which at last was able to show British and Americans getting on well together at an R.A.F. airfield. There were two memorable things about this marvellous film: a poem by John Pudney, 'For Johhny', full of a spirit unique to the R.A.F. – if your pal is killed, look after his wife, marry her if necessary – 'Do not despair for Johnny-head-in-air; He sleeps as sound as Johnny underground . . . Better by far for Johnny-the-bright star, to keep your head, and see his children fed'; and a tear-jerking moment when a very young Jean Simmons sang 'Let him go, let him tarry'.

John Mills and Rosamund John in *The Way to the Stars*, 1945

It was, of course, the Navy, commandeered by Noël Coward, that walked off with the honours. His friend Lord Louis Mountbatten had been torpedoed off Crete in H.M.S. *Kelly*; Coward would make his first film about it, playing the hero himself. *In Which We Serve* (1943), hailed in America as 'the first really *great* picture of World War II', a 'naval cavalcade' showing the entire life of a destroyer and its men, was almost ruined by the Films Division of the Ministry of Information, who objected to a film which showed a

Noël Coward (*below right*) in *In Which We Serve*, 1943

British ship being sunk as defeatist. Worse still, a cowardly stoker (Richard Attenborough) deserts and yet is not utterly disgraced. In America the Hays Office cut the words 'God', 'hell', 'damn' and 'bastard'; and then, repenting, reinstated 'bastard'.

From Hollywood came most of the sheer entertainment films, the singing, the laughter, the dancing, the innocence. Bing Crosby, Bob Hope and Dorothy Lamour saronging in *The Road to Singapore*, to Zanzibar, to Morocco, anywhere; Betty Grable in *Down Argentina Way* and *Coney Island*, in which, a critic said, Miss Grable exploited her 'virtually unprintable person'; Deanna Durbin's wonderfully hygienic voice in *Spring Parade*. And some of the best Disneys – *Dumbo, Fantasia, Pinocchio*.

Yet Hollywood also did bold, even experimental things in these years which had nothing to do with war. One evening I sat in a cinema in Durban, Natal, exhausted after seven weeks in a troopship, on leave until there was another troopship to take me to Bombay. The silhouette of a wedding-cake castle, swirling snowflakes in a glass ball, close-up of an old man's mouth saying the word 'Rosebud'. A series of flashbacks, a curious muffled echo so that you can't hear everything that is said (and does it matter?). Sometimes the lighting is so dim that you can't see people clearly either; sometimes it shines in your face and blinds you . . . I, tired soldier, fell asleep. I suppose I had expected a gangster picture – the title, *Citizen Kane*, gave little clue. I woke up again in the great room-wrecking scene and was riveted. I saw it round again; and five more times wherever it was revived. It said everything about the American Dream, about men like William Randolph Hearst, the mania for acquisition which hits the second generation of the hopelessly rich.

Equally un-Hollywood, and an astonishing film for wartime, was Hitchcock's *Lifeboat* (1944); an allegory, perhaps, of a shipwrecked world. Nine characters in one boat (including Tallulah Bankhead). A German (Walter Slezak) has a secret supply of water and a compass. An ex-surgeon, he amputates the leg of William Bendix (a ballroom dancer), takes charge of everything, sings *lieder* to cheer the others up. But the others find him out, throw him overboard and beat him to death with the amputated shoe. What now? The only Negro character, a religious man, says: 'We still got a motor'. You know he means God. Well, it had to have some kind of moral.

America's greatest war (or anti-war) film was probably *A Walk in the Sun* (1945) by Lewis Milestone, who had directed *All Quiet on the Western Front* fifteen years before.

(*above*) Bing Crosby, Dorothy Lamour and Bob Hope
in *The Road to Rio*, 1947

(*right*) Scene from *Citizen Kane*

(*below*) Walter Disney's *Pinocchio*

Among conventional war films, *Bataan* (1943), starring Robert Taylor, was probably an understatement of that particular three-month hell; and *This Is the Army!* had Joe Louis leading a Negro chorus, George Murphy (with Ronald Reagan as his son) bridging the gap between 1918 and 1941, Irving Berlin wheezing 'Oh how I hate to get up in the morning', and the entire cast of *Yip Yip Yaphank* (Berlin's World War I show recreated for World War II) marching, in a magnificent bit of tear-jerking corn, 'off the screen' and apparently through the audience to a waiting troopship. Similarly, *The White Cliffs of Dover* took us back to 1914, with C. Aubrey Smith and Irene Dunne, then forward to 1942, with Irene saying, over her dying son, as the American troops arrive

in Britain, 'God will never forgive us . . . if we break faith with our dead again.' (This and *Mrs Miniver* were studied closely by Dr Goebbels as masterpieces of propaganda.)

There were some good historical films, each making its propaganda point about the soundness of the British spirit, even when made in America – Robert Donat as *The Young Mr Pitt* (Britain standing alone but 'saving Europe by her example'), John Gielgud as Disraeli in *The Prime Minister*, and Vivien Leigh, with Laurence Olivier as Nelson, in *Lady Hamilton*; the Trafalgar sequence always made Churchill weep whenever he saw it, which was often. As victory approached, Olivier made his sumptuous technicolor *Henry V*, a great landmark in screen Shakespeare,

Vivien Leigh and Laurence Olivier in *Lady Hamilton*

Laurence Olivier, Felix Aylmer and Renée Ascherson in *Henry V*

with stirring music by William Walton.

Two splendidly awful films stand out in the memory: *Dangerous Moonlight* (1941) with Anton Walbrook as a Polish pianist, playing the 'Warsaw Concerto' as the bombs rained down (this near-Tchaikovsky fragment by Richard Addinsell was enormously popular and started a chain of Cornish Rhapsodies and such-like); and – how different! – Howard Hughes's Western, preceded by two years of publicity, *The Outlaw* (1943). Shot at ridiculous expense, mostly at night, because Hughes was busy designing planes for Henry Kaiser by day, it was remarkable for two things: for the first time in movie history a special press agent, Russell Birdwell, was employed to publicize Jane Russell's breasts; and the

climax of the audience's continual laughter, which was when Jane (as the half-breed Rio), nursing a wounded Billy the Kid (Jack Beutel), gets into bed with him 'to warm him'.

When Russia perforce became America's ally, Warner Brothers thought it necessary to 'put Russia on the map', and fast. The result, an adaptation of Joseph E. Davies's book *Mission to Moscow*, glorified Roosevelt and Stalin as brothers in arms; in it, wrote *Time* magazine, 'the Russians look like fur-coated Americans, and the Soviet Union is pictured as a land of magnificent food and drink.' The Russians replied with *The City that Stopped Hitler – Heroic Stalingrad*, containing the worst atrocity shots ever seen on a screen, and their new weapon, the Katyusha rockets.

Scene from *Casablanca*, 1943

The personality of Humphrey Bogart, for ten years cast as a villain, now underwent a change. Not yet partnered by Lauren Bacall, he emerged in John Huston's *The Maltese Falcon* (1941) as Dashiell Hammett's Sam Spade, tough yet vulnerable, sending down Mary Astor for murder – 'If they hang you, I'll always remember you.' In *Casablanca* (1943) he was Rick, another version of that odd wartime figure that pretends it doesn't want to know, doesn't care who wins the war, but secretly helps the good guys to escape persecution, drinking to forget his old flame Ingrid Bergman. The plot? No matter. What everyone remembers is the song, 'As Time Goes By'. The film owed at least part of its success to its title; for Casablanca, just after the film's New York première, was the scene of a famous conference between Roosevelt, Churchill and De Gaulle. By 1946 Bogart had found his screen and life mate, Lauren Bacall; they were together in *The Big Sleep*, in which he played another private eye, Raymond Chandler's Philip Marlowe.

When what was technically known as peace broke out in 1945, and Colonel Zanuck, Major Niven, Colonel James Stewart and Captain Clark Gable became ordinary film people again (Errol Flynn's main contribution to the war effort had been to send a lock of his hair to be auctioned for War Bonds), Hollywood looked at the returning servicemen and did an intelligent and compassionate thing: it made *The Best Years of Our Lives* (1946) showing soldiers of all ranks trying to adjust to civilian life, the embarrassed reunions, finding somewhere to live, a job to do – and what happens to a man whose hands have been blown off: the disabled seaman was played by Harold Russell, an ex-paratrooper who had lost his hands on D-Day.

In Britain, there was one studio that was actually making money, Gainsborough at Shepherd's Bush. Its stars were sadistic James Mason, nice Phyllis Calvert, lecherous Stewart Granger, fun-loving Patricia Roc, Dennis Price, Jean Kent – and Margaret Lockwood. Miss Lockwood was, in *Love Story* (1946), a concert pianist who, having been told she was dying, moved to Cornwall and fell in love with an airman who was going blind (this was where the 'Cornish Rhapsody' came in). In *The Wicked Lady* she, the symbol of all that was decent in British women, was a female highwayman, Lady Barbara Skelton, who

The Best Years of Our Lives, 1946

shot one lover, poisoned another and betrayed a third
to the gallows. Her dresses showed a splendid amount
of cleavage, which necessitated a little reshooting for
America. You never actually *believed* a Gainsborough
film: it was all rather like family charades, you knew it
was our Maggie all the time. There were moments
when one longed for the talking camel in *The Road to
Morocco* who turned to the audience and said: 'This is
the screwiest picture I ever was in!'

In *The Seventh Veil* (1945) James Mason who had
already been a Regency sadist in *The Man in Grey* did
a dreadful thing: he slammed a piano lid on to Ann
Todd's artistic fingers as she (or rather the unseen
Eileen Joyce, assisted by the London Symphony Orchestra) was playing Grieg's Concerto. There were
(and I would like to read a psychologist's report on
why there were) a good many post-war films about
beastly things happening to women. Anne Baxter an
alcoholic in *The Razor's Edge*, Jane Wyman a deaf

mute in *Johnny Belinda*, Joan Crawford mad in *Possessed*, Olivia de Havilland madder yet in *The Snake Pit*,
directed by Anatole Litvak.

The Snake Pit (1948), memorable for Miss de
Havilland's horrific screams, upset everybody. The
idea that mental illness, hitherto associated with fashionable psychoanalysis, 'can happen to anybody', as
Dr Kik (Leo Genn) said in the film, was thoroughly
frightening. Moreover, it was known that it had been
at least partly filmed in an actual mental hospital,
that the entire cast had visited such hospitals to get
the atmosphere, that actual night noises there had
been recorded. Britain had 'U', 'A' and 'H' certi-
ficates – how should this film be classified? ('X' did
not arrive until 1951.) In Britain a hundred and forty
nurses asked for the film to be banned because it
showed nurses as cruel; and the censor passed it only
on condition that its showing was preceded by a
notice saying that it was not to be shown to anyone

under sixteen, and making it clear that it was about *American* hospitals only, and that 'all the characters are played by actors and actresses'. With this kind of publicity, who needed advertising?

A much-repeated headline of 1949 was CRISIS IN BRITISH FILMS, when to a crippling entertainment tax was added the devaluation of the pound, and Pinewood Studios, built to produce twenty-five films a year, was producing barely one. We were not yet used to living in a permanently sick economy; but a sick film industry had long been with us. It was a pity, because, in the drabness of post-war social life, Cabinet ministers joined socialites at film premières, and there was now an annual Royal Command Performance at which the Royal Family were treated to innocuous fare such as Anna Neagle and Michael Wilding in *The Courtneys of Curzon Street*.

To the rescue came a flour-miller, J. Arthur Rank, surrounded by chartered accountants. As every businessman knows, all businesses are the same, aren't they, so what was so special about films? We had to export or die, and films were an export. But there was more to it than that. Mr (afterwards Lord) Rank was a millionaire and a Methodist – 'I am in films because of the Holy Spirit,' he said, as J.D. Rockefeller had claimed that God gave him his money. Films were a force for good, a channel for idealism and patriotism: Mr Rank uttered prayers before Board meetings, and taught in Sunday School. When Hollywood complained about the amount of cleavage revealed in British costume films, he replied in genuine perplexity: 'But in England bosoms aren't sexy.'

In November 1947 Mr Rank announced plans for making forty-seven films at a cost of £9¼ million. He would distribute them himself. Meanwhile the Chancellor of the Exchequer, Dr Dalton, suddenly slapped a 75 per cent customs duty on all imported films, which Mr Harold Wilson, President of the Board of Trade, soon lifted: he had the more realistic idea of setting up a National Film Finance Corporation, whose purpose seemed to be to counterbalance Rank. Unfortunately it ran out of cash too quickly. Some argued: did British films need to be as lavish as Hollywood's in these lean times? Hadn't Ealing Studios shown what could be done on a shoestring? And what about the new Italians, Rossellini and De Sica, producing realistic films out of the rubble of the post-war

world? Carol Reed, for one, wasn't to be confined by accountants: he exceeded his budget on *Odd Man Out* (1947), the first of several loner-on-the-run studies, and one of the best British films ever made, and he had to go.

Not that Mr Rank minded spending money at first. He started the J. Arthur Rank Company of Youth, popularly known as the Charm School or the Rank Starlets. Jean Simmons, Jane Hylton, Diana Dors, Barbara Murray, Sally Ann Howes, Honor Blackman, Zena Marshall, Lana Morris; all were groomed at the Charm School, and probably all would have made the grade anyway. Fan Clubs became big business (Jean Kent's was the first, and, with more than twenty-five thousand members, the biggest): it was possible to have a Fan Club before you had been given a sizeable role.

Ealing Studios, under Michael Balcon, was a friendly little studio, a touch amateurish, full of well-loved character actors, which was famous for a very British kind of farcical comedy, typified by the boyish high spirits of T.E.B. Clarke, one of its principal writers. *Hue and Cry*, a sort of Cockney *Emil and the Detectives*, filled the screen with hundreds of small boys tearing about in bombed buildings. *Passport to Pimlico*

Passport to Pimlico, 1949

postulated an independent state near Victoria Station, London. *Whisky Galore*, about salvaging a cargo of precious liquor off the Outer Hebrides, was an adaptation of a Compton Mackenzie novel; and *Kind Hearts and Coronets* had Alec Guinness playing eight characters in a black farce about multiple murder with one of the most polished scripts (by Robert Hamer) in the history of the cinema. All the last three films were produced by Ealing in one year – 1949.

It is said that British films grew up after the War. Well, there were good things in those years. Excellent films based on Graham Greene stories – *The Basement Room, The Fallen Idol, Brighton Rock, The Third Man; The Small Back Room*, Nigel Balchin's story of that new kind of tension, the interval between the initial tinkering with a bomb and the final defusing – or detonation; Peter Ustinov's *Vice Versa*; Noël Coward's *Brief Encounter*, a fragile novelette of unconsummated love which mostly happens in a railway station buffet: the absolutely authentic wartime touch was the sugar ration – a single lump which was always left in the slopped teaspoon. Other good films starred Moira Shearer in *Red Shoes*, with choreography by Massine and Helpmann, Vivien Leigh in a sumptuous *Anna Karenina* and that nice chap Ray Milland playing an alcoholic in *The Lost Weekend*.

Bernard Shaw, seduced by Rank, United Artists and a hypnotic Hungarian named Gabriel Pascal (who had made *Major Barbara* in 1940), at last allowed a spectacular *Caesar and Cleopatra* to be screened, with Claude Rains, Vivien Leigh, and Flora Robson as Ftatateeta. Shakespeare was enduringly committed to film in Olivier's athletic *Hamlet*, with Jean Simmons as Ophelia, and eccentrically by Orson Welles in *Macbeth*, whom he played (said a New York critic) 'like a dead end kid on the make', chopping and rearranging the text in a manner described as 'throwing good Shakespeare after bad'. Two films of Dickens novels remain indestructible classics to this day, David Lean's *Great Expectations* (1946) and *Oliver Twist* (1947): the latter's release in America was held up because the Board of Rabbis objected to Alec Guinness's portrayal of Fagin.

And Chaplin? Gone was the little tramp. In *The Great Dictator* (1940) he was a Jewish barber who happened to look like Hitler; in *Monsieur Verdoux* (1947) he attempted a black comedy on a Bluebeard-Landru theme.

From Italy and France, came two strangely contrasted legacies of the war and enemy occupation. The Italians were harshly realistic, almost documentary in *Open City, Bicycle Thieves, To Live in Peace*. No script, amateur actors, hand-held camera off-centre moving faster than a running figure because that is how the eye really sees it. *Open City*, which cost only $19,000 to make, took more than $5 million ($\pounds 1\frac{1}{4}$ million) in America alone. In no time Selznick was after De Sica, M.G.M. after Rossellini. So was Ingrid Bergman: 'If ever you need an actress with a Swedish accent,' she wrote to him, 'just call on me.' The result was the uncomfortable *Stromboli*, and their brief marriage, condemned by women's clubs all over America.

The French, stifled by German censorship during their claustrophobic Occupation and slow to recover afterwards, retreated into myths, romance, fantasy; Cocteau, Beauty and the Beast, Orpheus and Eurydice, Tristan and Isolde. Safe enough to make *Le Diable au Corps*, a torrid love story of World War I (Gerard Philipe and Micheline Presle), *Monsieur Vincent*, with Pierre Fresnay as a suffering priest in another century (much recommended by the Catholic Church); or to go back to Debureau and the Paris theatre in 1848 for *Les Enfants du Paradis*, directed by Marcel Carné and written by Jacques Prévert with Arletty reviewing all her lovers, Jean Louis Barrault superbly miming and a cast of three thousand – the greatest French film of these years, more than three hours long.

There was, in Cocteau's much disliked *Love Eternal*, a loathsome pop-eyed dwarf, horrific enough for people to say that the sequence should have been cut. The same image (only this time it is a sinister child gazing up a staircase, fooling the audience, because it is never seen again) occurred for a moment in *The Third Man*. It had no other function than to set a sinister mood of despair, in the existentialist sense that Hell is here on earth, surrounding us all the time.

The Third Man was born of Alexander Korda's vague desire to make a film about the four-power occupation of Vienna in 1949. Suppose Carol Reed, the director, had not had the idea of a single instrument, Anton Karas's zither, to provide the whole of the soundtrack. Suppose Graham Greene, the writer, had insisted on his original intention to have a happy

Great Expectations, 1946

ending. . . . How seriously would we have taken this thriller, with its melodramatic meeting of Joseph Cotten and Orson Welles in the Ferris wheel high above the Prater, Harry Lime the trafficker in black-market diluted penicillin (suddenly a superman as he argues his contempt for human life and – in the lines he wrote himself – for 'brotherly love and democracy' which in the long run produces, in a country like Switzerland, only the 'cuckoo clock'); the funeral of the wrong man, the dreary world of forged passports which is the daily life of Trevor Howard as the British security officer, the great chase in the sewers (based, I suspect, on the case of the Apache bandit Bonnot in the Paris of 1912)? A moment of pure comedy – Wilfred Hyde White as the oily British Council representative roping in Holly Martins, the pulp-writer of Westerns, to give a cultural lecture. A moment of deadly serious-

ness – the Greene Catholic bit – among the nuns of the children's hospital where Harry Lime's bad penicillin claims lives every day (a surgeon friend of Greene's said he had known two R.A.F. doctors who were in the penicillin racket). And the memorable ending – Alida Valli, Charlie Chaplin in reverse, walking alone from the cemetery after Harry's real funeral, along an endless avenue, slowly approaching the camera as Joseph Cotten waits for her. They do not embrace. He makes no move. She does not even look at him. You know that he will catch the next plane back to the States. They will never meet again.

CHAPTER 10

World of Sport

'A player whose stroke is affected by the simultaneous explosion of a bomb or shell . . . may play another ball from the same place. Penalty one stroke.' This solemn wartime rule assumed, like Harry Graham's verse, that neither air-raid, nor invasion, nor 'the thought of England's shame' would put any true golfer off his game. Some British golf courses, and cricket grounds too, were covered with Army huts or dug up for air-raid shelters or ploughed and planted with vegetables. Almost the only sport which survived was amateur, not to say amateurish; but you could still while away hours in an air-raid shelter doing your football pools. What, asked *Horse and Hound*, as the bombs rained on British cities, was the outlook for fox hunting? 'I am sure you will all be uplifted by this message,' it told its readers, 'flashed round the nation by news agency on Monday last – "The Quorn has started cub hunting".'

In America, Gene Sarazen tied with Lawson Little for the U.S. Open Championship, but lost to him in the end. Betty James was top woman golfer in 1940. War obscured the game for six years, though Byron Nelson, P.G.A. champion in 1940 and 1945, won eighteen tournaments in a single year; and in 1942 the veteran Chick Evans battled his way to the final of the Chicago city championship, only to be defeated by a much younger man.

After the war the British Open Championship was won by Henry Cotton for the third time. This great gentleman of golf was thought to have raised the status of professionalism (and golf, after the war, became extremely professional: in America, tournament purses were never less than $15,000). Cotton, Walter Hagen and Arthur Locke were the first three professionals to become honorary members of the Royal and Ancient. Ben Hogan and Sam Snead were now to the fore, Hogan winning the U.S. Open and

P.G.A. titles in 1948 (and seven other tournaments) before being incapacitated by a serious road accident. Hogan, from Fort Worth, Texas, son of a blacksmith, who had started as a caddy at 65 cents a round, was famous for 'assembly-line precision' and for his principle that 'putting is foreign to the rest of the game'.

Britain's woman champion in 1949 was Miss F. Stephens, who became Mrs Roy Smith; but it was of course America that produced the extraordinary girl of golf, Mrs Mildred ('Babe') Didrikson Zaharias. At seventeen she had thrown a baseball 296 feet. At eighteen she had been a gold medallist for athletics in the 1932 Olympic Games; and being shown a golf club for the first time in that year, took up the game and became a champion fifteen years later, and also the first American woman to win the British women's amateur title as well. With her, singing as it were in close harmony, were Patty Berg, Betsy Rawls and Louise Suggs, who won the U.S. Amateur Championship in 1947, the British in 1948, and the U.S. Open in 1949 respectively. Golf was no longer a rich man's game, and its democratization was helped by television.

Football, too, was increasingly professional; transfer fees grew bigger. There were changes of style, some due to foreign influences as, in the first flush of peace, international matches were played. In 1945 it was probably true to say that Arsenal, the most famous team in the world, was on the whole copied by the world, especially in their use of the W-formation; but it tended to be a defensive game. The usual tactic was to upset the enemy's centre-half and so penetrate the goal's first defences. But Manchester United, under Matt Busby, was experimenting with a more mobile centre-forward, at the risk of his becoming a prima donna. The Italian team in 1949, at Tottenham, which attacked England by using a V-formation with

Tommy Lawton, 1948

ageless 'wizard of the dribble'; Tom Finney, who had begun playing for Preston North End during the war; Stanley Mortensen, hero of England's victory over Italy at Turin in 1948.

The Russians did not seem to think there was anything wrong with British football. Hardly had Japan been defeated in 1945 when they sent their renowned Moscow Dynamos to Britain. Let their goalkeeper, Alexei Khomich (immediately nicknamed 'Tiger' by the British press), tell the story. None of the Russians had ever seen the British play football before, except Khomich himself, who had played against an Army team for the Shah's Cup at Teheran in 1944. It was known that he was capable of spectacular leaps to save goals. In twenty games with the Dynamos he had let through only twelve goals. They met the British (Chelsea) team at Stamford Bridge in the murky fog. The Russians presented the British with red and white carnations; the British presented the Russians with cigarette lighters.

'It is a Saturday afternoon,' Khomich reports. 'The stands are crowded. The spectators have various ways of showing their pleasure or dissatisfaction. They shout and whistle. They even sing songs. They repeat phrases in a chorus. They make good use of the rattles sold at the entrance to the stadium . . . I specially watched Tommy Lawton. They said there had never been a centre-forward like him since Drake – "Oh, Tommy – he is like a machine gun!" Lawton is tall and lean, moves quickly, and is always dangerous as

the centre-forward as spearhead, disconcerted their opponents but failed to beat them. Still, they had given them something to think about. In international matches there were often different interpretations of the rules; and so, in 1949, F.I.F.A. (the International Association Football Federation) asked Sir Stanley Rous, that very experienced referee, to draw up a code for referees in future World Cup tournaments.

Sports page headlines of these years used to ask: Is English football growing old? Are tactics stereotyped, does excessive caution rule the field? Continental teams went for youth, dash, attack. Why, we had even been beaten by Eire! It was no use blaming rationing; Britain seemed still to be thinking that Soccer players were born, not made by strenuous training. Britain had Tommy Lawton, 'greatest centre-forward of the age', with a kick like a cannon; Stanley Matthews,

Stanley Matthews, 1948

he can shoot hard from any angle. He is an excellent header. He is a typical prima donna. The entire team plays for him and creates opportunities for him . . . he can knock the ball out of the goalkeeper's hands with his head. English rules allow tackling the goalkeeper in this way. In our country such tactics would incur a penalty.'

Khomich always had a bottle behind the goal. What was it for? Soon after half-time the crowd began to chant: 'Khomich – whisky! Khomich – whisky!' It turned out that it contained only water; to wet his gloves so that he could get a better grip on the ball. Honour was satisfied all round when, before eighty-five thousand spectators, they drew 3–3. But four days later, Dynamos beat Cardiff 10–1. They gave the Welsh roses: the Welsh gave them each a miner's lamp.

Both Matthews and Lawton played with newer, younger men in the Great Britain team that faced the 'Rest of Europe', in May 1947 at Hampden Park. Two red-haired Scots (Forbes and Macaulay), half-backs; Billy Steel and Billy Liddell, of Liverpool (he was very much a man of his time, a miner's son who had been an R.A.F. pilot and was now training to be an accountant); Burgess and Hughes, both Welshmen; Hardwick from Middlesbrough, and Vernon from Belfast. 'Rest of Europe' did not include Germany or Russia, but comprised two Swedes, two Danes, and one each from France, Czechoslovakia, Belgium, Italy, Holland, Switzerland and Eire. Poor 'Rest of Europe': they were beaten 6–1.

The presence of a baseball star in the U.S. Army sometimes inspired commanding officers to say, of any forthcoming event, 'Orders of the Day – *Win*.' It wasn't too easy to keep track of who was where, but occasionally one read in a Californian newspaper that 'Private Joe Di Maggio is playing ball at Camp Santa Ana.' Returning to civilian life, Di Maggio, now thirty-one, hit twenty-five home runs in 1946: all was beginning to be right with the world again. By 1948 he was said to be earning $67,000 a year, and was part-owner of Di Maggio's seafood restaurant in San Francisco. His younger brother Dominic was playing for the Boston Red Sox. The seafood restaurant pleased their father, who had wanted them both to be fishermen, and regarded baseball as 'a bum's game'. The nation's youth, brought up to revere Babe Ruth, studied Joe curiously: Babe had always kept his feet

Joe Di Maggio, 1941

together, but Joe always stood with them a yard apart. He didn't diet, either; seemed to live on spaghetti, and smoked a pack of Chesterfields a day. Never mind: he was the eighth man in history to hit three hundred home runs.

He did much of it for the New York Yankees club, run by Casey Stengel from 1948 onwards. There was in Stengel a streak of madness that, when he wasn't fooling, made him talk like *Finnegans Wake*. It worked: he led them to victory in the World Series.

So far, baseball had been white. Boxers and athletes could be black: why not baseball players? It had happened once, when Jackie Robinson was asked to join the Brooklyn Dodgers (of course, he *had* been to college); and the story goes that he was hired only when manager Branch Rickey was satisfied that he wouldn't lose his temper if there were demonstrations against him. When Brooklyn played the St Louis Cardinals there was indeed trouble, but Brooklyn in the end whipped them. In 1948 the breakthrough was complete when Satchel Paige, from Mobile, Alabama, believed to be over forty, was signed up by Cleveland Indians. He had been playing for nearly a quarter of a century.

In post-war Britain village greens gave up their cabbages and returned to their proper uses, chief among them cricket; and from Lord's Pavilion, requisitioned as part of a training school for airmen, flannelled figures issued again, Yorkshire and Middlesex leading, with a newcomer, Glamorgan, joining the big league in 1948. Two great Middlesex names, Denis Compton and Bill Edrich, brought back some of the glory of Surrey's Jack Hobbs, whose total of runs and centuries Compton would beat.

There are those who remember 1947 as 'the summer of Compton and Edrich'; others for whom these years were 'the twilight of the all-rounder'. What, in an age of professionals and specialization, had become of the versatile amateur, good at more than one sport, able to play at several positions on the field, and usually also a man of coordinated brain power as well? It was a question often asked by old-stagers like R.C. Robertson-Glasgow, sports correspondent and an all-rounder himself. W.G. Grace had also been a passable golfer and an excellent hurdler. Walter Hammond, Captain of England cricket, had been good at both Rugby and Soccer, and his golf handicap was 2. C.B. Fry, also in his day Captain of England cricket, had as an undergraduate been President of athletics, had for some years held the world long jump record, and was besides scholar, author and wit: the ancient Greek ideal.

Compton had something of this quality. He went from council school to Lord's ground staff when he was fourteen, and to the Arsenal football ground a year later; then entered both county cricket and First Division soccer, and by the age of thirty was one of the very few who had played both games for England with speed, power and almost balletic grace. There was a little criticism of his sponsorship of Brylcreem in advertisements; but it sold an awful lot of haircream, and suited the elegant image of a man who was said to get through 'a hundred and fifty clean shirts, a hundred pairs of laundered flannels, two hundred clean singlets and two hundred pairs of clean white socks' in a season.

In 1947 the first M.C.C. side to visit Australia for ten years was led by an ex-professional from Gloucestershire, Walter Hammond, who had spent six years in the R.A.F. 'The old man', now forty-four, was a playing captain, famed and feared for his follow-through drive off either foot; a big, outgoing personality. Australia, as it turned out, was better prepared under Don Bradman, and won the Test. When Bradman brought his side to England the following year, England fared no better. The batting of Len Hutton, Compton and Edrich was formidable, but the united talents of the Australians – with three young stars, Arthur Morris, Keith Miller and Ray Lindwall the fast bowler ('Australia's revenge for Harold Larwood') – were too much for them. And yet – England *did* beat Australia; for one of those lest-we-forget footnotes to sporting history, obscured by sex discrimination, discloses that in 1948–9 an English women's cricket team, captained by Miss M. Hide (who herself made over a thousand runs and five centuries) toured Australia and New Zealand, losing only one of their twenty-eight matches.

One of the brave gestures of the War was the U.S. Lawn Tennis Association's resolution, taken just after Pearl Harbor, to carry on. Tournaments, using what talent could be mustered, would be used to raise funds for the American Red Cross and other war funds; meanwhile a new generation of players would be trained up through a 'Junior Tennis' organization for under-eighteens. There could obviously be no Wight-

Don Bradman in action, 1948

man Cup in wartime. To see first-class games, you had to live near Forest Hills, Long Island, where any player stationed nearby could be seen – and that meant Seaman Bobby Riggs and Lieutenant Fred Schroeder (both in the Navy), and, from the Army, Sergeant Frank Parker and Lieutenant Joseph Hunt. America was certainly readier for post-war tennis than any other country. The Davis Cup must not be allowed to stay in Australia: twenty other nations were agreed on that, and it was regained for America by Jack Kramer's team. Five of Europe's

Davis Cup candidates had been killed in action.

At Wimbledon, where the bomb damage had taken some time to repair, there were record crowds in 1946. The British were virtually written off, and although it was said by way of excuse that both Britain and France were still 'suffering from the effects of war', only France produced a worthy adversary for the Americans – Yvon Petra, who won the men's singles. The typical American male player was dedicated, ruthless, strained, crewcut, and wore barely adequate shorts.

When Kramer turned professional the new U.S. champion was Richard Gonzales from California, the boy with the big service. Was it the game or the personality we watched? Was not professionalism only a recognition that sport was show-business? Bob Falkenburg, winner of the Wimbledon singles in 1948, brother to the beautiful Jinx, used to irritate the crowd at Wimbledon by kneeling like a Muslim at prayer or lying down on the baseline to rest in the middle of a game, so much so that they began to cheer his double faults. Ted Schroeder, Wimbledon champion of 1949, a little bandy, nervously sucking his thumb, smoking his pipe before a game to overcome his stage fright. Czechoslovakia's Jaroslav Drobny – the left-hander with the formidable forehand, beaten by Schroeder.

And the women . . . Alice Marble, she of the 'masculine service', had won her fourth and last U.S. championship in 1940, defeating Helen Jacobs for the third time. (But she was beaten, after three years as national champion, in 1945 by Sarah Palfrey Cooke, one of the few tennis girls from the East of America, who came out of retirement to do it.) From California came cool, confident, blonde Pauline Betz, three times winner of the U.S. Women's Singles: 'I'm a retriever,' she described herself. Red-haired Margaret Osborne du Pont, blonde Louise Brough, Pat Todd and Doris Hart, all Wightman Cuppers, simply blew Britain's out-of-practice players off the courts. And what vision stands out more vividly than any of these in the memory? 'Gorgeous Gussie' Moran in her frilly pants.

Jaroslav Drobny, 1949

But Britain at last had a heavyweight boxer. Bruce Woodcock, son of a miner, was twenty-two when he first appeared at the Royal Albert Hall in January 1942, and earned £25 by knocking out Stoker Clark. Three and a half years later he was heavyweight champion of the British Empire, having knocked out the heavier (218 lb) Jack London in the sixth round at White Hart Lane, Tottenham, before a crowd of thirty-eight thousand. But from now on he became accident-prone. In May 1946 he fought Mauriello. At the ringside was Cary Grant, who shouted: 'Woodcock, you've got him! I'm from England too!' A moment later, Woodcock and Mauriello banged their heads together; Woodcock seemed dazed thereafter, and lost. He managed to beat Freddie Mills and Gus Lesnevich; but then, in April 1947, came the terrible fight with Joe Baksi, who broke his jaw in the first round: it was as if he had been run over by a bus. Somehow Woodcock remained on his feet for another six rounds. A fight was arranged with Lee Savold for September 1949. A month before, Woodcock drove a truck into a tree, badly hurting his right eye. Sportswriters, notably Peter Wilson of the London *Daily Mirror,* again sang the refrain about the amateurism of British sport: what professional would drive any vehicle anywhere just before a big fight? The fight was postponed for nine months, but it made no difference. One further defeat, and Woodcock retired to run a pub in Yorkshire.

Do boxers ever know when to retire? Joe Louis did, it seemed, when he ended his own record reign of twelve years in 1949, having defended his title twenty-five times, winning mostly by knock-outs. The great black gentleman only came back to face Ezzard Charles and bloody defeat because he owed a million dollars to the Government which taxed him on two purses he had donated to charity. In America boxing seemed to be getting dirtier. There was a featherweight named Willie Pep, who did nasty things to his opponents 'without actually cheating', as Stephen Potter would say; and a middleweight hoodlum named Rocky Graziano (by no means to be confused with Rocky Marciano) who just went at people like a mad dog. All the more reason to admire Sugar Ray Robinson (Walker Smith from Harlem), welterweight champion in 1946, cool, sometimes amused, conserving his strength, and not hurting people too much.

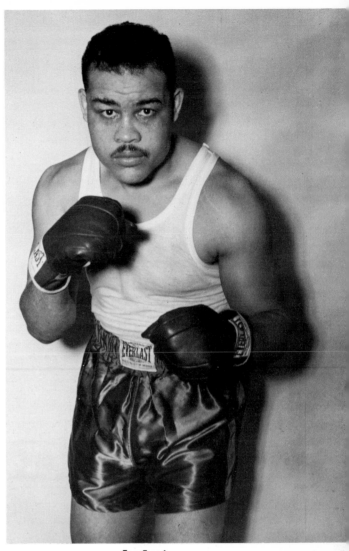

Joe Louis

Boxing looked good on American television, and ringside attendances fell off for a while, until it was clear that television was creating new publics for all sports. There were, indeed, freak events that seemed to have been devised specially for the new medium. A violent kind of free-for-all roller skating known as the Roller Derby. An all-in wrestler called 'Gorgeous George', who waved his hair, wore pink satin, and had the ring sprayed with eau de cologne before performing (was he invented by Liberace?). Women wrestlers, too.

The British, beaten to their knees by having won a war, were obsessed with their poor performance in sports. The King and Queen, at the first Royal Ascot since the war, when the Enclosure was open to the general public, saw the King's horse, Tipstaff, come in last. It was now quite usual to talk of 'the decline of the British horse'. Punitive taxation, owners claimed, was decimating their stables. Social critics complained that the daily food for one race horse could feed dozens of hens. Yet Britain needed to breed fine horseflesh to earn dollars. Huge prices were being paid: in 1945 the Gaekwar of Baroda had given

Sugar Ray Robinson

Spain was too far away for television; but here in 1949 there was a man really worth watching – forty-five-year-old Sidney Franklin, Brooklyn born, son of an immigrant named Frumkin, and now at the peak of his career as the only American recognized internationally by *aficionados* as a fully fledged matador. Friend of Hemingway, author of the *Encyclopaedia Britannica* article on bullfighting, fluent in Spanish, he had killed two thousand bulls, some in Mexico but most in Spain. He thought Hemingway romanticized the whole business; he didn't care for *Death in the After-noon*. The hot-blooded Spaniard, the so-called love affair with death – 'Death, shmeath, so long as I keep healthy!' Ever since his début at Seville in 1929, his approach to bullfighting had been absolutely cold: 'It gave me a feeling of sensual well-being to kill a bull – by killing bulls, I learned how to be interested in *life.*'

28,000 guineas ($141,000) for Sayajirao, who won the 1947 St Leger. How could humiliated France suddenly be winning almost everything? The answer was Marcel Boussac, the French textile millionaire who had financed the New Look. He owned Galcador and Asmena, won both Derby and Oaks in the same year; won the Ascot Gold Cup twice, with Caracalla and Arbar; won the St Leger twice; and in October 1949 broke records by winning £60,000 in stake money in one week.

But is it not the riders that we remember? Gordon Richards, indestructible at forty-five, in a single week of 1949 rode thirty races, won ten, and was placed in eleven. He had passed Fred Archer's record of 2,749 winners in April 1943; he was the greatest jockey of his age; but he had not yet achieved his life's ambition to win the Derby; for this he would have to wait until 1953, when he would also become the first professional jockey to be knighted. And students of jockey form noted a twelve-year-old boy named Lester Piggott, whose two grandfathers had both been jockeys, and who, as he rode a horse called The Chase to victory at Haydock Park, was cheered as the youngest boy to win a flat race within living memory.

Gordon Richards winning the Queen Anne Stakes on Pambidian, 15 June 1949

The torch of amateurism, the classical ideal, was carried from Greece to London in the Marathon relay that opened the first Olympic Games since the War. The 1936 Games in Germany had been polluted by racialism and political tension; the 1948 Games, the first to be held in Britain for forty years, would, must, express some kind of redemption, one felt, as a blond youth, looking truly god-like, carried the flame round the White City Stadium and ran lightly up to the 'fountain', touched it with his torch, and watched the symbolic flame flare up; as indeed it should, for it was gas.

British athletics, it need hardly be said, were in decline; you cannot, the excuse ran, train athletes on Woolton Pie. Great hopes were entertained of Macdonald Bailey, a West Indian, who, however, was subject to muscle trouble. Somehow Britain managed to get four silver medals. A horse named Foxhunter, owned by Colonel Harry Llewellyn, helped the British Olympic show jumping team to a bronze medal. It was, of course, America ('the steak-fed Yanks', their rationed hosts said nastily) that swept the board

with twelve gold medals; neutral Sweden got five; and invaded, starved Holland got four. They were all won, for the 100 metres, 200 metres, hurdles and 400 metres, by a strong lady called Mrs Fanny Blankers-Koen, who became 'the greatest all-round woman athlete of the century'. For America, Harrison Dillard, expected to win the hurdles, won the 100-metre dash instead: it was William Porter and Roy Cochran who won the hurdles. A seventeen-year-old Californian schoolboy, Robert Mathias, won the exhausting Decathlon (ten events in two days). Britain rejoiced in the successes of her Commonwealth – Australian John Winter's high jump, and Jamaican Arthur Wint's 400 metres. But the silhouette that stays imprinted on the memory is none of these; it is Emil Zatopek of Cezchoslovakia, who, in winning the 10,000 metres, broke Nurmi's 1920 record and years of Finnish domination of distance running by doing it in 29 minutes 59.6 seconds. His style was like nothing anyone had seen before, alternately sprinting and lolloping. 'He runs', one sportswriter said, 'like an upright turtle.'

Mrs Fanny Blankers–Koen (*right*) competing in a hurdles final at the Olympic Games in 1948

CHAPTER 11

Disunited Nations

It could not be pretended, as the war years receded, that Britain and America were getting on well together. The fact that neither was getting on well with Russia merely forced them into a shotgun marriage which, by 1949, did not look very secure. Britain was by then trying to blame her own perpetual economic crisis on an American recession. In London, at a tiny club theatre called the New Lindsey, a play called *49th State* had run for a few performances, and it was being seriously suggested by one economist that Britain should apply to join the United States, nipping in even before Hawaii and thus becoming the Airstrip One of *1984*. An American public relations expert, Edward L. Bernays, said that an Anglo-American committee for mutual explanation should be formed. Americans simply hadn't time to penetrate beyond what they thought of as British apathy, dirt, bad cooking, insolent service in hotels. As for America, it should lower its tariffs against British manufactured goods, and both countries should learn each other's history at school. Every American child, especially the majority who were not of British stock, grew up believing that Britain, even though she had once killed a tyrannical king, still bullied an Empire, and tolerated peers who were all too rich; and never forgot that 'Benedict Arnold sold out to the British'. In October 1948 *Time* magazine noted with relief that Britain and America had at last agreed about *something* – the standardization of screw threads.

But they were not agreeing about Israel. In March 1946 an Anglo-American committee had recommended the immediate immigration of a hundred thousand Jews into Palestine, which should become a United Nations trusteeship instead of a British mandate. Unfortunately the Americans were unwilling to share the military and financial burden of implementing this, so the British rather helplessly handed the problem over to the United Nations. By May 1947

a special United Nations committee was coming round to the idea of partition into separate Arab and Jewish states, which was violently opposed by the Arabs. America and Russia voted for partition; Britain abstained. The mandate was to end on 15 May 1948, and British troops were to be out by August.

There was never any prospect of avoiding violence. This had been clear since a day in July 1946 when a Chrysler truck, driven by Jews dressed as Arabs, had unloaded some milk churns at the King David Hotel, Jerusalem, which housed a large number of British soldiers and foreign journalists. The churns were full of T.N.T. which exploded in the biggest single act of violence within living memory. It was the work of the Irgun Zvai Leumi, an extremist group, led by Menachem Beigin, a Polish soldier who had deserted in Palestine, under the code name 'Gideon'. In America a Hollywood script writer named Ben Hecht, raising funds for Israel, informed the press that 'there is a song in my heart every time a British soldier is killed'. There were Jews who, because the Palestine immigration quota since 1939 had been only ten thousand a year, blamed Britain for the gas chambers.

British troops captured and flogged terrorists. The Irgun captured and flogged British troops. 'If we go down,' Beigin said, 'we will see to it that the state of Israel sinks with us!' A terrorist named Dov Gruner was sentenced to death for a raid on a police station. A Tel Aviv judge, Ralph Windham, was kidnapped in retaliation: the two men were exchanged. Windham's captors, who kept his wig as a souvenir, seemed to find a kind of poetry in violence: they talked to him like excited undergraduates about art and religion, and gave him Arthur Koestler's novel of *kibbutz* life, *Thieves in the Night*, to read.

Gruner was recaptured and hanged in Acre jail. The Irgun attacked the prison and opened it: more than two hundred prisoners escaped. The raiders were captured and condemned to death. In revenge, two British field security sergeants were hanged in a eucalyptus grove near Nathanya. One of the bodies was booby-trapped, exploding in the face of a British officer. Guerrilla bands of Arabs invaded from Syria and Lebanon. Into this setting of civil war the state of Israel was born. The United Nations sent the saintly Count Bernadotte of Sweden to mediate between Jews and Arabs. He seemed on the point of success when he was assassinated by the Stern Gang, a break-away group from the Irgun which had four years before murdered Lord Moyne, Minister Resident in Cairo. Bernadotte was succeeded by Ralph Bunche, who negotiated an armistice and became the first Negro to win the Nobel Peace Prize.

It is probable that Ernest Bevin, Britain's Foreign Secretary, never really understood the Palestine question: he had been opposed to the state of Israel on the grounds that Jewry was a religion, not a people; and when, in December 1948, a book left on Bevin's seat in the House of Commons was found to contain a bomb, the Stern Gang claimed that they had put it there.

In Manchester, Liverpool and the East End of London the news from Palestine had stimulated anti-Jewish demonstrations. Among the blitzed pubs and churches pamphlets bearing photographs of Sir Oswald Mosley, the pre-war Fascist leader, were dis-tributed by an organization calling itself the British League of Ex-Servicemen. Their meetings flew the Union Jack; there hadn't been much flag-flapping since VJ-Day, and in a sad way it warmed East End hearts. Rebecca West, reporting the meetings for the *New Yorker,* noticed 'ex-officers of a special type, sometimes handsome, but queer . . . mad about the eyes.' Some of the speakers appeared to be Irish. People marched through the shattered streets chant-ing: 'Two-four-six-eight. Who do we appreciate? M-O-S-L-E-Y.' The star speaker was a blond, extrem-ely Aryan young man called Jeffrey Hamm. Like Hitler, he seemed to have only one speech. He denounced, not Jews as a race, but Jewish financiers, black-marketeers and Bolsheviks. Hecklers were called 'pansies with pink toenails'. Much of his speech was about his own personal life, the miserable jobs he had had and been fired from. Some of the women in the audience found this self-pity appealing to their maternal instincts. He did not look like the father-figure Britain sought, now that Churchill was out of power. What about Mosley himself, who was starting up again with a new Union Movement? He was being more careful about anti-semitism; the voice was still hypnotic, but it no longer worked. His meetings and Hamm's were attended by a lot of adolescents. 'They don't mean any harm, you know,' a Jewish woman placidly told Rebecca West. 'You see, they all used to sleep down in the tube stations when the war was on, and they had a wonderful time then, with the concerts and all. And really, you know, the blitz and those rockets, they were very exciting, for all the harm they did. The boys and girls miss it all dreadfully, and this chasing around fills up the evenings for them. They'd forget it if anything else came along.'

In 1948 both America and Britain had elections. The British one, a less noticeable affair, brought back the weary Labour Government and was remarkable only for a pamphlet which, celebrating the housing, health and full employment achieved by Labour since the War, showed a photograph of an infant in a posh-looking pram: 'The prams of Britain,' it claimed, 'are filled with the bonniest babies in living memory.' The baby in the photograph, taken in 1936, turned out to be Prince Edward of Kent. However, the State Opening of Parliament brought back the first ceremonial since 1938, complete with Household Cavalry and the newly-polished State Crown. The King's speech announced plans for the nationaliz-ation of steel.

In America – indeed, the world over – people were asking: could the little man possibly get a second term? The Democrats only flourished in bad times, orthodox opinion ran; the Republicans were the nat-ural party to govern. Roosevelt had had four terms, but of course the times were unusual, this sort of thing could not go on, they must get back to normal. . . .

The 1948 Presidential Election was held during the Berlin Airlift, so what was normal? In June the west-ern allies had taken the decision that if the division of Germany were to be permanent, a democratic West German Federal government should be set up. Amer-ican atomic bombers arrived in Britain. The new Deutschmark was regarded by the Russians as a threat to their own East German currency. China was going Communist. Russia now had the A-bomb. NATO beginning, Marshall Aid, Churchill's talk of a United Western Europe – Russia felt the West was

The Anglo–American solution to the Russians' blockade of Berlin was the Berlin Airlift. Inside an aircraft, about to land, the crew loosen straps round crates to save time in unloading

ganging up on her. The toughness of Foreign Secretary Ernest Bevin, who had tried very hard to get on with the Russians, even persuading the stony Molotov to sing 'The more we are together' on the platform of a Moscow station, and expressing his growing disenchantment with Stalin by exploding, towards the end of 1947, 'Now 'e's gone too bloody far,' was a relief to everyone except the far left.

Bevin, the great commoner, attacked Vishinsky, prosecutor in many 'purge' trials, at the United Nations in Paris, with wonderful fury: 'If atomic war should happen, it could only be the fault of *one* nation. . . . If the Soviet representative had any feeling for the simple people of Europe or the world, if he were animated by anything but out-of-date, backward, unscientific doctrine, he would be the first to applaud the great unselfish contribution of the United States to world recovery. . . .' And then the terrific peroration: 'Open up the world and let light and knowledge come in!'

Russian retaliation to the West German Federal Government took the form of an act which, at most, looked warlike, and at least was an attempt to drive Britain and America out of Berlin. The Russians blockaded the city by refusing to allow land or water transport between western Germany and the Berlin enclave. This meant that Britain and America could no longer feed the 2½ million people in their sectors of Berlin. The Anglo-American solution was equally warlike: a massive airlift, based on lessons learned in war, of five to six thousand tons a day of food, coal, machinery, medical and other supplies, twenty-four hours a day until further notice.

The Airlift (called by Germans *die Luftbrücke*) was the result of General Lucius Clay, commander-in-chief of U.S. forces in Germany, convincing Harry Truman that America must stay in Berlin at all costs. Four-engine transport planes were used, mostly C-47s (known in peacetime as DC-4s and by the British as Dakotas): they landed at three West Berlin airfields and on the Havel river, and, to avoid returning empty, often carried Berlin exports on their return flight, including, on one occasion, the seventy-strong Berlin Symphony Orchestra. New runways were built at Tempelhof and Gatow, and a new airfield at Tegel, in the French sector. The British called their part of the operation Plainfare; the Americans called theirs Operation Vittles (though food was not more than a third of the load). There was a great shortage of flying personnel, and staff officers gladly volunteered to leave their desks. Weather conditions, especially in winter fog, were often vile, but the number of accidents was kept very small by recently-developed radio and radar techniques. Among the thousands of different things carried by the Airlift were vitamin tablets, machine tools, snowploughs, police uniforms, bicycle parts, dried banana flakes (for three German babies who could not assimilate any other food), ladies' underwear, and T.N.T. for demolishing the results of Allied air-raids.

To Berliners, sceptical at first, it was strange to be brought manna by the very airmen who, four years ago, had wrought the greatest destruction the pre-Hiroshima world had ever known. It was a staggering demonstration of Anglo-American efficiency and united air power. It made the Russians lose face. Its propaganda value rubbed off on Anglo-American relations: suddenly the two countries liked each other again. In May 1949 the Russians called off the blockade. The Airlift, which had so far cost $170 million, went on, gradually diminishing, until the end of September, by which time 2,324,000 tons of supplies had reached Berlin in fifteen months. For better or worse, it is to the Berlin airlift that we owe the world of Konrad Adenauer and Ludwig Erhardt, the 'economic miracle', and all that followed.

But this was not foreseeable in the months leading up to the 1948 Presidential Election. What, asked Walter Lippmann, was Truman doing about anything? His generals were running it all. 'There is not even an attempt to pretend that the President is directing affairs, is making the decisions, is forming or conducting policy.' The Republicans put up Tom Dewey, Governor of New York. The southern Democrats, thinking Truman hadn't a chance, suggested Eisenhower, whose politics were unknown (although in 1947 he had told friends he supposed he was 'just a good Kansas Republican') but whose popularity was

at its height. Truman himself did not, at first, take his chances seriously, and at Potsdam three years before had said jokingly to Eisenhower: 'How about the White House in 1948?' In the deep South, where it was known that Truman favoured full citizenship for Negroes, a new 'Dixiecrat' party nominated Governor Strom Thurmond of South Carolina. In the North, a 'Progressive' Democratic wing nominated Henry Wallace.

It was the last real whistle-stop campaign before television took over. The British, reluctant to admit that politics, like the Royal Family and the Established Church, is a branch of show business, have never really understood American elections in which candidates play one-night, one-hour or even five-minute stands on the back of a railroad car like a fit-up theatre, with splendid motorcades at important centres. Truman and Dewey toured the country by rail. Truman's train went via Pennsylvania, Rock Island (Illinois), Denver and Rio Grande Western, Union Pacific and Southern Pacific railroads to Los Angeles, which took just over a week. Dewey's train went up the West Coast to Seattle, then east by Northern Pacific, Great Northern and Milwaukee lines. It was hell for reporters, who in those days had to send their stories by telegram which local stationmasters had to tap out in Morse code.

Dewey's campaign at first sight looked more professional. He had a smarter press office (run by James Hagerty), he brought more messages of goodwill from movie stars. He drank, and offered, cocktails. He played sophisticated bridge. The style of his speeches was described as '*Reader's Digest*'. He sometimes sang 'God Bless America' in his mellow baritone voice. He was apt to say, patronizingly, 'Of course, Harry *knows* he can't win!' Harry was only in the White House by accident, look at his great 'Fair Deal' manifesto, with all that expensive social security, going even farther than Roosevelt: no wonder it had become the 'Do-Nothing' policy, since nobody wanted it.

Truman, by contrast, seemed amateurish – in the words of Richard H. Rovere, who covered the whole whistle-stop, he was a 'coal-stove griddle' compared to Dewey's 'pop-up toaster'. His daughter Margaret waved and smiled a lot. Truman was applauded, but there were no actual ovations. Like Dewey, he had a speech writer, one Clark Clifford, but seemed more at ease when, to the consternation of his press office, whose handout was thereby invalidated, he threw away his prepared notes and spoke off the cuff. Actually, he didn't speak much at all: not about politics, anyway. After about five minutes, he became extremely folksy: 'How d'ya like to meet the family?' Now was there, or was there not, an assumed Southern drawl as he went farther south? Rovere quotes a particular sentence (his italics): 'And now I'd like *for* you to meet *Miss* Margaret.' And he always got a laugh by referring to Mrs Truman as 'the boss'. He drank Kentucky Bourbon, and played plebian poker.

One of the campaign gimmicks was a 'panty doll', obtainable at Moss Stores, California. Some dolls had 'Dewey – Warren' embroidered on them, others had 'Truman – Barkley', and the 'Dewey – Warren' doll was outselling its rival by eight to five. The opinion polls, and 85 per cent of the press, and all the commentators (even Alistair Cooke on transatlantic radio!) were certain Dewey would win. The Chicago *Tribune* even risked an edition headlined DEWEY DEFEATS TRUMAN, and there is a famous picture of a victorious Truman reading it. Why did Truman win? Impressions of the campaign vary widely: some witnesses say Truman was 'vigorous' and Dewey 'listless' (or maybe over-confident). Was it that the man from Missouri knew his America better than the man from Michigan? Or was it simply that the band played 'I'm just Wild About Harry'?

Almost the first problem of his second term was China. Three years before, he had sent General Marshall to try to make peace between Generalissimo Chiang Kai-shek's nationalists and Mao Tse-tung's Communists. Marshall spent a frustrating year or more before returning home with the recommendation that America should stop military and economic aid to the Nationalists. Now, in December 1949, Chiang's government fled to Formosa (Taiwan) as Mao's armies came south from Manchuria. Many Americans were confused. Republicans attacked Truman, saying he had sold out to the Reds; and weren't there known and named officials in the State Department who sympathized with the Chinese Communists, saying they were not like Russian Communists at all, but were merely 'agrarian reformers'? Wasn't China an old friend, perhaps not recently a very grateful one, to whom America had been sending missionaries for generations, and whom America had tried to protect from the Japanese by sending first Colonel Clair Chennault's Flying Tigers, and then General 'Vinegar Joe' Stilwell, who called Chiang 'Peanuts' and 'the little bastard' and seemed not at all impressed by his beautiful wife, the 'first lady of China' who wrote such eloquent propagandist books about her country? Hadn't Roosevelt, or someone, called Chiang 'the George Washington of China'? Why, *everyone* had read *The Good Earth*. . . .

China now had two Governments – the People's Republic of China, proclaimed to two hundred thousand people in the Square of the Gate of Heavenly Peace in Peking; and the Nationalist Government, now exiled to an island about a quarter of the size of England and Wales. Russia recognized the first; so, embarrassingly, did Britain. America and the United Nations did not. Next year the Korean War would begin, and Chiang would call it the start of the Third World War.

CHAPTER 12

Necessary Journeys

As my troopship nosed into Durban, Natal, one April afternoon in 1942, a large woman, all in white but for a red hat, had sung 'Land of Hope and Glory'. Dodging tin-fish, we had zigzagged about the North Atlantic, making believe we were going to put in at Newfoundland, the Azores, Rio, before we got to Freetown. (This was 1942, when the U-boat attacks were at their worst.) Then, in a mad dash, we made for the Cape, and the convoy split up, half to Cape Town, half to Durban. The wonder of blazing lights and gleaming American automobiles, and girls in thin summer dresses, and a pervading smell of fruit that our rationed nostrils had picked up at sea long before we could see the city. Soon we would be paid out with ten shillings and a V.D. pamphlet and let loose on the town. The large white woman, whom everyone loved, stood on the roof of the Cape Sugar Company and sang and sang. We wept, because she was Mother, because we had been so lonely. Years later I learned that her name was Perla Siedle, a retired Wagnerian soprano, daughter of a South African shipowner: she had sung to five thousand ships, 'God Bless America' for the Americans, the *Marseillaise* for the French.

They took us in cars to their homes on the Berea, to open-air nightclubs; only the Country Club was officers-only. They filled us with fruit salad, and Van der Hum; we were waited on by enormous Zulus in splendid sashes. They didn't care whether we were officers or not; the Imperial Army, we were told, treated its soldiers like dirt; what mattered was that we were white. It was a great country, full of opportunities: why didn't we come out and live here after the War?

Then in the *Ile de France* to Bombay, minus a number of deserters who were either lost in the shebeens or had hitch-hiked to Johannesburg to get jobs in gold mines; and a five-day crawl across India, lying on the floor of a horse box, to the Maharajah of Jaipur's summer place in Northern Bihar. Two of our brigades, detached to take Madagascar, had there contracted so virulent a strain of malaria that we were unfit for Burma and were asked by the Indian Government to go away before we infected everyone else. We spend the monsoon under canvas, the first Division ever to do so; we are so sick that it doesn't matter. Then by motorcycle back across India, in heat above bloodheat, into a stinking ship called the *Yoma*, rats running over our hammocks at night, up the blistering Persian Gulf to Basra; miles of squat date palms, eternal sickly oil smell. By rail to Baghdad, via Ur Junction, past a mound they said was Babylon; then to our motorcycles again, living on biscuits, weevilly blocks of dates and chlorinated water, lurching over the Paitak Pass, peering at each other through dust, into Persia, to Kermanshah: the only twelve miles of tarmac in the country, like a ceremonial carpet leading to the Anglo-Iranian Oil Company.

The sewage stink of Persian villages, the mountain tribes who silently stole the tents from over our heads as we slept. On to Qum, holiest of Persian cities, the cupola of its mosque made of pure gold: here we dig in for the winter, tents over dugouts walled in with snow, thirty degrees below zero. Over against Teheran, 95 miles away, the pink-tipped Demavend, Persia's Fuji-yama, regards us contemptuously, looking much nearer in the clear mountain air. We have nothing to do but sit on the oil wells in case the Germans should come down through the Caucasus, or we should decide to invade Turkey.

But El Alamein has happened, and there is a movement west. Back down the Paitak Pass to Baghdad, and then over the desert, following the southern oil pipeline into Syria. The only place with a name is

Rutbah; the others, where we meet encampments of men going mad with solitude, are pumping stations known as H2, H3, H4. ('Couldn't you stay a bit longer?' a medical officer begs. 'I could show you some fascinating Palaeolithic remains near here. . . .') At Dera'a, where the body of Lawrence of Arabia was outraged, the first green trees and grass seen for months; and so to the wonder of Damascus, where we live in the old French Foreign Legion barracks at Mezze.

My job is now to write a 'security report' on the whole area. This involves 'liaising' with two police forces, one of them French, hostile and loyal to Vichy; patrolling the hill villages with a boon companion named Lance Corporal Prince Nicholas Obolensky (you get all sorts in the Intelligence Corps – our gas instructor at Winchester Depot was Sergeant the Comte de Chamois); and drinking endless cups of Turkish coffee with the *mukhtar* or mayor of Mezze, to listen to his complaints about the behaviour of our troops. It is all too good to last. A visiting Captain from Army Public Relations turns out to be someone I know from Fleet Street: it seems they need an editor for a new military magazine in Cairo, 500 miles away. I am to leap on my motorcycle, take the rank of Sergeant, and report immediately. At Rosh Pinna, a few miles inside the Palestine frontier, I see the whole Bible laid out before me: Galilee, the Jordan valley, the depression where I know the Dead Sea lies.

There really is a place called Nazareth, and you can buy Coca-Cola there. Jerusalem, where I spend the night, is as I always imagined it. After Beersheba the wilderness begins: the road across Sinai is simply tar sprayed on sand, sand which drifts with any puff of wind: my motorcycle slithers, I fall off, I hobble along in first gear, using my feet, I am frightened. I somehow get to Ismailia before dark. And in Cairo my motorcycle is taken away from me: it is one of the happiest moments of my life.

'Is your journey really necessary?' asked a wartime Government poster. These were some of my necessary journeys.

At home in England, many would have envied me. From the beginning of October 1939 petrol had been rationed to 200 miles per month per car. No more brands: only 'Pool'. There were various illegal ways of getting round this: buying black-market petrol at 6s. 6d. a gallon (the normal price was 4s. 2d.), burying cans for the future in the garden, putting naphthalene mothballs in the tank to make it last longer, wangling a businessman's supplementary allowance, which varied according to size of engine – four gallons for an Austin 7, ten for a Rolls. Sometimes a doctor's certificate of lameness could get you an extra ration.

In July 1940 the manufacture of new cars was stopped, and two years later allowances of petrol for private motoring ceased. Motorists, since there was no used car market any more, drained their sumps and kept their cars raised on wood blocks in the garage until better times. There were experiments with coal-gas trailers and gas bags on the roof, and some buses ran like this, but it could not be done on a large scale. Fearsomely publicized prosecutions of people, especially in show-business, who used petrol for luxury purposes showed how seriously the authorities took rationing: thus Jack Hylton, band leader and impresario, was fined £155 for using his special allowance as a farmer for taking some friends from a theatre to the Savoy Hotel; and poor Ivor Novello was jailed in Wormwood Scrubs (where he became prison librarian) for a month for driving home from the Adelphi theatre to Maidenhead after the evening show on petrol supplied by an admirer. For doctors the ration was never enough, and in country districts the old world was revived when they visited patients on horseback. Not until May 1950 was petrol de-rationed, although in April 1949 a 'holiday allowance' came with the end of sweet rationing and (from Austerity Cripps) a penny a pint off beer. There was nervous talk of a 'world surplus of oil', and fuel prices fell, even in Britain, where half a penny was knocked off the gallon.

In America gasoline, like most other things, was rationed from 1 January 1942. There was no attempt at gradualness, and it came as a considerable shock. Three gallons a week was actually tougher than the British allowance, but at least it continued. There were rackets, of course; but somehow Americans managed, not only to keep many private cars on the road, but to go on manufacturing a few: even so, from 1943 onwards there was a used-car boom. Thus, when the War ended, the American automobile industry was able to roar ahead on a policy of new models every year. There was even a new manufacturer – Kaiser-Frazer. Gadgets became standard design features – cigar lighters, clocks, heaters, power-operated

A Cadillac of 1949, which although not a typical Cadillac, as it has a French body, gives an idea of the more extreme styling features of the period

Clark Gable at the wheel of an XK 120 Jaguar

windows; and as early as 1940 Chrysler had proudly announced 'two-speed wipers'. The word 'silhouette' was much used in car advertisements – 'long, low and very luxurious' – 'sparkling beauty of the rear-engine grill and individualized exhaust pipes' (this was the 1948 Tucker Torpedo, which also had a 'steerable Cyclops Eye headlight'). And, in 1949, tail fins came in. In America there was a new use for cars as drive-in cinemas spread across the country.

General Motors' 1949 million-dollar show of new cars, in the Grand Ballroom of the Waldorf-Astoria, implied a prosperity which did not exist anywhere else in the world. (That prosperity, said veteran advertising man Bruce Barton, was America's weapon against Russia: he seriously suggested 'bombing Russia with Sears Roebuck mail-order catalogues'.) Everything was longer, lower, wider, more powerful: some cars looked like floating boudoirs. Buick had what they called a 'doctor's car', professional and not too expensive; and their 155 h.p. Roadmaster had 'revolutionary Dynaflow' automatic transmission: Chrysler were also selling 'Gyromatic automatic fluid drive'. Chevrolet, Pontiac and Oldsmobile had models with either snob-appeal or its opposite – modest good taste. There were four 'sleek and sybaritic' Cadillacs at $30,000. Plymouth had a new metal station wagon called Suburban.

Yet America was also buying British cars. Morris in 1948 launched the highly successful (and convertible) Morris Minor, designed by Alec Issigonis, the 'British Volkswagen' that lasted for ever. But otherwise Morris still offered pre-war models such as the Morris 8. Not so Leonard Lord, who used to work for Nuffield, but was now at Austin's, where, in 1949, he sold $22 million worth of post-war models in America and Canada. In the middle price range was the curvaceous Standard Vanguard (1948), sturdy, yet sporty, but cramped in the back seats, and the first Ford Consul and Zephyr. And for those with £1,263 to spend there was the famous XK120 Jaguar (1948) whose top speed was 120 m.p.h. (And where, in Britain, could you do 120 m.p.h.? There were no new roads until 1954.) The custom-built limousine barely survived the war; but something of the kind was prestigiously attempted by the British Aircraft Company – the Bristol 400, aerodynamically styled, capable of over 100 m.p.h., a great rally performer. I knew an American couple who had two – His 'n' Hers.

Morris Minor saloon, 1948

If you had enough petrol to get to a port, or an airport (preferably the slapdash, cheerfully amateurish one run by a girl called Audrey at Ferryfield, on Romney Marsh) which carried cars, you could make a £25 – or even a £35 – holiday allowance go a long way, for once abroad you could buy foreign petrol. The claustrophobic British drove through the almost empty roads of France, staying at one-star hotels, eating and drinking themselves sick, scoffing a whole week's ration of eggs in one hors d'œuvres, and acquiring new tastes for scampi, bouillabaisse, sea urchins and blackbird pâté.

Package tours began modestly in 1947: Cook's sent you to France and Switzerland, Major Ingham sent you to Austria, and soon Horizon Holidays were starting up to send you to Corsica. You went mostly by train, sitting up all night, and the glory of arrival in Switzerland was breakfast on Basel station with cherry jam and a fortnight's ration of butter to put on your rolls.

Capri was rediscovered by tourists in 1949, after Princess Margaret had been for a much-publicized holiday and Gracie Fields settled there. Saint Tropez began to attract people who spoke a little French and didn't like package tours. The Americans, led on by Milan millionaires and Alan Moorehead, the Australian writer, discovered the 'fine, earthy squalor' of Portofino, once the haunt of painters and still a fishing village where the fishing was done at night by acetylene lamps.

There were no new transatlantic luxury liners until the *United States* in 1952 – and she was designed with a view to her immediate conversion to a troopship in case of war. France's unlucky *Normandie* was burned out and capsized in New York harbour in February 1942 while being converted to a troopship. Britain's two *Queens, Mary* and *Elizabeth,* after doughty war service, still ploughed the waves, while most of Britain's shipbuilding, with acute shortages of steel and dollars, went into making up the fearful losses of tonnage from U-boat sinkings. Yet there was something of the old romance about Cunard White Star's R.M.S. *Caronia* (34,183 tons), designed to take Americans on Caribbean trips: she made her maiden voyage to New York in January 1949, and, carrying 932 passengers, boasted thirteen air-conditioned lounges painted in four shades of green to reduce sun-glare.

Railways, having toiled their way through the war, seemed to be yielding wearily to road and air. 'Is your journey really necessary?' It was not to be supposed that anyone in Britain would travel by rail in wartime unless he had to. There were about seventy thousand special trains a year for the Forces, and they went at snail's pace by weird routes. It could take ten hours to go 200 miles. If you had a forty-eight-hour leave, you could spend half of it travelling. Corridors were full of soldiers and kit bags, and if you wanted to go to the lavatory (and there wasn't always a lavatory) you had to pick your way through them and then join a queue of people already waiting. This could take two hours. Sometimes, especially if you were a girl, you would be handed overhead by cheering soldiers: 'Can you hold it till you get there, love?' At night there were no lights but a tiny blue bulb, because of the blackout, so you couldn't read. If there was an air-raid, the train stood still until it was over. You never knew where you were, because station names had been obliterated lest they should be of help to the enemy. If a child was sick, it was sick. There was no food unless you had brought your own.

One wartime picture remains forever in the memory: the soldier going away again after home leave, or abroad after embarkation leave, the girl following the departing train with fluttering handkerchief, walking right to the end of the platform, standing there, not turning round so that no one shall see her face.

British railways never really recovered from the War. After 1945, said a contemporary magazine, they had a new battle against 'age, dirt, congestion and financial loss'. In the first year of nationalization, 1948, they lost nearly £5 million. They had also lost £7 million worth of passengers, who were taking to the road: why not, when you could go from London to Brighton and back for only 5s. 9d. ($1.38)? Perhaps diesel engines, electrification, double-decker coaches would help. There were still relics of the pre-war world in the Trianon Bar attached to the Golden Arrow; but now in 1949 the new Railway Executive, taking some mad marketing man's advice, tried to democratize luxury with a Travelling Tavern in mock-Tudor style with high lattice windows and bogus brickwork. Nobody liked it, and it was withdrawn.

More purposeful was the ballyhoo surrounding the inauguration, in September 1949, of America's new

Twentieth Century Limited at Grand Central Station, New York (another one was simultaneously launched at Chicago). It had a streamlined lookout lounge, which sounded more fun than 'observation car'; double bedrooms each with its own lavatory and circulating ice water; and a 'club car' with shower, barber, valet, bar, stenographer and radio telephone. The ceremony was performed by Beatrice Lillie with a bottle containing, not champagne, but a mixture of water from the Hudson and Mohawk rivers and lakes Erie and Michigan.

The future was in the air. In America the scramble for post-war routes began as early as 1944, when fifty-four nations met at an international aviation conference in Chicago to draft agreements on air rights, and established the International Civil Aviation Organization in preparation for the tremendous expansion expected when peace came. Until 1939 Pan American Airways had been the leading carrier, but now there was competition. Had flying boats really any future? America had the Glenn L. Martin Company's *Mars* which carried more than three

The Saunders-Roe, SR/A1 jet-propelled flying-boat fighter, July 1947

hundred people in one flight: a large beast with a 200-foot wing-span which flew regularly between California and Hawaii. The British had a turbo-prop ten-engine seaplane, the Saunders-Roe SR/45 'Princess' on the drawing-board, designed for a luxury passenger service between London and New York, but the Government lost faith in it. Howard Hughes designed an eight-engine *Hercules* flying boat with a wing-span of 310 feet, all in moulded plywood because of the shortage of aluminium; but it never went into service. When the War began, flying boats had seemed to have a great future: there were two a week from London to Australia, and one to Durban. Not until June 1940, with Hitler in Paris, did Britain abandon hope of a transatlantic service using three romantically-named flying boats, the *Golden Hind*, *Golden Fleece* and *Golden Horn*, and trying to tie up with the Pan Am Clipper service to Lisbon via Horta in the Azores ('only 23 hours to Europe'): this was difficult because General Franco would not let foreign planes fly over Spain.

During the War everyone gained a lot of experience in flying over water. Aircraft design and engine power had increased, navigation was more sophisticated. In October 1945 it became known that TWA (then known as Transcontinental and Western Air Inc.) was buying thirty-six Lockheed Constellations, sleek 340 m.p.h. airliners. Air Transport Command (U.S. Army) had started a weekly round-the-world service in Douglas C.54s, taking just under a week to fly Washington D.C.–Azores–Cairo–India–China–Guam–Honolulu–San Francisco. In 1946 American scheduled airlines carried more than 13¼ million passengers, ten times more than in 1938, at an average speed of 200 m.p.h.; and in 1945, local short-haul flights, almost as informal as bus rides, began with the Houston–Amarillo (Texas) service. Soon there were 'coach' and 'family plan' reduced fares and night 'sky coaches' for inter-city travel.

By the 1946 Civil Aviation Act, all British air transport was nationalized. Britain now had three airlines (compared to America's fourteen), British Overseas Airways Corporation (BOAC), British European Airways (BEA) and British South American Airways (BSAA). BSAA was short-lived, and merged with BOAC. Because the British aircraft industry was slow to convert from war to civil production, the first airliners were uncomfortable converted bombers and

troop transports, usually unpressurized Yorks and Lancasters: to cross the Andes, passengers were given oxygen masks. The Vickers-Viking twin-engined transport was the first plane that really opened up the civil market. This was the aircraft that left daily for Paris and Europe – from Northolt, for Heathrow was still a-building. There were already reports of an even better plane, about two years away, the turbo-prop Viscount 700, which would fly at an almost unbelievable 600 m.p.h. with 'so little vibration that you can stand a penny on edge for 20 minutes'.

That 600 m.p.h., only 100 m.p.h. less than the speed of sound, showed where air travel was leading. In October 1947 the Bell Aircraft Company had produced the X-1, air launched at 30,000 feet from a B-29 which carried it in its belly like a kangaroo: piloted by Chuck Yeager, it had, after fearful buffeting, made the first supersonic flight. A year later, John Derry flew a DH-108 jet at 40,000 feet over southern England, diving at nearly 700 m.p.h. into what became known as a 'supersonic bang'.

For long hauls, there was the de Havilland Comet, which took three years to create. In August 1949, after two trial hops off the runway at Hatfield aerodrome, Hertfordshire, the first commercial aircraft in the world to be powered by jet engines was flown, climbing to 8,000 feet, for thirty-one minutes by Group Captain John 'Cat's Eyes' Cunningham, night-fighter pilot of the war and now Sir Geoffrey de de Havilland's chief test pilot. The Comet, designed to 'sell air travel at a profit', was silver and beautiful: for Sir Geoffrey, who had built the famous Moth biplane and had lost two sons in the cause of aviation, it was the culmination of his career. The *idea* of the Comet went back to 1943, when the Government had set up a committee under Lord Brabazon to decide what types of commercial aircraft would be needed after the War. Britain had got there first, for once: America had no jet airliner. The Comet cruised at 500 m.p.h. and could fly at an altitude of eight miles. It burned 120 imperial gallons of kerosene per hour, so it had to have 6,000 gallons in its tanks. True, it carried only twenty passengers on a long flight against the DC-6's forty-four; but it could cut the London–New York trip by about half to six or seven hours, and in four hops could make London–Sydney in thirty-six hours. Moreover, it was 'almost sound-proof'. BOAC bought fourteen Comets. There were mishaps due to metal fatigue, and America never bought any, but the Comet warmed British hearts all through the Fifties. It was so much better than the Bristol Brabazon which, in April 1949, had had some difficulty in leaving the ground at all.

Meantime, BOAC had to buy American planes, Argonauts, Constellations and Stratocruisers. What if it took twelve hours to reach New York? If there was any turbulence you were sick as a dog; but the charm of flying at only 20,000 feet has been lost. There was time for talking to people, even for shipboard romances. There was a bar on the lower deck, with windows placed so that you could see ships, cities, rivers below. Flying across America, I saw the Mississippi, the Grand Canyon, the Rockies, less than four miles away. A man from North Dakota, as we flew over the Midwest, pointed out what appeared to be an endless grid of squares. 'Those squares are roads, and in each square is a farm, worked maybe by a Czech or a Pole or a German, all growing food – and *that* is the true wealth of America!'

The BOAC service to New York was called the Monarch. The British were not yet very used to flying; BOAC public relations people were fond of telling passengers that 'every year more people are kicked to death by donkeys than lose their lives in air accidents.' All the way across the Captain spoke soothingly over the intercom saying how safe it was: 'You'll notice that the engines look red hot behind, but it's quite normal, they won't drop off or anything. . . . We're flying at 19,000 feet and the weather's pretty good over Newfoundland. . . .' We shall come down at Gander, where it will be 4 a.m.; here we shall wait forty minutes, and there's time for a shower, and those of us who have no Canadian dollars will be given two free cups of coffee. Above our heads are bunks like luggage racks with doors: you climb into them by ladders. From the forward cabin come shrillings and cheepings of small children being put to bed; a stewardess takes charge of everything: 'Go to sleep, darling – you're going to wake up in America.' Dinner has eight courses, with one free glass of champagne. Women passengers are given free Elizabeth Arden beauty kits, and in the men's washroom there is free hair tonic, cologne, talcum and the use of the ship's electric shaver, a bit of American technology that hasn't come to Britain yet. . . .

In those days every younger woman's magazine had a story about an air hostess. Generally, just before THE END, the pilot proposed to her. It was the most glamorous career imaginable. BOAC girls wore an elegant navy-blue uniform that made them look like WRN officers. They came from Good Families and few were chosen out of the thousands who applied. They walked like mannequins. In mufti they wore twinsets and pearls, and they were ambassadors for what remained of the British Empire. They packed long dresses for evening dates in New York, if they weren't too tired: in 1946 there were only fourteen of them, one per plane. They were paid £6 10s. od. ($26.00) a week. One or two were fired for smuggling nylons, but mostly they were too busy. Asked by a reporter what was the most trying part of her job, one replied: 'Those Hollywood filmstars! You had to warn them half an hour before serving breakfast. They were in each other's bunks all the time.'

CHAPTER 13

Loyalties

'I am become Death, the shatterer of worlds.' This line from the Bhagavad-Gita was the only thought present in the mind of J. Robert Oppenheimer after the blinding flash that announced the success of the first atom-bomb test at Los Alamos, New Mexico, on 16 July 1945. From this date forward, war, peace, patriotism, loyalty all had to be redefined. Nothing would ever be quite the same again. Especially loyalty: loyalty to what? To one's country? To one's friends? To humanity? Dr Oppenheimer might well wonder: in 1949 he was to testify before the Committee on Un-American Activities about his friend, Dr Bernard Peters, and his mistress Jean Tatlock (a Communist); he was to learn that his mail had been opened for ten years and that there was an F.B.I. file on him.

Almost a month before that first test a scientist working on the bomb project, Dr Klaus Fuchs, had met, at Santa Fé, a small man of about forty whom he knew as 'Raymond', whose real name was Harry Gold, born Heinrich Golodnitsky. Gold, whose motivating passion seems to have been sympathy for underdogs everywhere (including students who failed examinations – 'everybody should pass, they deserve it'), had for nine years been carrying out small industrial espionage jobs for the Russians, among them the handing over of processes and formulae from the laboratories of the Pennsylvania Sugar Company where he worked. The Russians had suffered more than any other country in the War. Moreover, the Russians had paid $600 towards the expenses of his further education at Xavier University, Cincinnati. At Santa Fé Dr Fuchs handed over to Harry Gold all that was known of the atom bomb. None of this would be suspected until 1950, by which time Dr Fuchs was working at Britain's atomic research plant at Harwell, Berkshire.

However, Gold was not unknown to the F.B.I. In May 1947 a chemical engineer named Abraham Brothman was being investigated through information supplied by Elizabeth Bentley, a self-confessed Communist and courier for Russian espionage: Brothman had contact with one Jacob Golos, a 'Soviet spy-master'. Brothman had given details of chemical processes to Elizabeth Bentley, whom he knew as 'Helen' only. It so happened that Gold at this time was working in Brothman's laboratory, and was subpoenaed to testify before a special Federal Grand Jury in New York, called to hear evidence of possible acts of espionage by various people Miss Bentley had named.

Plump Miss Bentley, who was headlined as a 'beautiful spy queen', a graduate of Vassar, where she had been a member of the university Communist cell, had fallen in love with Golos, a Russian who had become a naturalized American. For him she had been collecting, from 1941 onwards, information on the Army, the Air Force, the State and Treasury Departments. She had sometimes posed as a 'researcher' for *PM* newspaper. Miss Bentley's name dropping seemed to make everybody suspect: she had talked to Earl Browder; well, you might expect that; but, among about thirty people, she also named William Remington of the War Production Board, Lauchlin Currie (one of Roosevelt's advisers), Nathan Silvermaster of the Board of Economic Warfare, and, for heaven's sake, Harry Dexter White, Assistant Secretary of the Treasury. Sometimes she was 'Helen Johnson' and sometimes 'Joan', and the subjects she had asked questions about included the wartime Office of Strategic Services, the B.29 aircraft and the date of D-Day. The chemists came out of this unscathed, because they were not deemed to be doing anything against the law; but Elizabeth

Bentley had touched off the biggest spy scare America had ever known.

Britain had nothing quite like the atmosphere America was to know between 1947 and the end of Senator McCarthy. Britain had her disappointed Communists, those for whom the god had failed, who were now often journalists and sometimes comfortable civil servants; but they had collapsed into melancholy. In the Fifties we were to discover an absolutely top-drawer, Rolls-Royce, Establishment, old-boy-net type of spy, linked together by a silver cord of homosexuality, who had no truck whatever with underlings, idiotic code names and piddling details, who had no need to steal information from Government sources because they *were* the sources.

The scare in America was bad enough for President Truman, in 1947, to order a check on the 'loyalty' of all government workers. In two years 2,351,097 federal employees were investigated, of whom seventy-six (0.03 per cent) had been discharged because of suspected disloyalty. Another 2,149 (less than 0.1 per cent) had resigned while under suspicion. Nobody had been charged with treason, and none of them seemed to be members of the 159 organizations listed by Attorney General Tom C. Clark as subversive, such as the American Veterans' Committee, a liberal serviceman's organization intended to challenge the conservative American Legion. Some had resigned because they could not afford to live without pay while the investigations went on, and some because they couldn't afford lawyers to argue their cases before a Loyalty Board. People who occupied 'sensitive posts' in the government got quite used to being questioned about each other: it became a kind of joke – 'Say, I've been telling the F.B.I. about you!'.

William Remington, now (in 1948) a Department of Commerce economist, was a worm who turned. Accused by Miss Bentley of both being a Communist and having (in 1942 and 1943) given her confidential war production data, knowing that she was a Soviet spy, Remington, having been exonerated by the Loyalty Review Board, claimed reinstatement by the Department of Commerce, and $5,813.72 in back pay. He also brought a $100,000 libel suit against Miss Bentley, General Foods and the National Broadcasting Company, because Miss Bentley had repeated her charges on an N.B.C. television programme sponsored by General Foods. Remington himself showed little indignation: to a reporter he said, 'The procedures ought to be changed so that the burden of proof doesn't rest with the defendant. Hearsay and rumors oughtn't to be treated as facts, and a man ought to be able to confront his accusers.' The whole of his past was thrown up against him: why had he lectured to C.I.O. workers? Why had he given money to help the Loyalists in Spain? Could one feel guilty about having subscribed to send milk to orphaned Spanish children? Why had he belonged to Peace Committees while at college? Was he having a romance with Miss Bentley?

Miss Bentley in fact failed to appear at Remington's Loyalty Review Board. She had been converted to Catholicism by Mgr Fulton J. Sheen and was busy lecturing on religion. In the fullness of time Remington was cleared. He was almost starving, and when he was reinstated in his old job, his back pay cheque went entirely to pay off debts. The worst effect of the whole business on him, he said, was that for ever after he would be sceptical of other people's motives. 'I used to assume indiscriminately that one man always took another man's decency for granted.'

Hollywood had for ten years been suspected of harbouring pinkos if not outright Reds. In 1947 the House Committee on Un-American Activities (the very name is replete with farce to British ears), chaired by J. Parnell Thomas (Republican, New Jersey), had 'examined' a number of film stars in an atmosphere of ugly levity made worse by trivial reporting. The appearance of Hollywood personalities such as Robert Taylor, Adolph Menjou, Robert Montgomery and Gary Cooper as witnesses attracted a mindless mob of bobbysoxers who seem never to have stopped cooing and whispering throughout the hearing. Ronald Reagan's appearance, said the *New York Times*, amid 'the continuous explosion of flash bulbs', drew 'a long-drawn-out *oooh* from the jam-packed, predominantly feminine audience.' The *Journal-American* printed its headlines in red: MENJOU EXPOSES REDS. ROBERT TAYLOR PLEADS: *Fire Communists, Ban Party*. 'How do you identify Communists?' asked Parnell Thomas of a witness named Rupert Hughes. 'You can't help smelling them,' said Hughes. (Laughter.) Leading questions, *non sequiturs*, bullying – any tactic seemed permissible to rid the country of Reds. You could stand firm, plead the 5th Amendment and your right to be represented by counsel, but the mud would stick. Suspicion became more important than fact: it was like the nightmare world of Kafka: 'Some-one must have been telling lies about Joseph K., for without having done anything wrong he was arrested one fine morning.'

The script writers were deemed the most dangerous, and ten of them were fired eventually.

Professors were dismissed from the University of Washington: loyalty to the Communist Party, said the president, disqualified a teacher for the main purpose of a university, which was the search for truth. Let it stand to the credit of General Eisenhower, who had just succeeded Nicholas Murray Butler as President of Columbia University, that he said quite firmly that the strength of a university lay in freedom to examine *all* ideas – and Columbia had been mentioned many times as a hot-bed of intellectual redness.

In September 1949 the U.S. Atomic Energy Commission announced that an 'atomic' explosion in Russia had been detected. (This was four years earlier than the West had expected, and two days after China went Communist.) There were others. Russia at first denied that she had the atomic bomb, saying that the bangs had been caused by 'large-scale blasting operations'. General Bradley, chairman of the American Joint Chiefs of Staff, said that if no agreement on international control of the bomb could be reached, America would have to spend enormous sums on defence.

And on counter-espionage. The Americans were in awe of Soviet intelligence work, which seemed to be winning hands down all over the world, and they had been meek pupils of the British Secret Service during the war years: General 'Wild Bill' Donovan, of the O.S.S., admitted as much. Counter-espionage for more than forty years had been the province of the F.B.I. America had never, since the Declaration of Independence, had a comprehensive intelligence service embracing everything from security to 'dirty tricks'; but she had Allen Dulles, an exceptionally well-trained secret agent, a veteran of two world wars in the second of which he had headed the O.S.S. European network in Berne. In 1947 Dulles sent President Truman a memorandum designed to get intelligence out of the hands of soldiers and policemen: 'To create an effective intelligence agency,' he wrote, 'we must have in the key positions men who are prepared to make this a life work. . . . The agency should be dir-

ected by a relatively small but élite corps of men with a passion for anonymity and a willingness to stick at that particular job. They must find their reward primarily in the work itself. . . .'

So was born the Central Intelligence Agency (C.I.A.). Some weeks before this memorandum, ex-Lieutenant General Reinhard Gehlen, once a servant of the Weimar Republic, then chief of all Hitler's intelligence ('controlling all espionage, subversion, sabotage and psychological warfare against the Soviet Union', says his biographer), had surrendered his entire organization, agents and files (which he had buried in the mountains of Bavaria) to the G-2 Intelligence branch of the U.S. Army. Gehlen was ready to serve his former enemies as he had served his Fuehrer. To what, in any study of loyalty, was Gehlen loyal? Not to any country, not to humanity, but to the great game of intelligence, to its mystery, glamour and safe bureaucracy. What made him acceptable to the Americans, who financed him with $20 million a year and allowed him to recruit former Gestapo and S.S. officers into his organization, was the one common thread that ran through all his activities: total dedication to the destruction of Communism. This dime-novel genius, who loved disguises, dark glasses, false moustaches, was proud of the £100,000 offered by the East German government as a reward for anyone who assassinated him. The fatal attraction of espionage for those who do not have to do the dirtier jobs is its approximation to the worst spy fiction. The British always try to hide who is the head of its secret service, but in America he has both the publicity and the accountability of a Cabinet minister. Allen Dulles enjoyed being 'the third most powerful man in the world', and his agency claimed to have saved Europe from Communist subversion.

Britain's own intelligence resources were not impressive at this time. Britain, it seemed, had other priorities. One was the refusal to admit, amid all her paralysing problems, that she was no longer a first-class power. You do not ask fifty million people, bound and gagged by rationing and four-page newspapers, whether they *want* their own atomic bomb. Nanny knows best. And so it came about that a Labour Government, whose mandate was the nationalized Welfare State, took the decision that Britain should manufacture its own nuclear weapons. Military opinion, especially Field Marshal Montgomery, was mostly for it: 'We *must* have the Bomb!' No argument: mind made up: will to power. Labour men had been the dreamers, the idealists, the disarmers, the pacifists. Now they were in power for the first effective time, and what were they about to do? The decision was taken in January 1947 by a secret committee of the Cabinet (known as Gen 163) consisting of Prime Minister Attlee, Herbert Morrison, Ernest Bevin, A.V. Alexander, Addison and Minister of Supply John Wilmot. It would cost £140 million over seven years, and this amount would be wrapped up in Ministry of Supply appropriations. A short announcement was made in the House of Commons in May 1948, and Honorable Members discovered that questions about how the Bomb was getting on were not popular.

Why did Britain make the Bomb? Because she felt inferior to America, because America wasn't being appreciative enough of Britain's scientific know-how, because the British were sick of being Poor Relations. The British were listening to generals, not to scientists such as Henry Tizard who said: 'We are a great nation but if we continue to behave like a Great Power we shall soon cease to be a great nation.'

The Campaign for Nuclear Disarmament, and its first propaganda march from the year-old Atomic Weapons Research Establishment at Aldermaston, Berkshire, began in 1948. Teenagers dressed in black shouted 'Ban the Bomb'. Britain's witch hunt would not come until the flight of Burgess and Maclean in 1951. Elizabeth Bentley, in her great naming of names, had never named them; but in 1948 someone else was confirming some of Miss Bentley's names and also naming some new ones. This was Whittaker Chambers, forty-seven, a senior editor of *Time* magazine, who admitted having been a paid functionary of the Communist Party from 1924 to 1937. In his soft, rather flabby voice, he accused Alger Hiss, forty-three, of having supplied him with military secrets for the Soviet Union while he, Hiss, was in the State Department. Hiss denied this and said he had never seen Chambers before. Later he identified Chambers, whose underground name had been 'Carl', as 'George Crosley'. In all his evidence Hiss, a lawyer by training, prefaced each statement with 'to the best of my recollection'.

Clearly one of them was committing perjury, and this, not espionage, was eventually the charge against Hiss. To defend himself, Hiss had to sue Chambers, and he did so for $75,000.

President Truman at first angrily dismissed the whole thing as a 'Republican red herring', but had to bow to public anxiety. Chambers was supported by Congressman (soon to be Senator) Richard Nixon, who in after years never ceased to be proud of his part in securing Hiss's conviction. Hiss's donnish precision obviously irritated Nixon: at one point Hiss cut through one of Nixon's questions ('Are you inferring . . .?') with 'No, I am not. *You* are inferring. *I* am *implying*.'

Alger Hiss before the hearing of the House Un-American Affairs Committee, 1948

That line of dialogue contained something of the businessman-versus-egghead, Republican-versus-Democrat, Midwest-versus-New England atmosphere of the hearings, and of the two leading actors. Whittaker Chambers, described in his own *Time* magazine as 'unprepossessing as a baker – a calm, pudgy little man,' was a Quaker who milked his own cows on his Westminster, Maryland, farm. On that farm was a yellow pumpkin containing three aluminium capsules of microfilm which Chambers said he had put there lest 'Communists should break in and search the farm'. The microfilm was alleged to show 'papers' passed by Hiss to Chambers in the Thirties. Hiss, who was not allowed to see the film, contended that it was deliberately made to incriminate him: he did not believe that it dated back to the Thirties.

At his perjury trial in 1949, which aroused the strongest liberal passions since Sacco and Vanzetti, the jury failed to agree. The Government then produced new evidence, including 'documents', said to have been copied on Hiss's own typewriter, whose authenticity were never proved. At a second trial Hiss was found guilty.

It seemed a victory for right-thinking Middle America, to whom Hiss appeared as a New England snob, a Harvard graduate born to privilege. He was a friend of Dean Acheson, Secretary of State, in whose department he had served at the office of Far Eastern Affairs. He had been at San Francisco when the United Nations idea had been born, at Yalta with Roosevelt. He was pro-British, elitist, bought his suits in London. He was head of the Carnegie Endowment for International Peace. Guilty or innocent, he was a useful scapegoat at a show-trial. Suppose he had ad-mitted knowing Chambers; suppose he had said calmly: 'Yes, a lot of us felt that way in the Thirties. Okay, we were wrong.' Would the Committee on Un-American Activities have hounded him less? Would the Pumpkin Papers have stood as evidence?

In December 1948 the name of Whittaker Chambers had disappeared from the staff list published weekly at the beginning of *Time* magazine. He survived to write a best-selling book about the Hiss case. Hiss went to jail for five years, of which he served almost four, and was disbarred from practising law.

Richard Nixon was not the only man whose career was advanced by the Hiss case. The stage was now set for Senator Joseph McCarthy, of Wisconsin, to do his worst. In the Fifties he would attack 'communist-coddling' everywhere. At last he had a cause. He had served in the Marines, and liked to be known as 'Tail-gunner Joe'. He had made out a case that 250 (there were actually seventy-one) American prisoners of war had been massacred by German S.S. troops at Malmedy during the Battle of the Bulge in revenge for the 'brutality' of American troops: he got his facts wrong, but the hue and cry he started in the Senate probably affected the sentencing of S.S. officers for war crimes. In 'Communist infiltration' he now had a long-term campaign that would cover up his ignorance of issues that really mattered. Too late would he be censured for abuse of senatorial privileges. He was as rude as, but less clever than, Huey Long, who often emptied the Senate when he rose to speak; why did they stay to listen to McCarthy? From him dates the first use of the expression 'character assassination'. And it was television, revealing the man as he was in everybody's home, that eventually destroyed him.

(*opposite*) Ralph Richardson as Falstaff in Shakespeare's *Henry IV*, Old Vic Company at the New Theatre, London, 1945. Costume design by Roger Furse

Henry IV

Sir John
Falstaff

Ralph Richardson

Hurse

King Lear 1st Costume
Laurence Olivier.

CHAPTER 14

Curtain Down and Up

Of course, the London theatre could never survive in a modern annihilating war. . . . For two weeks after 3 September 1939, London theatres closed. Then, in mid-September, the Prince of Wales reopened, followed by Herbert Farjeon's *Little Revue*; then *Me and My Girl* resumed its seemingly endless run at the Victoria Palace, to be revived twice before the War ended. Somehow, with desperately little money and much of its best talent in the Forces, the theatre learned to live with bombs, closing when the raids were too heavy for either cast or audience to get to the theatre, reopening when the German Air Force held off for long enough to justify the risk. This was not so stop-go as it sounds: except during the very worst destruction, there was always a show on somewhere. Some theatres brought the evening performance forward to 5 p.m. so that people could get home safely to the suburbs, improvising ways of doing so if public transport was out of action. There was never any heating: in winter one sat in overcoat, muffler and gloves while the cast caught their deaths of cold.

What do people want in wartime? You must cheer people up, thought some managers; make them laugh; can't risk anything highbrow. . . . So musical shows became ruder and girlier. George Black gave us *The Little Dog Laughed*, with members of the Crazy Gang, introducing to Britain the song 'Franklin D. Roosevelt Jones', *Black Vanities* and many others. Firth Shephard began with musicals – *Shephard's Pie, Fun and Games*, with well-loved comics like Sydney Howard and Arthur Riscoe – and then went on to a policy of bringing to London established New York successes such as *The Man who Came to Dinner* (with Robert Morley in Monty Woolley's old part as Sheridan Whiteside). Not all of them transplanted: some Londoners walked out of Robert E. Sherwood's *There Shall Be No Night*, starring Alfred Lunt and Lynn Fon-

tanne, at the Aldwych – it was too tragic, too close to their own experiences; yet it ran for 220 performances in 1943, nearly twice as long as its New York run at the Alvin three years before.

Revue, cheap to produce, flexible, topical, generating togetherness in small theatres, flourished in wartime, and grew more sophisticated. From mild Farjeon it went to sharp Alan Melville at the

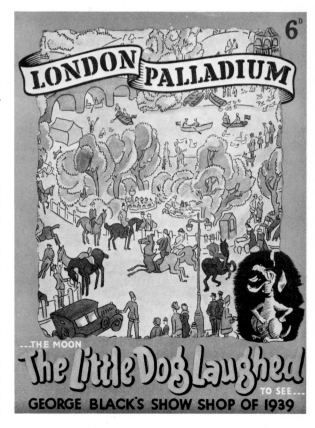

(*opposite*) **Laurence Olivier as King Lear in Shakespeare's *King Lear*, New Theatre, October 1946. Costume design by Roger Furse**

Hermione Gingold as Britannia in *Sweeter and Lower*, **Ambassadors, 1945**

Scene from *King's Rhapsody*, Palace Theatre, 1949

Ambassadors, beginning with *Sweet and Low* (1943) through *Sweeter and Lower* (1944), which ran for more than two years, to *Sweetest and Lowest* (1946). Melville, a B.B.C. writer-producer, somehow managed to write most of these shows in the intervals of the daily chore of writing the B.B.C.'s first radio soap-opera, *The Robinsons* (later *The Front Line Family*). His revues, which became a wartime institution, brought together the talents of Hermione Gingold who was in all of them, Henry Kendall, Bonar Colleano and Walter Crisham; and if there were rather too many theatrical 'in' jokes for visiting provincial audiences, who were not necessarily to know that 'Binkie' referred to Hugh Beaumont, big boss of H.M. Tennent Ltd., there was enough well-timed foolery to convulse them.

That World War II was really only Part 2 of World War I may perhaps explain the enormous number of revivals of very old musical shows: there was a special kind of management that plumped straight away for these.

Escaping into the past is what people harmlessly do in times of national stress to reassure themselves, and the means of doing so is what Ivor Novello was sent to earth to provide. But he could not return to Drury Lane, which had become the headquarters of Entertainments National Service Association (E.N.S.A.), founded by Basil Dean in 1939 to provide entertainment for the troops, corresponding to U.S.O. in America. Novello's *The Dancing Years* was revived at the Adelphi and ran for 969 performances before going on tour; a new show, *Arc de Triomphe*, came to the Phoenix in 1943, and the much more successful *Perchance to Dream* to the London Hippodrome in 1945. This kind of lavish British-Ruritanian

Mary Martin in *South Pacific*

operetta never succeeded in crossing the Atlantic, and there were brilliant new things going on in New York which would have quickly shouldered it out of the way. Novello did it once again in *King's Rhapsody* (Palace Theatre, 1949). Christopher Hassall wrote lyrics which were tasteful but never likely to become part of folklore, to Novello's music. In this he brought together the famous Dare sisters (Zena and Phyllis, respectively sixty-two and fifty-nine, Edwardian picture-postcard beauties) as 'Queen Elana of Murania' and 'Marta Karillos' the King's mistress. It ran for 941 performances.

There is another reason for travelling back to the past in wartime: to draw strength from the imperishable. Shakespeare, Shaw, Congreve, Sheridan, Wilde, Ibsen, Chekhov, were well served. Gielgud's 1943 production of *Love for Love*, with himself as Valentine, ran for a year. Laurence Olivier, whom New York had seen in his own production of *Romeo and Juliet* at the 51st Street Theatre in 1940, became director in 1944 of the Old Vic Company at the New Theatre, with Ralph Richardson, whom the Fleet Air Arm had just released with the rank of Lieutenant Commander, and John Burrell. Together they made the Old Vic Company 'West End box office', with *Peer Gynt*, *Arms and the Man*, *Richard III*, *Uncle Vanya*, *Henry IV* (both parts) and *Oedipus Rex* and *The Critic* in an astonishing double bill, taking some of these productions to New York's Century Theatre and the Comédie Française in Paris. *Henry IV*, described as a 'smash revival', was a particular success in New York, with Ralph Richardson as Falstaff, and Sybil Thorndike as Mistress Quickly ('I love the bawdy old bitch and the way she tells off Falstaff').

It seemed that Olivier could do everything: what would he make of *King Lear*, last attempted, magnificently, by Donald Wolfit in 1943? *Lear* is traditionally regarded as unactable. It opened at London's New Theatre in October 1946. Somehow, in alternate raging madness and gentle terror, set off by Alec Guinness as a touching Fool, Pamela Brown as a steely Goneril and Margaret Leighton as a softly sadistic Regan, he did it.

While the bombs were falling, the Old Vic Company dodged them like anyone else. Once, in Bristol, all their costumes were blitzed: in twenty-four hours students at the local art school made them new ones.

Despite the beliefs of commercial managers the arts became important in wartime. This was recognized by Dr Thomas Jones, C.H., Secretary of the Pilgrim Trust, founded by Edward S. Harkness of New York 'for the benefit of Great Britain'. Dr Jones and others wished to prevent 'the blackout of the Arts' in wartime. The result was C.E.M.A. (the Council for the Encouragement of Music and the Arts) which afterwards became the Arts Council. C.E.M.A. took the arts to factories, mines and air-raid shelters, financially assisted by the Board of Education. Its director of drama was Lewis Casson, who with his wife Sybil Thorndike took a company to South Wales. The C.E.M.A. organizers asked them what play they would do. '*Macbeth!*' said Casson, a Welshman. The organizers looked perplexed: a tragedy, for miners who needed cheering up? 'I know my countrymen', said Casson. 'They like *drama*.' Rehearsals in London had to be abandoned because of the blitz, and Tyrone Guthrie, the Old Vic administrator, announced that they would continue in Newport, Monmouthshire: 'We leave Paddington Station at noon – if Paddington is still there.'

London and New York, West End and Broadway, were almost out of touch during the war. Any communication tended to be one-way, west to east. Thus Irving Berlin's *This Is The Army*, with its New York cast, was a sell-out at the London Palladium. Broadway never had an acute manpower shortage, even of chorus boys; yet it too was disrupted. Some of its best critics joined the forces and went overseas. There was an undercurrent of dissatisfaction with the theatre as it was: it should develop in new ways, get beyond the curtain and the proscenium arch, experiment. Mike Todd's *Hamlet*, for example, with Maurice Evans playing the gloomy Dane as a tough guy in nineteenth-century dress, which opened at the Columbus Circle in December 1945, might be a symptom.

But something else had happened, and it had happened to the musical play, and it was called *Oklahoma!* 'It smells of hay mown up over barn dance floors, steps around like an apple-faced farm-hand, rolls along like a good wagon slicked up with new axle-grease!' cried Carl Sandburg, enraptured. Sentiment was in again. This adaptation of an old play, *Green Grow the Lilacs*, brought together the talents of the composer Richard Rodgers, whose partnership with Lorenz Hart (he of the slick intellectual lyric with daring Gilbertian rhymes) was just breaking up, and Oscar Hammerstein II, who had had a series of flops since his late-Twenties heyday of *The Desert Song* and *Show Boat*. 'It was Oscar's sincere belief,' said Rodgers of his new partner, 'that someone had to keep reminding people of the vast amount of good things that are in the world.' Likewise, 'only a poseur can be anything but sentimental about falling in love.' Hence 'People Will Say we're in Love,' and, later on, 'I'm in Love with a Wonderful Guy', as distinct from 'Falling in Love with Love – is falling for make-believe'. Hammerstein was not only romantic, he was accurate: before writing the line, 'The corn is as high as an elephant's eye', he went to both the local zoo and a maize field with a tape measure. Poor Hart, in an alcoholic nervous crack-up, died not long after that unforgettable first-night at New York's St James Theatre on 31 March 1943.

Oklahoma! was the first 'total musical', integrating story, songs, music, and an Agnes de Mille ballet, woven together into a whole of which each part was indispensable. Since it was sponsored by the Theatre Guild, it was intended from the start to be art; and it ran for 2,278 performances. No wisecracks (but plenty of folksy humour); no chorus line. Not one of the actors, singers and dancers in it was a star. Here was the idealized America a million G.I.s hoped they were fighting for. *Oklahoma!* could not arrive in London until April 1947, and when it did, it introduced a nine-year run of Rodgers and Hammerstein musicals at the refurbished Theatre Royal, Drury Lane. How to describe the impact of *Oklahoma!*, innocent, hopeful, clean, folksy, on the grime and corruption of postwar Britain? A great, warm gust of Midwest air and colour, a sense of illimitable space and freedom in the claustrophobic ruins and dreadful littleness of grey rationed lives. *Oklahoma!* ran for 1,543 performances.

Musicals could never be the same again after it. *Carousel* (1945 in New York, 1950 in London) went to Molnar's *Liliom* for its story, weepy yet earthy, with a last-minute ghostly appearance of the hero who has died at the end of the first act. *South Pacific* (1949 in New York) did not reach London until 1951: in this strange account of the American experience of the Pacific war, amid a dozen memorable songs, while 'Some Enchanted Evening' is the song you hum on the way home, it is 'A Cockeyed Optimist' that contains the soul of Oscar Hammerstein.

Annie Get Your Gun (New York 1946, London 1947) found Ethel Merman – Dolores Gray in London – brandishing a beautifully inlaid rifle somewhere in the Midwest. Irving Berlin's songs, such as 'The Girl that I Marry' and 'Doin' What Comes Naturally', and Helen Tamiris's choreography, showed that the *Oklahoma!* lesson had been learnt. *Brigadoon*, with songs provided by the newer team of Frederick Loewe and Alan Jay Lerner, persuaded us to believe that there was a time-travelling Scottish town that reappeared once every hundred years. And there was a new look about Cole Porter, too, in *Kiss Me, Kate* (New York 1948, London 1951), a play-within-a-play about a production of *The Taming of the Shrew*; yet the songs, 'So In Love', 'Always True to You in My Fashion', 'Too Darn Hot', could have fitted into almost any Porter show, and he was unable to resist topical allusions to the Kinsey Report.

Broadway was calling Cole Porter a has-been, a man who, in *Something for the Boys*, was 'tailoring his tunes to the brash Merman'. He needed the success of *Kiss Me, Kate*; yet nobody thought it would succeed. It was Shakespeare's lousiest play, and even his best plays were box-office poison in New York. There were casting difficulties, solved eventually by choosing the almost unknown Patricia Morison as Kate. It all ended in rave notices and 1,077 performances. *Panama Hattie* (New York 1940, London 1943), a rowdy show which took Ethel Merman to the Panama Canal as a nightclub queen, was never like this; nor, for heaven's sake, was his melancholy involvement with Billy Rose's revue *The Seven Lively Arts* (1944), in which he found himself associated with Stravinsky on the music and writing songs for a cast of one hundred and fifty including Bea Lillie, Alicia Markova, Bert Lahr and Benny Goodman.

When the first air-raid sirens sounded, Charles B. Cochran, the veteran impresario, had kissed his Young Ladies goodbye for the duration (the floor show at the Trocadéro was his only enterprise at the time). For him the war years had been years of failure and illness. His last two revues, *Lights Up* (1940) and *Big Top* (1942) were far from his best. Now, in 1946, he came back with *Big Ben*, Vivian Ellis and A.P. Herbert providing the music, book and lyrics. This gentle satire on Parliament scraped together only 172 performances: but Cochran followed it quickly with the same team's *Bless the Bride* (1947) which, opening

(opposite) Programme for *Oklahoma!*, St James Theatre, New York, 31 March 1943

Act I, scene 2 of *This Happy Breed*, Haymarket Theatre, 1943

at London's Adelphi Theatre four days before *Oklahoma!*, ran for over two years. It was young, it turned Lizbeth Webb from a dance-band vocalist into a West End star, and it had the infallible attraction of a young French singer, Georges Guétary, who was immediately offered a Hollywood contract but turned it down because it would have meant an operation to straighten his nose. Night after night audiences rose to the two show-stopping songs, 'This Is My Lovely Day' and 'Ma Belle Marguérite'. No composer not born in Europe could have written these songs, which, uninhibited in their romantic sentiment yet full of life-devouring gaiety, had an extraordinary ability to make people happy.

From Noël Coward, a revue, *Sigh No More* (1945), all rather pre-war but yielding two memorable songs, 'Matelot' and 'Nina'; then the spectacular *Pacific 1860* with which bomb-damaged Drury Lane re-opened in December 1946. It had Mary Martin as a prima donna who falls in love with a younger man on a South Seas island. On stage, in an Arctic temperature, the cast strove to create in the unheated auditorium the fantasy of tropical heat. It was not a very good show; even the music fell flat, and was damned by one critic as 'faintly reminiscent of Ivor Novello'. Other, less friendly critics, re-christened it *Soporific*.

No, the strength of Coward was still in comedy. *Blithe Spirit* (1941) ran for 1,997 performances, the longest run (at that time) of any straight play in London's history, even longer than *Charley's Aunt*. This story of an author and his second wife haunted by the ghost of his first wife was felt by some people (among them Graham Greene in the *Spectator*) to be in bad taste: one should not be flippant about death in wartime. The medium Madame Arcati, played unforgettably by Margaret Rutherford, stole the play as Coward was writing it and the show when it was performed. In New York the bicycle-riding medium was played by Mildred Natwick, and the author Charles Condomine by Clifton Webb. Together they filled the Morosco Theatre for eighteen months.

Present Laughter (1943), a comedy of self-indulgence in which Coward, as Garry Essendine, virtually played himself, was presented at London's Haymarket Theatre with *This Happy Breed* on alternate nights in what was called 'The Coward Season'. It was sufficiently self-mocking to reveal the author as a man who could not bear to be alone, and my endur-ing memory is of Coward-Essendine, alone and silent, gloomily emptying ashtrays after all his guests have gone.

If *Blithe Spirit* was in bad taste, what about *Arsenic and Old Lace*, by an ex-professor of music named Joseph Kesselring, which ran for three and a half years in both New York and London? Two gentle old ladies with a mad brother, who thinks he is Theodore Roosevelt, killing off people as an act of kindness? Is that funny? (Oh, but it *is*!) Or *Harvey*, a comedy about an alcoholic whose imaginary friend is an out-size rabbit? Elwood P. Dowd, the drunk, was played in New York by Frank Fay and afterwards by Joe E. Brown, and in London by Sid Field and again by Joe

Kay Hammond, Margaret Rutherford and Cecil Parker in *Blithe Spirit*, Piccadilly Theatre, 1941

Tom Tit caricature of the cast of *Harvey*, Prince of Wales, 1949

Scene from *The Linden Tree*, Duchess Theatre, 1947

E. Brown – all three from vaudeville and all pestered by letters from admirers asking 'Do you *really* get drunk every night before you go on?' Sid Field, well known in the provinces as a multi-mimic who could catch any accent, had burst upon the West End in a wartime revue, *Strike A New Note*, drawing from James Agate, the *Sunday Times* critic, a heartfelt 'At last the stage has an actor who knows how to exuberate.'

But there were more serious matters afoot. In J.B. Priestley's *An Inspector Calls* (1946), since performed all over the world, the mysterious Inspector Goole (Ralph Richardson), investigating a girl's death, calls on the Birlings, an apparently respectable family, and reveals a world of collective guilt. And in *The Linden Tree* (1947), another family play which has been called 'the best domestic play of our time', the conflict is between an elderly professor dedicated to teaching at a third-rate university (played by Lewis Casson), his ambitious wife (Sybil Thorndike) and rich, fast-buck-making son Rex. Here, as in other plays of these years, there is a suppressed fear of the materialism of the post-war younger generation and a radical apologia for what the Government was trying to do: 'Call us drab and dismal if you like, and tell us we don't know how to cook our food or wear our clothes – but for heaven's sake realize that we're trying to do something that is as extraordinary and wonderful as it's difficult – to have a revolution for once without the terror, without looting mobs and secret police, sudden arrests, mass suicides and executions. . . .'

From Thornton Wilder, *The Skin of Our Teeth,* an allegory of mankind; 'like a philosophy class conducted in a monkey house', said *Time* magazine of the Antrobus family, with Fredric March and Florence Eldridge as the parents, Montgomery Clift as their Cain-like son, and Tallulah Bankhead as Sabina, the *ewig weiblich* maid: there was a nightly gasp when Tallulah reached her line, 'I *hate* this play!' In London Sabina was played by Vivien Leigh.

From William Douglas-Home, something still more daring: a realistic study of prison life, with implications of homosexuality, in *Now Barabbas. . .* (1947), which took a revolutionary anti-Establishment view of murder by seeming to show more sympathy with the killer than with the dead policeman. Douglas-Home had undergone twelve months'

Tallulah Bankhead as Sabina in the American production of *The Skin of Our Teeth,* **Plymouth Theatre, 1942**

imprisonment after a court-martial for refusing to obey what he considered to be an immoral order.

In the greyness of post-war London poetry returned to the stage. Born in small, unfashionable theatres, Christopher Fry's *A Phoenix Too Frequent* and *The Lady's Not for Burning* (with Alec Clunes as Thomas Mendip) played with language in ways that had not been used since the Elizabethans. High spirits, but an underlying loneliness. Gradually critics began to accuse Fry of 'typewriter facility'. Even T.S. Eliot's comedy, *The Cocktail Party,* in verse so blank that for long spasms one thought it prose, was not universally admired, though one had to be careful, because the author had just won the Nobel Prize, and received the Order of Merit and honorary degrees from three universities. No matter: after its début at the 1949 Edinburgh Festival it ran for nearly a year on Broadway. Brooks Atkinson thought it 'verbose and elusive'. The argument? Edward and Lavinia, unhappily married, both with lovers, give a cocktail party for Celia who is in love with Edward. A psychiatrist-confessor, Sir Henry Harcourt-Reilly, explains everything as we go along. What is to be done about life? Hang on to established institutions, such as middle-class marriage, it's all we've got. Celia prefers despair: she alone has a sense of sin: she goes off to a savage country called Kinkanja and dies horribly, crucified near an ant-hill. (Why? I never could make out.)

From America came news of Bertolt Brecht, the epic theory of 'alienation' by which the audience was not supposed to become emotionally involved in the play. *Mother Courage, Galileo, The Good Women of Set-zuan* – they could be read, but not yet seen, unless one lived in Hollywood, where, in 1947, *Galileo* was produced by Charles Laughton a year before Brecht, a lifelong Communist, went to live in East Germany.

However, one was allowed to become emotionally involved with Danny Kaye. In show business since 1929, though intending to be a surgeon, he had been

Bud Flanagan, Chesney Allen and Danny Kaye, London Palladium, 1948

a soda-jerk and a summer-camp cheerer-upper in the Catskills before being 'discovered' by Moss Hart in 1940 at La Martinique nightclub, New York. Hart, dazed by Kaye's parlour trick of reciting fifty-four Russian composers' names in forty seconds, engaged him for *Lady In The Dark*. On his 1948 and 1949 visits to London Danny Kaye began his relaxed mass hypnotism of London audiences. He, one man, could hold them for more than an hour, sitting on the edge of the stage, making people sing silly songs; after a motor accident he walked about the stalls showing them his X-rays; suddenly he would say, 'My, that's a pretty hat!' to a blushing dowager; then turn to her neighbour, introduce them to each other, borrow a cigarette and then sing 'Candy Kisses'. Friend of the Royal Family and of Ambassador Lewis Douglas, he now had the status of goodwill ambassador himself, and at a reception for him in the Lincoln Room of the Savoy Hotel the Lord Mayor of London said so. Kenneth Tynan, who had just succeeded Ivor Brown as dramatic critic of the *Observer*, compared his diction to Olivier's and Barrault's; and Geoffrey Gorer the social anthropologist said, 'He makes love to his audience.'

Where were the new playwrights, those who had been in the War or who could not bear the peace? The rebels would not break through until the mid-Fifties. The younger established craftsmen were still wedded to 'naturalism', whatever it was. Terence Rattigan, an air gunner in the R.A.F., used his service experience well in *Flare Path* (1942) about the wives of a bomber crew waiting for their husbands to return from a mission. Near to tragedy, it was criticized as 'bad for morale' – but it ran for eighteen months. In *While the Sun Shines* (1943), he went back to popular topical comedy, with jokes about Spam, shortages, and the new superficial classlessness of society – an earl serving as an ordinary seaman engaged to the daughter of an impoverished duke, a rich girl who has become a typist, comic American and Free French officers doing and saying the things you would expect them to . . . it never got to New York, but in London it ran for 1,154 performances.

In *The Winslow Boy* (1946) a deeper, more tender Rattigan emerged, in a tale based on the case of an Osborne naval cadet accused of stealing a five-shilling postal order, in its pre-1914 day a kind of mini-Dreyfus case. The play was almost stolen (in London) by Emlyn Williams as the famous barrister who defended the boy. New York enjoyed the play, though Wolcott Gibbs in the *New Yorker*, not a noted anglophile, found it no more than 'good, presentable entertainment, suitable for all the family'. *Adventure Story* (1949) with Paul Scofield, an attempt to put Alexander the Great upon the stage, deserved more marks for trying than it got; and *The Browning Version* (in *Playbill* 1948) was a moving study of a failed, pedantic schoolmaster unable to communicate or make himself liked, beautifully played by Eric Portman. Not until 1952 would Rattigan write his greatest play, *The Deep Blue Sea*, which would cause one critic to say that he had a fundamentally tragic outlook, and was the only British dramatist who understood love.

At Malvern they were holding, in 1949, the first drama festival for ten years, to present ninety-three-year-old Bernard Shaw's *Buoyant Billions*, a 'comedy of no manners' about the plans of Junius Smith to improve the world, which include a visit to Panama, where he meets, not Panama Hattie, but Babsy Buoyant, a billionaire's daughter who lives in a shack and charms snakes with her saxophone. 'Forgive it,' Shaw told the public. The old boy had just over a year to live.

We have cleared the way for two big new talents, both American. If Tennessee Williams and Arthur Miller had anything in common, it was the ability to probe painfully into human beings, to make them tear themselves to pieces on stage. Williams's staple material was the Southern Belle (in Britain, the name of a railway train; in America, a tragedy left over from the Civil War). She figures in both *The Glass Menagerie* (1945) and *A Streetcar Named Desire* (1947), ageing in the first, nubile in the second; Laurette Taylor in the first, Jessica Tandy in the second. Was Williams writing the same play over again? Both are concerned with the pathos of nostalgia for times that perhaps never were, of the escape into fantasy and lies which, in *Streetcar*, erupts into violence seldom seen before on the stage. We know, as the curtain rises on that only scene, a basement apartment in New Orleans in summer, where four men play poker, that the hot claustrophobia is going to explode, as the mindless Kowalski (played by Marlon Brando in New York, Bonar Colleano in London) knocks the poor, deluded sister-in-law Blanche (played in London by Vivien Leigh) about, because he has no words. She

hates his violence, wants her sister to leave him. She keeps maddeningly switching on the radio. He smashes it, and suddenly the whole room is being wrecked, they are shrieking at each other; then lust takes control as he picks her up and carries her upstairs, baying like an animal. Passion had returned to the stage.

Like *Streetcar*, Miller's *Death of A Salesman* was directed by Elia Kazan. 'Less an indictment than an elegy' was one verdict on Lee J. Cobb's performance as Willy Loman, the sixty-three-year-old travelling salesman who is put on commission by his firm, and eventually fired. (In London he was played by Paul Muni.) We see everything Willy believes in collapsing. His sons disappoint him; by being found with a girl in a Boston hotel bedroom he disappoints his sons; he can't keep up the payments on the electric ice box ('God, for once I'd like to own something before it's broken down!'); he keeps crashing his car, he is losing his grip, talking to himself – and so we get flashbacks into the illusions and false values of his past life. He believes, as so many salesmen believe, in popularity: he wants (like Babbitt) to be loved by men more than by women: 'Be liked and you will never want. You take me for instance; I never have to wait in line to see a buyer. . . . Call out the name of Willy Loman and see what happens!' His ideal salesman was a man who was still on the road at the age of eighty-four and died the true death of a salesman – in the Pullman of a train just going into Boston – 'hundreds of salesmen and buyers were at his funeral.'

Broken, Willy decides on suicide – the family will somehow survive on the money from his insurance. But nobody comes to his funeral. British and American audiences reacted differently to the play. For the British, the naked emotion was almost indecent: they thought they were looking at a foreign country. But Americans were shaken to the core. Geoffrey Gorer sat in the stalls at the Morosco and was amazed to hear sobbing all round him – from men even more than women. The women, when the lights went up, were clearly thinking: 'This is the man I've been married to all these years!' And the men were seeing – themselves. I have never quite believed the story that, of the many professional salesmen who went to see the play, one was heard saying to another as they left the theatre: 'That New England territory never was any good.'

(*above*) 'The Messerschmitt in Windsor Great Park', 1940, by Paul Nash
(*below*)'. . . Meanwhile, in Britain, the entire population, faced by the threat of invasion, has been flung
into a state of complete panic . . . etc., etc., etc.', cartoon by Pont, 14 August 1940

In the Picture

What, asked Sir Kenneth Clark, Director of Britain's National Gallery, would art be like after the War? He was asking it in *World Review*, in November 1940. Since the Renaissance, art had depended on a small privileged class which had a high level of taste. Even in the nineteenth century painting had survived by unearned increment. Sir Kenneth Clark was not, like Cyril Connolly, defeatist; but if, as everyone seemed to think, the War would remove unearned increment, some other patronage must be found. Would it be the State? If so, the artist of the future might have to please 'a very large audience and a number of committees', and to do that he must work in a style that wouldn't upset people. This was already happening in Nazi Germany and Soviet Russia, and in America under the Federal art project. There might not be room for such an artist as Henry Moore, undoubtedly Britain's greatest.

In war, meanwhile, art must be taken to the people and artists must be chosen to record the war. Sir Kenneth Clark was the man who organized the War Artists' scheme; who had the imagination to set painters to work in surroundings utterly unlike their usual material – John Piper and Graham Sutherland to war-damaged areas, Henry Moore to the Tube railway shelters to draw huddled, sleeping forms, Epstein to model the heads of Service chiefs, Edward Ardizzone to North Africa and Italy to sketch the scenes that war correspondents Alan Moorehead and Christopher Buckley were describing in words. Strangest of all was the prising of the visionary Stanley Spencer out of Cookham village to record shipbuilding on the Clyde. Paul Nash, who had painted World War I, produced a memorable picture of the Battle of Britain, a wild tangle of vapour trails and smoke from dead or damaged aircraft falling among clouds and barrage balloons. The Henry Moore drawings and some of his sculpture were shown at the Buchholtz Gallery, Man-

hattan, in 1943, introduced by Sir Kenneth Clark, who, having heard the sculpture described in London as 'morphology, not art', felt it necessary to explain that the holes in the stone 'connect one side with the other, making it immediately more three-dimensional.'

Many painters were recruited by the Army for camouflage, and here they were surprised to meet illusionists like Jasper Maskelyne, who was in charge of a camouflage unit in Cairo. Among the experts of 'disrupted patterning' were Oliver Messel, the stage designer, and Basil Spence, who would one day design Coventry Cathedral. I do not quite believe the art historian who claims that camouflage was influenced by 'the amoeboid shapes of Jean Arp'.

Feliks Topolski, a descriptive draughtsman admired by Augustus John, drew in Gibraltar, Africa, Persia and Britain: whether his subject was bombed-out families or Russian peasants, the keynote was pathos. As for John, he painted a portrait of the Queen, and an unflattering one of General Montgomery, which was shown in the depressing Royal Academy exhibition of 1944, with Dame Laura Knight's interiors of bombers and aircraft factories, and 'subject pictures' by various hands, among them 'The Week's Ration' in which a butcher was gloomily looking from two lamb chops to a 1s. 2d. meat allowance.

Most of the treasures of London's National Gallery and the best of the King's pictures had been stored in caves 300 feet deep near Bodnant, North Wales, where they were kept at the right temperature by special heating; and the Gallery itself was used mainly for lunchtime concerts. Towards the end of the War single pictures were brought out of hiding to be exhibited: one of the subjects of this experiment was El Greco's 'Christ and the Moneylenders in the Temple'; another was the Rokeby Venus, which probably started the joke about the American soldier's first reaction to it: 'Boy, what an ass!' When, in May 1945, the Gallery reopened, the old favourites returned first: Rembrandt's 'Woman Bathing', Rubens' 'Judgment of Paris' and forty-eight others.

The Metropolitan Museum, Manhattan, also hid its treasures, four hundred and fifty of them, in Whitemarsh Hall, the 147-room Philadelphia mansion of Mrs E.T. Stotesbury the society hostess: Breughels, Raphaels, Titians, Rembrandts, medieval tapestries and Sèvres pottery, all guarded by an electric signal system. America was not asking who would patronize art after the war: there was no need, as long as there was Peggy Guggenheim. 'Today is the age of collecting, not of creation,' she once said. She had cheerfully lost $6,000 a year on 'Guggenheim Jeune', her *avant-garde* London gallery in the Thirties; then, during the Phoney War, tried to start another gallery in Paris, until the Germans came; decided that it was no use trying to found an artists' colony on the Riviera for the duration of the War; and then, in New York in 1942, started her 'Art of This Century' gallery. She launched three new painters, William Baziotes, Robert Motherwell and Jackson Pollock, then two more, Mark Rothko and Clifford Still. She had married Max Ernst, with whom she had escaped from Europe through Lisbon. 'Art of This Century' occupied the top storey at No. 30 West 57th Street. Designed by Frederick Kiesler, it had curved walls like a subway ('a kind of artistic Coney Island', said one critic), used spotlights, hung unframed pictures on strings or mounted them on baseball bats. Seven Paul Klees were exhibited on a revolving wheel. Among many exhibitions was one of 'The Negro in American Life'

(*opposite*) One of the canvases entitled 'The Furnaces – Shipbuilding on the Clyde', about 1940, by Stanley Spencer
(*below*) 'Submarines in a Dry Dock', 1940, by Eric Ravilious

(*above*) 'The Manufacture of Battle Dress', 1940, by A.R. Thomson
(*opposite*) 'Somerset Maugham', 1949, by Graham Sutherland

which Mrs Roosevelt came to see (but she refused to look at the Surrealists). Miss Guggenheim had no doubt that Jackson Pollock ('Jack the Dripper'), whom art critics labelled 'Abstract Expressionist', was 'the greatest painter since Picasso', and that he 'alone justified her effort'. He seems to have been the first to practice what is now called 'action painting' ('the painting has a life of its own – I try to let it come through'), exemplified in a wall canvas 23 feet by 6 feet, using splash-drip instead of brushes, which decorated the entrance hall of 'Art of This Century' and was afterwards given to the University of Iowa for its students' dining hall.

Miss Guggenheim, who lost her husband, Max Ernst, to another of her protegées, Dorothea Tanning, gave up her gallery in 1947 and went to live in Venice. Jackson Pollock had another big exhibition in 1949

which was said to 'reflect an advanced stage of the disintegration of modern painting ... but with a liberating and cathartic effect.' The 'New York School' of Abstract Expressionists now had a new headquarters at the top of a house in East 8th Street known as 'the Club'.

The Museum of Modern Art had shows of 'eye-witness war paintings', many of them commissioned by *Life* magazine (the general opinion was that they weren't as good as *Life* photographs), and an exhibition of forty-six 'war pictures by Chinese children' which were even livelier than *Life*. Who shall say that art lacked patronage? The Pepsi-Cola Company held an annual United States Art Exhibition at which, in 1948, it somehow came about that every one of 156 entries won a prize, like the Caucus Race. Heaven help anyone who painted recognizable objects or people. 'Cézanne made an apple important,' cried Samuel M. Kootz in his book *New Frontiers in American Painting*. Painters like Thomas Hart Benton could 'make a lynching trivial'; Benton's lurid anti-Axis paintings were 'cheap melodrama', he and his kind were mere nationalists painting 'postcards heavy with facts'; all this was absurd now that 'Picasso frees us from . . . our bondage to nature.'

As the Allies closed in on Berlin, the Whitney Museum held an exhibition of 'European Artists in America'; the two most memorable pictures were Kisling's 'Nude Reclining' and Yves Tanguy's 'Un Lieu Oblique'. And from France came portfolios of Matisse and Picasso prints, printed during the German occupation on black-market paper by twenty-five-year-old Maurice Girodias, a one-man artistic Resistance who would publish and then disappear from Paris while the Gestapo tried to find the source.

As the dust of peace settled on stricken Europe, artists wondered, not only what to paint, but *how* to paint. At studio parties you actually heard them asking each other: 'What style are you working in now?' Where was the new movement? In Paris the French Surrealists were still at it, holding exhibitions and attacking functionalism in everything. In London, open-air sculpture became the thing: pensive Henry Moore ladies with small heads were seen by the lake in Battersea Park. They had been presented by the London County Council after a memorable outdoor exhibition of forty-three sculptures organized by the L.C.C. and the Arts Council: art was indeed being taken to the people. The 'two Roberts', MacBryde and Colquhoun, surrealized in new ways. John Minton excelled in watercolours, and in 1949 Francis Bacon had his first nightmare exhibition.

In France, Georges Rouault, at seventy-seven, brushing greens and yellows so thickly on to his canvases that they seemed three-dimensional, felt a new ecstasy; and he was found, one day in 1948, wearing a bowler hat, burning more than three hundred of his early paintings, which he had recovered from the heirs of Ambroise Vollard the dealer on the legal grounds that, since he had not signed them, they were therefore unfinished.

It was a relief to turn to the primitive and the serene. At her Eagle Bridge farm in Hoosick Valley, New York State, an old lady of eighty-six was painting jolly little landscapes, rather like the Douanier Rousseau or L.S. Lowry without the chimney stacks, mostly of her farm and its surroundings. In her bedroom, heated by a wood stove, she had painted about seven hundred pictures between 1940 and 1947, when she was given a comprehensive exhibition in New York City, for which Louis Bromfield wrote an introduction to the catalogue. 'Grandma Moses, American Primitive', he claimed, was to be ranked with Peter Breughel. Anna Mary Moses saw her own work as documentary, 'so people will see how we used to live.' She could paint five landscapes a week and sell each for $3,000. Her skies were always pink. To the dozens of callers who came to watch her paint she would answer all their silly questions with: 'Why did I start to paint in my old age? Well, to tell the truth, I had neuritis and arthritis so bad I could do but little work, but I had to keep busy to pass the time away, so. . . .' One of her earliest callers (in 1941) was Cole Porter, who bought twenty canvases from her and sent them to friends as Christmas cards. One, a farm scene with red chickens all over it, was given to Ethel Merman, who thought it was a child's daub and gave it away. In Britain, a much stranger 'primitive' named Scottie Wilson had a brief vogue in 1949: he lived in Kilburn, a dingy quarter of north-west London, and earned between £5 and £15 a picture – 'enough money for cigarettes and kippers' on which he mainly lived.

Old Masters became confusingly new when, in 1948, 625,000 people went to see an exhibition of cleaned pictures at the National Gallery. We learned that nineteenth-century varnish and sheer dirt had discoloured Rubens' *Chapeau de Paille*, Rembrandt's *Woman Bathing*, Velasquez's *Philip IV*, and that some of our ideas about lighting had been wrong; and were reassured that the pictures would not crumble to dust after this new method of restoration.

What should a modern art gallery look like? Frank Lloyd Wright's plans, first seen in 1945, for 'The Modern Gallery of Non-Objective Painting' aimed at being 'democratic': the visitor must not be made to feel insignificant. As it was apparently inspired by an Assyrian ziggurat, which seldom makes one feel significant, this was not easy to realize; but inside the ceilings were to be never more than twelve feet high, so you could almost feel you were in your own apartment, except that rooms would be connected by spiral ramps so you could almost drive in. (Peggy Guggenheim thought it looked like 'a huge garage'.)

'Two Sisters', 1945, by Robert Colquhoun

'Functional', an illustration by Osbert Lancaster to *Homes Sweet Homes*, by Osbert Lancaster

Eventually known as the Guggenheim Museum, it was completed fourteen years later.

How to express, in building materials, the new determination to wrest some kind of international order out of an unpromising post-war world? A slaughterhouse had been razed, with unconscious symbolism, to help clear a site in New York for the new United Nations headquarters on Manhattan's East Side. The plans, first seen in 1947, were likened to 'a sandwich on edge and a couple of freight cars'. The blue-green glass windows held by a tracery of aluminium could look mighty pretty, but as there were 2,700 of them in each of the east and west walls, the effect of a single bomb, even a non-atomic one, didn't bear thinking about. Lewis Mumford disliked both site and design, which were of course the work of a committee. The forty storeys of the Secretariat Building would be rendered insignificant by the neighbouring R.C.A. Building and the Chrysler Tower.

Why was there no better provision of trees and gardens? Why was the Secretariat allowed to dominate the design – was it not a symbol that 'the managerial revolution has taken place and that bureaucracy rules the world'? The architects argued that it wasn't meant to be a symbol – it was 'a workshop of peace'. But Mumford was not to be mollified: 'these buildings,' he said, 'should be as beloved a symbol as the Statue of Liberty, as powerful a spectacle as St Peter's in Rome.'

In Manchester, England, the Ministry of Town and Country Planning rejected the appeal of an architect, Joseph Sunlight, who wanted to introduce 'vertical development' by building, in Quay Street, a thirty-five-storey building 380 feet high with room for one thousand offices. If the University of London Senate House could be 210 feet high, could not Manchester have as dominant a feature? No; the present height limit of 80 feet, laid down in 1890, must stay.

Skyscrapers would exclude light; there could be no 'vertical development' unless the width of streets was quadrupled. Anyway, nobody wanted to *live* in a skyscraper: the 1949 nostalgia for everything Georgian was nearer to the sort of hearth and home we had been fighting for. Perhaps only Osbert Lancaster foresaw the horrors of the future: in *Drayneflete Revealed* (1949), a joyous satire on architecture and design, he looked forward to a multi-storey Drayneflete whose Municipal Offices would include a psychiatric clinic, a crèche, a helicopter landing strip on the roof, and a Floating Concert Hall.

The British at this time had no very ambitious ideas for their own homes; many of them didn't have homes. But in America people aspired to apartments with thermostatic central (space) heating, all-electric kitchens, two bathrooms for every four rooms, and even an 'adequate sub-basement atomic bomb shelter'. An architect named Martial E. Scull designed a house which could withstand an A-bomb raid: it used a lot of concrete and lead, had sealed doors and windows and was terribly expensive. Design was often 'free-flowing', and the 'open plan' was coming in: the theory was that if you have air-conditioned central heating you don't need doors and windows. You don't need a fireplace either, so that the television set becomes the focus of the room. There was even talk of harnessing solar energy.

In Britain design was cramped by 'utility'. This had begun in 1943 when Hugh Dalton, then President of the Board of Trade, had called in Charles Tennyson, the poet's grandson, to chair a committee of social workers, furniture manufacturers, architects and a housewife. Six months later the first 'utility' furniture was on sale: seventeen essential pieces had been designed in forty-five different sizes, using wood for legs and struts and hardboard ⅛ inch thick for flat surfaces. All 'utility' things carried a symbol like a double-disc with one segment missing. (I still have my utility bookcases – they never wear out.) In New York City the Museum of Modern Art in 1947 held an international competition of low-cost furniture design in which more adventurous things were to be seen, such as Charles Eames's 'aerodynamic' designs using moulded fibreglass and other new materials.

Britain Can Make It (1946) was a brave, backs-to-the-wall exhibition supervised by the new Design Council under Gordon Russell. It showed Spitfires

being beaten back into saucepans, gadgets galore, and an extraordinary optimism. The Victoria and Albert Museum, in which it was held, had had most of its windows smashed by bombing, but using the dictatorial powers of those days, Sir Stafford Cripps diverted London's entire supply of glass to mend them in time for the opening.

Nothing dates so quickly as advertising; nothing re-creates an age so sharply or so sadly. In 1943 America was still spending about $440 million a year on advertising. Side by side with American Airlines's 'No spot on earth is more than 60 hours from your local airport' was the Hood Rubber Company's 'How to make your rubber footwear last longer', while Del Monte was keeping its brand name alive by urging people to grow Victory Gardens. In Britain Guinness, knowing perfectly well that they could sell every pint they brewed, had one of their fanciful posters showing a 'Wheel, for putting shoulder to; Socks, for pulling up; Stone, for not leaving unturned; Brass Tacks, for

Stacking chairs by Charles Eames, 1940

'Dust cart', by Ethel Gabain

getting down to . . . Guinness for Strength.' 'Too tired to sleep?' asked Dr Hiram A. Jones of the Office of Physical Fitness, New York State War Council, in a series of government advertisements; and, like Britain's Radio Doctor, he was full of homely health hints. 'Vimms,' gleefully announced a manufacturer of vitamin pills, 'require no points at all!' 'Every woman in a vital civilian job is a *Soldier.* . . .' Government propaganda? Not at all: those women 'find delicious Beech-Nut Gum refreshes them.'

In Britain the biggest wartime advertiser was the Government. It ordered the nation to 'Go to it!' In Tom Eckersley's 'Long Hair is Dangerous' poster it told factory girls to cut it short and keep it out of the machinery. It asked idle girls: 'Are you living a selfish life . . . spreading complacency? . . . Russian women in slacks and smocks are fighting in the trenches . . . Join the ATS!' 'Careless Talk (three officers gathered round a fascinating blonde) Costs Lives'.

BEWARE

HE WANTS TO KNOW YOUR UNIT'S NAME,
WHERE YOU'RE GOING, WHENCE YOU CAME,
EVEN ALONE OR IN A CROWD
NEVER MENTION THESE OUT LOUD.

Famous commercial advertisers like Barratt's Shoes, who could not promote their inadequate supplies, chatted to their customers about shortages, and the makers of a famous cold remedy said: 'If you have any Vapex please make it last.' – 'Unfortunately Cadbury's are only allowed the milk to make a small quantity of chocolate . . . *do* save it for the children.' – 'Won't it be nice when we have lovely lingerie, *and* Lux to look after our pretty things?' And Rose's Lime Juice advertisements, featuring the butler Hawkins and his master Mr Gerald, looked back in Wodehouse dialogue to the days before the War when a gentleman could actually have a hangover.

As peace broke coldly on the world, advertisers fanned the embers of the better life. 'They're coming back, those 57 Varieties, one by one!' Grey's Cigarettes, still featuring a bear-skinned, grizzled officer, still dedicated to well-bred understatement, still muttered something about 'Just honest-to-goodness tobacco.' 'How does she get that pre-war feeling?' (You'll never guess, so I'll tell you: she drinks Hall's Tonic Wine.)

The Government, through a peacetime organization called the Central Office of Information, was still shouting at people to do things and not do things. Join the R.A.F. Train to be a nurse. Protect your child by Immunization. Don't listen to the Traffic Jimp (a sort of gremlin tempting you to take risks). Beat the Squanderbug – National Savings. And a notorious poster, 'Keep Death Off the Road,' showing a 'black widow', which had to be withdrawn because it made people *want* to throw themselves under a bus. There was also a notable campaign *against* the Government, or at least against nationalization. The Government having threatened to nationalize sugar, Britain's leading sugar company, Tate & Lyle, asked its publicity adviser, Warwick Charlton, to invent a Mr Sugar, a Sugar-Daddy, somebody like Mr Therm of the Gas Board, a cartoon character who could get across to the public the idea that they would be better off if sugar remained free. Tate, in fact, versus State. Mr Charlton had been editor of the *Eighth Army News* during the War and had seen fit to criticize Winston Churchill in some of his leading articles, for which he had not been reprimanded by General Montgomery. He now got together in the bar of the Savage Club with a *Daily Express* artist, St John Cooper, who, on the traditional back of an envelope, sketched a little man with huge surprised eyes and christened him Mr Cube. It worked: sugar was not nationalized.

America was far ahead of all this: in a 200-page issue, under the slogan 'America Believes in Competition!' the *Saturday Evening Post* displayed such a wealth of ham, steaks, refrigerators and washing machines, and eight-cylinder automobiles in full colour that one reached simultaneously for bicarbonate and blood-pressure pills.

Advertisements still used a high proportion of drawings, as if in deliberate contrast to the 'editorial' effect of photographs. (But not for fashion: fashion photography literally leapt ahead as Richard Avedon made his models move, laugh, jump; for they were as important as the clothes they wore.) Yet photography was the 'relevant' art of these years, and so sophisticated had picture journalism become that almost all photographs had a propaganda effect. The British Army Film and Photographic Unit had proportionately higher casualties than any other arm of the services. *Life* photographers, in the forefront of battle, suffered similarly, and Carl and Shelly Mydans were in a Japanese prison camp at Santo Tomas in the Philippines. The unforgettable photographs of the War are a subject for an over-fifties competition. Cecil Beaton's picture of St Paul's Cathedral, seen through bombed masonry and rubble in which willow herb is growing. The planting of the Stars and Stripes on Iwo Jima. A tender little picture of Winston and Clementine Churchill, average man and wife, sailing down the Thames in a boat. Bill Brandt's air-raid shelter pictures, a strange counterpart to Henry Moore's drawings, and his romantic-sinister studies of London in the blackout and by moonlight.

Deep in the earth, all over Europe, treasures of art were stored for six years. In the old Aldwych Underground station in London, in kapok-lined crates, was the newly found treasure of Sutton Hoo, in Suffolk – a Saxon 'ship burial' of thirteen centuries ago, the most dazzling archaeological find since Tutankhamun's tomb; a 90-foot rowing boat with, amidships, not the body of a king (for this was a memorial only) but all his regalia – a gold-and-garnet-inlaid helmet, a round shield, a gold-and-garnet-decorated sword with a solid gold buckle wrought with intertwined serpent and animal forms, drinking horns made from the horns of aurochs, innumerable silver vessels and jewels. Whose memorial? Probably Redwald, greatest of East Anglian kings, or one of his sons; he flourished before *Beowulf* was written; perhaps he *was* Beowulf. Nobody but archaeologists and museum officials saw any of this glory until 1946, when it made the most brilliant exhibition of the decade.

The Nazis had a quasi-military art-looting organization called the Reich-Leader Rosenberg Task Force for Occupied Territories. Many of this organization's depredations were destined for Hitler's hometown at Linz, or for Hermann Goering's private collection which was buried in a cave at Unterstein, Austria. (It was discovered there by the American 101st Airborne Division and thrown open to G.I.s, who, since it consisted largely of nudes, were appreciative.)

The Task Force was advised as much by art crooks as by art experts, and so it came about that the greatest single craftsman in paint of these years was the world's greatest exposed forger. Hans van Meegeren had been producing bogus Vermeers for some years, certainly since 1937, when his 'Disciples at Emmaus', passed as a genuine Vermeer by the art historian Dr Bredius, sold for £52,000. Three more 'Vermeers' were 'discovered' between 1940 and 1943, and in 1944 Goering paid (yes, *paid*) £165,000 for 'The Woman taken in Adultery'. In 1945 Van Meegeren was arrested by his fellow Dutchmen and charged with 'collaborating with the enemy' in that he had sold the 'Vermeer' to Goering. To prove his innocence, Van Meegeren, who suffered from the paranoia of artists who have more technique than creativity, and whose satisfaction was that he had revenged himself on the critics, undertook to forge a Vermeer under supervision. It was called 'Jesus Among the Doctors'. Only chemical analysis of paint, frame and canvas could have proved it a forgery if the 'experts' had not seen him paint it with their own eyes. Van Meegeren was sentenced to a year in prison, but died nineteen days after his sentence began.

St Paul's Cathedral seen through bombed masonry and rubble by Cecil Beaton

177

Prayers, Boffins and Flying Saucers

'Almighty and most merciful Father, we humbly beseech Thee . . . to restrain these immoderate rains,' General Patton intoned one day when things weren't going too well in Belgium, taking upon himself a duty normally performed by a Senior Chaplain of the Forces. In wartime each participating nation has to assume that God is on its side. Prayers are requests for big, simple things: victory, survival. There is little time for refinements of doctrine, and moral dilemmas are fewer. The commonest, in Europe, was probably: 'Ought I to pray that the bomb won't hit me? What if God then makes it hit someone else, and is it my fault if it does?'

The right sort of padre did a good job in the War. My memories are of a Nonconformist and a Roman Catholic chaplain squatting on the deck of a troopship playing housey-housey or Crown and Anchor with the men, with the Church of England padre averting his gaze; and it was the Church of England padre who covered his face with his hands and walked out when the camp concert jokes became too blue. In air-raids clergymen did innumerable unrecorded heroic things, far beyond the usual requirements of their calling, not the least of which was the absolutely basic thing of organizing community singing among frightened people in bomb shelters. In both the R.A.F. and the U.S.A.A.F., chaplains said: 'May the good Lord grant you happy landings.' I have never met a parson who did not think the War the most rewarding time of his life; and some older ones, confined to the gentle routine of country parishes, are still homesick for it.

It was difficult to be a devout Jew in the Army. Canned Kosher foods were available in America, but there were never enough of them, and prayer shawls and Passover prayer books were not easy to carry around. Jewish boys in my intake unit brought little attaché cases full of *gefillte* fish with them, and gave us dormitory feasts after lights out; and I had an arrangement with one of them by which I swopped my cheese for his bacon.

In 1942 the American business magazine *Fortune* temporarily forsook its glossy materialism to set up a symposium on the body and soul. Jacques Maritain, the French Catholic writer, the British scientist Julian Huxley, the Harvard philosopher William Ernest Hocking, the Columbia philosopher William Pepperell Montagu, and the theologian William Learoyd Sperry argued, as the Battle of Stalingrad raged 7,000 miles away, whether the body and the soul were one. Yes, they were, said Huxley, alone in his certainty; therefore he reasoned the soul could not leave the body.

Certain sects, such as Jehovah's Witnesses, having registered as conscientious objectors, went before tribunals in Britain to decide whether they should be forced to join the Forces or go to jail. Moral Rearmament members in America, applying for 1-A classification on the grounds that their work was more important than military service, usually lost their appeals.

Are people more or less religious in wartime? In Britain, Mass Observation in 1943 published a two-year survey which found that, while apathy was general, the *desire* for belief was increasing: the 16 per cent who had said in 1941 that war had strengthened their faith had grown to 26 per cent in 1943. Or, as a wayside pulpit in a much-blitzed area put it, 'If your knees knock, kneel on them.'

To American Protestants it seemed that Catholics were taking a long time to make up their minds about the war. *Time* magazine in 1943 thought that 'Pope Pacelli (Pius XII) . . . is one of the world's most hardened statesmen,' and made much of the fact that he owned a solid gold telephone. And why should Monsignor Fulton J. Sheen, Professor of Philosophy at the

Catholic University of America at Washington, as late as 1944 make such a point of stressing the need to pray daily for Stalin? Monsignor Sheen was often heard on the radio, talking about War and Guilt, Peace and War, God and Peace, in many permutations. When Cardinal Spellman visited sixteen countries, flying 15,000 miles, *Time* guessed that this meant that 'the Vatican expects and desires a United Nations Victory'; and soon Spellman was broadcasting to Hungarian Catholics urging them to ignore and resist the new anti-semitic laws, for 'spiritually *we* are Semites'. Nearer home, the Cardinal attacked Walter Wanger's government-sponsored film *To the People of the United States*, which was propaganda about syphilis and yet contained 'not one word of condemnation of unchastity'. The Public Health Service thereupon withdrew its support.

Did God mean us to hate the German people or only the Nazis? And how should they be dealt with after the war? Dean Inge, incorrigible at eighty-four, said 'don't blame Hitler, blame Luther for the miseries Germany has brought to the world!' Dr Cyril Garbett, the leftish Archbishop of York, who with the new Archbishop of Canterbury, Dr Geoffrey Fisher, had each halved his salary for the duration, thought there should be 'no sensational public trials' of the leading Nazis who had ordered crimes against humanity: 'Those who catch them should at once put them to death.' It was the obedient subordinates who should be tried. After the War Dr Garbett was to say that it was possible to be both a Christian and a Communist, but not a *Marxian* Communist. His predecessor Dr Temple had never had any doubt about war aims: 'We are fighting for Christian civilization,' he said; and thirty-three American Protestant leaders signed a document agreeing with him. At the same time he was convinced that 'all our values are wrong. . . . We shall not come to order and peace until our price-tags tally with God's.' Dr Barnes, Bishop of Birmingham, always odd man out, thought the blockade of Germany should be relaxed, but was overruled by Canterbury. Total pacifist (even refusing to take part in national days of prayer), opponent of the atomic bomb, leader of Modernism and the scientific approach to religion, in 1947 Barnes published a book, *The Rise of Christianity*, which caused his Archbishop to ask him to consider whether he was really fit to be a bishop at all. Two years later it seemed that Barnes

had succumbed to the sin of despair: 'large families', he was understood to say, 'are selfishness'; they were justified only by Catholic propaganda and the need for cannon fodder.

There was one great scientist who would have disagreed with Barnes. 'Only the churches stood squarely against the path of Hitler,' said Einstein. The churches, and certain individuals who were mown down by him. Three weeks before Hitler's suicide, a tough, moon-faced man named Dietrich Bonhoeffer, the nephew of a German general, had been hanged by the S.S. in prison. The last Englishman to see him alive had been Dr G.K.A. Bell, Bishop of Chichester: they had met in Stockholm in 1942 and had talked of the anti-Hitler forces in Germany, of which Bonhoeffer was a part. A few months later Bonhoeffer had been imprisoned. This was the theologian who had dared to use Nietzsche's phrase 'the death of God', adding: 'What God is teaching is that we must live as men who can get along very well without him.' God is not all-powerful, he is suffering in his weakness, and this is how he can help us. God is not in church or 'up there', he is here in the world. Our view of him is still medieval.

Moreover, trying to be an atheist is *hard work*. In 1942 people were reading C.S. Lewis's *Screwtape Letters*, in which the fiends plot against God the Enemy, fighting for the soul of a young Englishman who keeps 'backsliding into faith' and is finally saved by a bomb.

These ideas ran parallel with the revival of interest in Existentialism, which particularly recommended itself to post-war France, where relief, defeat and guilt rallied round it. The novels of Sartre and Camus were said to be influenced by it, and an 'existentialist' lifestyle grew up along the Boulevard St Michel, where young people seemed to interpret it as a kind of fatalism which needed no ethics, authorized promiscuity, had something to do with not bothering to wash one's hair, vintage jazz and bars with names like Whiskey-à-Gogo.

In Oberammergau, Bavaria, the villagers were rehearsing for the 1946 Passion Play, with Alois Lang as Christus – not without difficulty, for some of the cast awaited release from American Army prisons, and all had been Nazis except Hans Zwink, who was to play Judas. In Rome they were preparing for mass pilgrimages in Holy Year, 1950. In the Protestant world, the pendulum swung back to a fringe of evangelism. The Reverend Brian Hession flew over to Hollywood to try to persuade someone to make a film of the life of Christ. Father Divine ('people call me God') after Hiroshima claimed: 'I am the author and the finisher of atomic energy. I have harnessed it.' But the new force was Dr Billy Graham, a Baptist minister from North Carolina. Without the vulgarity of Aimée Semple Macpherson, claiming little more than that he was an instrument to make you go and talk to your own parish priest, he came into the news in 1949. It was of course in Los Angeles, where some three hundred thousand people went to listen to him in a tent. Among the modest 2 per cent of conversions, it was claimed, was a gangster named Mickey Cohen.

Billy Graham had a British counterpart in The Reverend Bryan Green of Birmingham, who toured America and Canada and drew congregations of six thousand a night for a week to Manhattan's Cathedral of St John the Divine: 'Have you opened the door? Has He come in? Will you thank Him for coming?'

If evil is the opposite of good, yet the one begets the other as if they were different aspects of the same thing, then it is a paradox clearly demonstrated by war. For war stimulates technology, releasing vast sums of money to finance it, and does it through fear. We have seen the dilemma of scientists like Robert Oppenheimer: ought we to share the secrets of atomic energy, and won't all nations who can afford it have atom bombs sooner or later anyway? America wanted international control with inspection of all countries' establishments. Russia wanted complete outlawing of the bomb and *no* inspection. Maybe we can devise an A-bomb that will simply destroy without polluting: we'll call it a *clean* bomb. But in July 1946 the American Navy held 'strategic' tests at Bikini Atoll in which forty-two thousand men (at a safe distance), sixty-seven expendable ships and quantities of goats, pigs and rats (on the spot) took part. The sailors were appalled at the fouled-up world they saw after two bombs (above and under water) had been exploded. The first was dropped from a B.29 Superfort which carried a picture of Rita Hayworth on its side, and was called 'Gilda' after her latest movie. Two years and three months later, fifty-seven of the vessels were found to be still contaminated and were sunk. In California the San Fernando Goat Association held a memorial service for the goats which had died in the

experiment. Norman Cousins, editor of the *Saturday Review of Literature,* wrote a book called *Man Is Obsolete*; but a few optimists went around saying that the A-bomb was a good thing because it had taken the profit motive out of war. War was no longer inevitable: war was simply ridiculous. Bikini island inexplicably gave its name to an exiguous two-piece bathing costume.

Soon Britain had her own nuclear reactors, and in March 1949 Harwell announced 'our first homemade plutonium'. There was a joke about atomic piles – 'they're what you get from sitting on a cold war.' British scientists had contributed enormously to the technology of war, prodded by amateurs like Churchill (Mulberry Harbours) and Mountbatten (PLUTO – Pipe Lines Under the Ocean, which pumped oil supplies to the invasion forces in France). Churchill is also thought to have inspired the idea of FIDO (Fog Investigation Disposal Operation) to help aircraft to land safely in fog. Mountbatten had been helped, as chief of Combined Operations, by J.D. Bernal and Solly Zuckerman; Churchill by Lord Cherwell. Donald Bailey had invented an all-purpose bridge; Barnes Wallis had devised a bouncing bomb tailor-made for blowing up dams. But now the War was over, there was a new trend by which science fiction was eventually to become fact, and it was going to happen in America and Russia.

Which of them had captured the best German rocket engineers? The V2 rocket was destined to become a spaceship, but it was going to be a guided atomic missile first. The rounding up of German scientists by the Americans was known as Operation Paper-clip, and its triumph was the capture of Professor Wernher von Braun, who had been in charge of Hitler's Peenemünde Rocket Station. Von Braun saw far beyond the V2 weapons with which his name had been associated, and from his teens had belonged to space-travel societies. In 1949 he became an honorary fellow of the British Interplanetary Society, and was halfway through writing a science-fiction novel called *Mars Project*.

At White Sands Proving Ground, 250 miles south of Los Alamos laboratory in New Mexico, in territory hitherto associated with Billy the Kid and rattlesnakes, where water was so scarce that gas stations charged 25 cents a gallon for it, there were launchings every few weeks, often attended by bus-loads of

Boy Scouts, students, and Rotarians. Small children rushed about yelling 'Whoosh!' Fruit flies and other small creatures were sent up in rockets to study the genetic effects of cosmic rays. It was not yet thought that the human body could withstand a speed of 3,600 m.p.h. Meantime the Germans walked around in ten-gallon hats, spoke with a Texan twang and seemed thoroughly at home.

In 1944 Harry Harper, spokesman of the Combined British Astronomical Studies group, had envisaged a 20,000 m.p.h. spaceship, propelled by 'a series of rockets jettisoned as they are used up', which would reach the Moon in forty-eight hours. By 1949 it was thought that the ship would use an atomic reactor while cruising round the Moon, but would be shot there by liquid oxygen and hydrogen. No doubt it would all be watched through Mount Palomar's new 200-inch telescope which, however, had been designed to probe more than nine hundred light years into space, being assisted by a wider-eyed Schmidt telescope, which, though it could see only three hundred light years into space, could tell the other one what to look at.

I was, about this time, trying to start a science-fiction magazine in London. Our first colour-spread was to have been a 'Mars Ship' which would roll slowly round on its eight-and-a-half-month journey to create artificial gravity. It would, we felt, be especially suitable for luxury cruises and must therefore have a ballroom, bars and recreation decks. It couldn't happen in this century, of course; but, on the best available scientific advice at the time, we were confident that the first manned flight to the Moon would be in 1973, and had the magazine ever seen the light of day, we were going to launch it with a stunt offer of free tickets as prizes for a competition.

Was outer space as interested in us as we were in it? On 24 June 1947, a pilot named Kenneth Arnold took off from Chehalis, Washington, in a high-altitude plane to look for a lost C.46 transport that had crashed in the Cascade Mountains. He reported 'two bright flashes and nine gleaming objects' flying at a vast speed towards Mount Rainier: they resembled 'saucers skimming over water'. There had been a number of previous sightings of what came to be called U.F.O.s – unidentified flying objects – including one near Oklahoma City and another at Manitou Springs, Colorado. There would be many more.

On 7 January 1948, Captain Thomas Mantell became the first man to die in his plane while pursuing a U.F.O. near Fort Knox.

Were they optical illusions caused by weather balloons? Were they Russian secret weapons? Were they stray rockets from White Sands? Surely not, since two or three had been reported from White Sands itself. Why didn't they land? Because the Venusians, or whoever they were, who were always presumed to have a higher ethical and technological civilization than our own, were afraid of us, afraid we would not believe they had come in peace; they knew we had discovered nuclear fission and would soon be attempting space flight, so we must be watched.

The U.S. Air Force, wishing to avoid another national panic like Orson Welles's radio version of *The War of The Worlds*, were cautious in their press releases. By 27 April 1949, they were prepared to say: 'The mere existence of some yet unidentified flying objects necessitates a constant vigilance. . . . The saucers are not jokes. Neither are they cause for alarm.' On 27 December the Air Force suddenly denied the existence of flying saucers; then three days later revealed part of a secret 'Project Saucer' report which seemed to admit the possibility of peaceful visitors from outer space.

Drafting men and women into the Forces opened British and American eyes to the health of the people. Teeth, for example: if an Army dentist found only five cavities in a recruit's mouth, he rejoiced. Britain has always lacked comprehensive dental statistics, but the U.S. Army throughout the war dealt with eighteen million cavities a year. Six per cent of draftees were found to have some form of V.D. Some had never had a medical examination before.

Most Army medical officers were very young and had no experience of tropical disease. If a man had a shivering fever, was it malaria or dengue or black-water? In 1943 all young British doctors with three months' experience were called up for field dressing stations, leaving a serious shortage of doctors on the home front. Curiously, there was also a shortage of corpses for dissection at teaching hospitals.

Britain and America still had different standards of hygiene; indeed, many American troops arriving in Britain thought the British had none at all: so afraid were they of British milk, 6 per cent of which was still not tubercle-free, that they brought their own. And doctors were uncertain whether the prevalence of jaundice in Middle East officers' and sergeants' messes was due to the nervous strain of responsibility or to the lower standards of cookhouse hygiene. In British cities, there were epidemics of gastric 'flu.

It was during these years that the word 'allergy' became fashionable (so did 'virus'). Skin doctors, it was discovered, knew almost nothing. You picked up athlete's foot in a communal shower, and this was thought to lead to other skin troubles. Gently nurtured girls dived into air-raid shelters and some days later developed a body itch. It surely couldn't be scabies, that was not a middle class disease . . . but it was. While there was a school of thought that believed Britain had never been healthier than in war, there was a low resistance against disease, especially skin troubles and conjunctivitis, sometimes attributed to lack of fat in the nation's wartime diet.

In the tropics our skins were under attack all the time: there was seldom a billet that did not have bugs. You stood the feet of your bed in tobacco tins full of paraffin; but the bugs were smarter – they crawled up the wall and dropped on to you from the ceiling. D.D.T. did not arrive until 1945 – too late.

In World War I you could be shot for cowardice; but in World War II the 'trick cyclist' was king, or at least a brigadier. Soldiers, like civilians, could be exhausted. Just as, in British trains, one saw people fall asleep, sometimes standing up, as soon as they had boarded, so a condition for soldiers known as 'battle fatigue' was diagnosed. 'The idea that the Army is making the boys crazy is not so,' said General Norman Kirk, head of the U.S. Army Medical Corps. 'It's just finding out those that are.' There was also a phenomenon called psychoneurosis, said to be caused by the long separation of husbands and wives, so that soldiers cracked up on receiving letters from home saying: 'It wasn't wise for us to get married. . . .'

New drugs, new uses for old drugs. The greatest immobilizer of manpower, malaria, was controlled by spraying the stagnant pools where the anopheles mosquito bred; and in 1944 two young Harvard chemists, Woodward and Doering, achieved the 'first total synthesis of quinine'. For dysentery, sulfaguanadine; for Churchill, when he had pneumonia, another sulfa drug. For pneumonia, penicillin too, which made it no more menacing than influenza; and

in all field hospitals penicillin was keeping down the horror of gangrene and amputations. New drugs from the glands and bile of animals: A.C.T.H., hailed in 1948 as a 'wonder drug' against arthritis, gout, rheumatic fever; cortisone against these and leukaemia. Benzedrine and dexedrine had a certain glamour because the air force had used them for keeping awake on long flights. We took them as pep pills and to counteract hunger and depression; not for a long time did anyone suggest they were harmful or addictive. As there were 'benzedrine inhalers', so there were also 'penicillin dust inhalers' for colds. Only you didn't say you had a cold: the in word was 'virus'. It is not easy, at the time, to identify new complaints caused by war, but the American Army found one which was due to continuous riding in a Jeep. It was called a 'pilonidal cyst disorder' or 'congenital cyst at the base of the spine'; the chief symptom was much simpler – 'it hurts to sit down'.

Life, birth, death. The birthrate went down, then up. There was much discussion about painless childbirth: could it be achieved by injections of metycaine at the base of the spine, or by Dr Grantly Dick Read's psychological overcoming of fear, and his relaxing exercises? In 1946 Dr Blackwell Sawyer of Lakewood, New Jersey, tried Dr Read's methods on 168 patients and claimed 90 per cent success. Artificial insemination was beginning to be talked about, and in 1949 a House of Lords debate on the subject was headlined in the *New York Daily News*, 'British Lords Lash Lab Love.'

Strange that, while the flower of youth were being slaughtered all over the world, so much progress should have been made in helping the old to get older. Gerontology, geriatrics – they were new words to the layman. Dr Martin Gumpert was already known for such cheerful advice as 'pay no attention to formulas against drinking, smoking or worry. Moderate indulgence is often beneficial.' Rejuvenation by 'monkey glands', associated with a Dr Voronoff, had been a Twenties joke. Now here was a doctor who believed that, with proper medical care, old age could be life's happiest season. America was crazy about youth: he would rather live in China, where the old were almost holy. In Germany, which he had fled as a refugee from Hitler, he had been known as a poet, and for him there was poetry in senescence. Old people were much better than young people – they had more sense of responsibility, more wisdom, they were more out-spoken and honest, more serene, even more beauti-ful. People died of diseases, not of old age. Dr Gum-pert's book *You Are Younger Than You Think*, was one of the bestsellers of 1944. The population was ageing, he pointed out: 'Are we going to convert ourselves into a gigantic old-age asylum – or are we going to have fun?'

The health of Britain, it was claimed in two 1949 reports, was better than it had ever been before, what with full employment, Government orange juice and free school milk. The average child of thirteen was said to be six pounds heavier than a child of the same age in 1932, and the average British woman measured 41 inches round the hips as against 38 inches before the war. Socialists claimed this as a victory for their health policies.

In 1944 Henry Willink, Health Minister in the National Government, had presented a White Paper called *A National Health Service*. The British Medical Association had been campaigning for such a service for several years before the war. The chairman of their Council, seventy-five-year-old Dr Guy Dain, and its secretary, Dr Charles Hill (nationally known as the Radio Doctor, afterwards successively Chair-man of Independent Television and Director Gen-eral of the B.B.C.) became aggressive opponents of Labour's Health Minister, Aneurin Bevan, who (without consulting the B.M.A.) published his own National Health Service Bill in 1946 which came into operation two years later. Newspaper headlines spoke of a 'Doctors' Rebellion'. It was as if both sides want-ed a fight about the means of achieving what every-body wanted. Aneurin Bevan brought in his Health Service on a wave of class hatred by his inability to forget the poverty and unemployment of his youth in South Wales, and the fact that his miner father had died of pneumoconiosis. It had been the fault of the Tories, who were 'lower than vermin'. This was said in a speech at Manchester which, though not widely reported at the time, lost Labour a lot of votes in the next election.

The Health Service, born at a time of seemingly endless crisis at home and abroad, included dentistry and spectacles and wigs. Its critics said, and some have continued to say, that it neglected preventive medicine and encouraged people to think of health as something you can buy in a bottle. In the first year of the Health Service, which cost £260 million (£1 mil-lion a week more than was estimated), 187 million prescriptions were written by eighteen thousand doc-tors, who found themselves filling in thousands of forms and were run off their feet by the 47½ million people who were treated. Providing spectacles for 5¼ million myopic Britons cost six times as much as any-one had dreamed. An average one hundred and sixty patients a week thronged the waiting room of each dentist, 40 per cent of them needing dentures. A Scot-tish dentist was found to be earning at the rate of £16,000 a year. The Health Service was the biggest undertaking next to the armed forces. It was soon discovered that foreigners were popping across the Channel to have free confinements, false teeth, spect-acles and wigs, and the resident funny-men of nat-ional newspapers had a new target. There was a Gov-ernment pamphlet to explain the Health Service to children and morons which showed a funny owl with a funny stethoscope listening to another funny owl breathing. A large number of working people, proud of having 'paid their way all their lives' and bewild-ered by having to pay national health insurance, re-fused to go to free doctors, who couldn't possibly be as good as doctors who sent in bills. Unfortunately the Health Service did not include the possibility of dying, and funerals grew more expensive than ever.

One thing which couldn't be alleviated with a bot-tle (well, not much) was sex. We really didn't know much about normal people's sex lives, if anyone could be considered normal. In 1943 a team from Indiana University questioned boys in a Midwestern city, and found that by the age of eighteen half of them had had sexual experience, some of them 'hundreds of times'. Braggadocio? By way of contrast, in 1949 there was a row in Yorkshire about sex education. It started when a thirteen-year-old schoolgirl refused to eat her breakfast egg because she had been told at school the facts of life, not about human beings, but about how eggs were – er – *made*. Her Mum got up a furious petition.

Indiana University, in cahoots with the Rocke-feller Foundation and a special committee of the National Research Council, had in 1939 started a project which, it was thought, might take thirty years. It would investigate marital and premarital sex, for men and women, prostitution, and segregation of men and women in prisons and other institutions.

The first results were seen in a volume of 804 pages, compiled by Dr Alfred C. Kinsey, a zoologist, and two associates, entitled *Sexual Behaviour in the Human Male*. Talks with more than twelve thousand people had been analysed, and of these 5,300 white males had contributed data to the present book. A further ninety thousand interviews were contemplated. 'The Kinsey Report', said the *New Yorker*, 'probably contains more dynamite than any other scientific document since Darwin's *The Origin of Species*.'

Dynamite indeed: in some cities the police tried to stop the interviewing, a medical association accused Kinsey of practising medicine without a licence, a teacher was dismissed from his school for helping. Among the findings were the unrealized pervasive power of the sex impulse, the lies and hypocrisy of everyone about sex, the wide disparity of sexual activity in individuals, the fact that it begins earlier and ends later than anyone admits. More specifically, 85 per cent of married men were not virgins when they went to the altar, 50 per cent were unfaithful, and one third of all men had had homosexual relationships at some time or other. Semi-skilled labourers had more sexual activity than any other group, with professional men second, and white-collar workers last. 'The book is intended,' said the publishers severely, 'primarily for workers in the fields of medicine . . . and allied sciences.' Ho hum; anyway it was a bestseller.

The word 'computer' was not yet in general use, though by about 1946 we knew that there was something called ENIAC, popularly called an 'electronic brain', and the study of its application was called Cybernetics. When Professor Niels Bohr, the Danish physicist, had a theory that the nucleus of the uranium atom was like a drop of water and split *unevenly*, he proved it by using 'Papa', Harvard University's Selective Sequence Electronic Calculator, which came up with the answer in 103 hours, which was quick for those days.

Technology hustled on. In a Nottingham (England) laboratory they were trying to solve the problem of the ladderless nylon stocking. In 1942 an engineer named John McGay of Tulsa, Oklahoma, invented a tubeless tyre. Within months of VJ-Day there was a boom in America of household machines, dishwashers, driers, garbage disposal units. In 1949 the Bridgeport Brass Company brought out an 'aerosol' (new word) for eliminating household odours. By now most smokers were using petrol (but not yet gas) lighters. In Britain local councils were trying to stop the sale of contraceptives from slot machines. London's first launderette, in King's Road, Chelsea, arrived in the summer of 1949.

It seemed that nothing could stop the march of science – unless you lived in Russia, where the object of science was to enable man to control nature – *totally*. If you can turn radium into lead, you can turn wheat into rye. Environment was all, and Western (Mendelian) genetics were based on heredity. Trofim Lysenko, who headed the environmental school in Russia, had the satisfaction of having his theory accepted by both the Soviet government and the Communist party in 1948. For a few years Lysenko was almost the dictator of Soviet biology, and anyone who disagreed was a fascist-deviationist.

Professor Julian Huxley disagreed so strongly that he wrote a book about it. If Lysenko was right, he said, then this was the end of science. Political ideology had nothing to do with science, yet in Russia they were closing down agricultural laboratories which had been run on Mendelian lines. One of Lysenko's most dogmatic assertions began with the words 'Dialectics show that. . . .' All over the Soviet Union Mendelians were being called bourgeois reactionaries and sacked from their jobs. Britain's most embarrassed scientist was Professor J.B.S. Haldane, a lifelong Communist. He was reduced to the judgment that 'there is a lot to be said on both sides.'

CHAPTER 17

Crime Club

We have long needed an Anglo-American dictionary to eliminate misunderstandings about how we use our common language. We have already commented on the word 'fiddle'. 'Fiddling' was almost a way of life in Britain just after the War. It was fashionable and amusing to outwit the Government in small particulars, and 'fiddle' sounded better than 'black market'. People 'fiddled' extra coupons. There were 'currency fiddles' for getting enough foreign money to take a trip abroad; and the most successful was run by a man called Max Intrator. His very name was improbably sinister. In 1947 nobody was allowed to take more than £50 out of Britain: this was enough to finance a two-week package holiday, but if your position in society or business was such that you could not be seen as a common tourist, you had to use your 'contacts'.

Most contacts sooner or later brought you to the Hotel Lincoln, off the Champs Elysées in Paris, and to a man affectionately known as Black Max. In these 'austerity' years he was a welcome relief after the headmasterly rectitude of Sir Stafford Cripps. Mr Intrator would supply you with francs if you could somehow supply him with pounds; and he was particularly good at rescuing people who had lost everything at casinos. Suddenly, in April 1947, his picture was in every paper: occasionally he wore a tarboosh, for he had spent some time in Egypt; he had a number of business associates, some of whom appeared to be stateless Poles or Hungarians, who were in touch with Tel Aviv, which led to reports that Black Max was behind the illegal immigration into Palestine; and who were his mysterious contacts in Panama and New York and Geneva? He hinted at his 'files', which contained eminent, even royal, names. 'I am a financier,' he claimed. 'I have never peddled pound notes like a vulgar black market man.'

Sidney Stanley, on the other hand, called himself a 'business agent', though those who knew him used the expression 'contact man'. The 'contact man' was a feature of post-war Britain, throttled by restrictions which people would do almost anything to circumvent; and when, in the late autumn of 1948, the activities of Mr Stanley almost pushed the birth of a male heir to the British throne off the front pages, those advertising agencies which still used the expression hastily renamed their carnation-buttonholed young men 'account executives'.

Hearing through the C.I.D. allegations of wholesale corruption at the Board of Trade, Harold Wilson, then its President, ordered a tribunal of inquiry under Mr Justice Lynskey. It seemed that Mr Stanley, whose real name was never discovered, had been born in Poland, had at various times used the names Kohsyzcky, Rechtand and Wulkan, and had been bankrupted under the curious name of Blotts. He claimed, as contact men do, to know everyone in the Government, and did actually know forty-three-year-old John Belcher, an ex-railway clerk who had become Parliamentary Secretary to the Board of Trade. Operating from a luxury apartment in Aldford House, Park Lane, Stanley was said to have 'helped' a great many people – a football pools firm needed an extra paper ration; an amusement arcade needed an import licence for fruit machines; a paint firm needed a building licence. In an age when business expense accounts flourished untaxed, Stanley was a big spender. He had spent £89 on a dinner for six people. He claimed to be paying Belcher £50 a week because the poor chap was so hard up, and had given him a gold cigarette case. He had sent Ernest Bevin some cigars. He took many of his contacts to the races. He claimed to have letters from Dr Dalton, Chancellor of the Exchequer, beginning 'Dear Stan'. He sent his friends bottles of whisky, and not only at Christmas. He had sent the Belcher family on holiday to Margate,

Sidney Stanley

which Mr Justice Lynskey, a man of humour, seemed to encourage. Stanley endured fifteen hours of examination by Attorney General Sir Hartley Shawcross without ever losing his smiling *chutzpah*. It seemed that Belcher was indeed guilty of small favours to the friends of Stanley, mostly through sheer inexperience, and he resigned from the Government and went back to a railway job. Gibson resigned and died five years later. Teper emigrated to Florida. Stanley, after giving a party for all the reporters who had covered the tribunal, sold his memoirs to *The People* and was deported, via Paris, to Israel. The whole affair should have brought the Government down, but it didn't. The Government set up a Committee on contact men whose report yielded almost nothing. The 50,000-word report on the tribunal, price 1s. 6d. was a sell-out.

Are there crimes of which we can say that they essentially belong to the Forties? Beside the unspeakable crimes of the concentration camps, all other crimes looked petty; even Dr Marcel Petiot, guillotined in May 1946 for the admitted killing for profit of sixty-three people at his house at 21 Rue Lesueur, near the Etoile, Paris – people whom, as a self-styled member of the Resistance, he was 'helping to escape' – by the standards of Auschwitz was a smaller monster. The notable crimes of the decade were perhaps treason or treachery, as shown in the vengeful trial of William Joyce, espionage, un-Americanism, and the newly-defined genocide. In these years the expression 'juvenile delinquency' crossed the ocean from America to Britain: it came to be recognized that young people committed crimes because they came from 'bad homes', homes where the father had been killed in the War, where parents had been divorced, or (in Britain) no home at all because it had been bombed. So a number of real-life 'West Side Stories' began, and (in Britain) a trend towards juvenile gangsterism which in the Fifties would culminate in Craig and Bentley and a particularly nasty stabbing on Clapham Common.

Murdering women for profit belongs to no particular age. In 1912 it had been Brides-in-the-Bath Smith. In 1949 it was thirty-three-year-old Raymond Fernandez of Grand Rapids, Michigan, and his plump partner and mistress Martha Beck, twenty-eight. For some years Fernandez, a Spanish-American from Hawaii, had run a bogus 'Lonely

picking up the bills himself. He had had suits made (without coupons) for both Belcher and George Gibson, a trade union official who was also a director of the Bank of England, by a West End tailor named Hirsch Teper.

The tribunal, held in the solemnity of Church House, Westminster, had a good deal of comedy

Hearts' club which enabled him to seduce and fleece numerous middle-aged women. It was Martha Beck who suggested killing them as well. Posing as brother and sister, they killed at least twenty women in two years. It was the disappearance of Mrs Delphine Dowling, a widow, and her two-year-old daughter at Grand Rapids that caused a police inquiry. A search of the house revealed the bodies buried under the cellar floor. The couple freely admitted three murders in New York and Chicago, apparently believing that since there was no death penalty in Michigan they would escape the chair. After a legal wrangle, their trial was transferred to New York where, on 22 August 1949, they were condemned to death.

There was a sad lack of good old-fashioned triangle murders that average readers could identify with; or at least they didn't make the news. Connoisseurs of family homicide noted with regret the passing, at the age of eighty-four, in Fall River, Massachusetts, of a sweet old lady named Lizzie Borden. On both sides of the Atlantic murder went sexual, psychiatrists gave evidence, some of which was unpublishable; or else it went coldly gainful. You could blame juvenile delinquency, the War, the subconscious mind, and still get nowhere. When twenty-year-old De Witt Clinton Cook of Los Angeles went prowling on moonlit nights with a piece of wood known to carpenters as a 'two by four', sometimes burgling, sometimes raping, always hitting women with the 'two by four', was that piece of wood a symbol of his sexual inferiority feeling? Why did Charles Floyd, a large cretinous truck driver, at intervals between 1942 and 1949, kill and rape (in that order) red-haired girls around Tulsa, Oklahoma, sometimes (but not always) after peeping through windows while they undressed? In 1945 an eighteen-year-old student of Chicago University, William Heirens, was arrested after a series of mutilation murders. One of his victims was an ex-Wave named Frances Brown: after killing her he wrote in lipstick on her bedroom wall: 'For God's sake catch me before I kill more.' Another was a six-year-old girl whom he dismembered. All this, it appeared, had begun in a compulsive urge to steal women's underwear. Heirens blamed, not himself, but an *alter ego* called 'George'. Headshrinkers could find nothing wrong with him. He went to prison for life.

Why did Mrs Nina Housden, of Highland Park, Michigan, chop up her husband Charles, giftwrap the pieces in Christmas paper and prepare to drive back to her native Kentucky to dispose of them? 'Charles wasn't a bad sort,' she said. 'It was just that he ran around with other women.' And who was the other moonlight murderer, armed with a revolver, who terrorised the Texas-Arkansas border in the spring of 1946?

In wartime Britain, many crimes went undetected. Violence hides violence. Karl Hulten, known as Ricky, a deserter from the U.S. Army, in 1944 met a striptease girl called Elizabeth Jones. They saw themselves romantically as a sort of Bonnie-and-Clyde team. Using a stolen Army truck, they drove around attacking and robbing in the blackout, finally killing a cleft-chinned taxi driver, George Heath. Hulten was hanged, but Jones was reprieved. All over the country women furiously demanded the rope for her, and women in an arms factory went on strike in protest. It was a letter to the press from Bernard Shaw that pointed out the waste of killing a 'a Welsh scholarship girl of eighteen'. Miss Jones did ten years in jail and sold her memoirs to a Sunday newspaper.

H is for Horror; H is for Hitler, Himmler, Hess, Heydrich, Hoess; H is for Heath, Haigh and Hume. Supernature has not yet offered an explanation for the prevalence of this initial in the Forties. Heath and Haigh may well go down in history bracketed together like Hengist and Horsa. Neville Heath, ex-Borstal boy, recently cashiered from the R.A.F. (and previously cashiered from the Army, somehow managing to enlist in the South African Air Force in the meantime) was always quick to gain acceptance as an officer. He had degenerate good looks, and passed dud cheques to the manner born. He attracted women easily, and among his girl friends was a filmstar. Behind him was a long career of petty crime. He haunted various sleazy clubs, and at one of them, on 20 June 1946, he picked up Mrs Margery Gardner. They went to an old haunt of Heath's, Room 4 of the Pembridge Court Hotel, Notting Hill, and stayed the night as 'Mr and Mrs Armstrong'. Next day her body was found with mutilations that have been catalogued often enough.

Heath then went to Worthing, calling himself 'Colonel Heath', because that was the name by which he was known to a Miss Symonds, who lived there and regarded herself as his fiancée. She, too, had stayed with him in Room 4 at the Pembridge Court Hotel.

He told her that he had seen the body of Mrs Gardner: her murder must have been the work of a 'sexual maniac'. He then wrote a long letter to the officer in charge of the case, Superintendent Barratt of Scotland Yard, offering information and saying that he had the whip which had been used on her. This done, he moved on to the Tollard Royal Hotel, Bournemouth, staying there under the improbable name of Group Captain Rupert Brooke. Meeting a girl named Doreen Marshall who was on holiday at Bournemouth, he took her for an evening walk in Branksome Chine from which she never returned. Her body was found, naked and mutilated, some days later. With one of those ghastly practical touches often shown by murderers, he sold Miss Marshall's watch to a local jeweller. Again, Heath telephoned the police and volunteered information.

John George Haigh

His trial at the Old Bailey was remarkable for an attempt to defend him on the grounds of 'partial insanity'. Expressions such as 'moral defective', 'morally insane' and 'psychopath' were tossed about, and an expert witness, Dr de Bargue Hubert, who was psychotherapist of Broadmoor Criminal Lunatic Asylum said that Heath's sadism was (to Heath) morally right because it was the only means by which he could satisfy his lust: 'He was doing what he wished to do.' This did not impress either judge or jury, and Heath was hanged at Pentonville Prison.

There was a semi-serious attempt to plead insanity in the case of John George Haigh, three years later; indeed the main suggestions came from himself. Mrs Durand-Deacon, who disappeared from the Onslow Court Hotel, South Kensington (where Haigh also lived, and where, by a mad coincidence, the judge at his trial, Sir Travers Humphreys, had also lived for some time), was interested in Haigh's scheme to manufacture plastic fingernails and willing to invest in it. He took her to a factory at Crawley, Sussex, shot her and tried to dissolve her body in a bath of sulphuric acid. What remained of Mrs Durand-Deacon was referred to as 'sludge'. The cash he obtained from her handbag and the sale of her jewellery was enough to pay off some of his immediate debts. What he did not know was that human body fat, gallstones, false teeth and plastic handbags are not completely destroyed by acid.

It appeared that he had done this before with the McSwann family, a Dr Henderson and his wife, and perhaps others, making about £8,000 out of them in the past five years, selling their property and forging relevant documents. He saw to it, however, that the Hendersons' dog found a good home.

Haigh had been brought up in a family of strict Plymouth Brethren, who believed that all entertainment and most reading was sinful. He had won a scholarship to Wakefield (Yorkshire) Grammar School, and also a choral scholarship at Wakefield Cathedral. Some of his apologists, including Haigh himself, thought that this sudden contact with grand ritual and gorgeous vestments unbalanced his mind. Once under arrest he encouraged the idea of insanity. He had not killed for gain but to drink the blood of his victims. (A premature headline in the *Daily Mirror* containing the word Vampire caused the editor to be jailed for three months for contempt of court.) He claimed that before each murder he had a recurring dream about 'a forest of crucifixes which changed to trees dripping with blood'.

Twelve doctors examined him in prison. Three eminent psychiatrists were consulted for the defence; the words 'schizophrenia' and 'paranoia' were mentioned, but none would say that he was not responsible for his actions. One of them, Dr Yellowlees, said at the trial that Haigh was mentally ill but knew what he was doing. To him Haigh wrote an extraordinary letter from the condemned cell: 'I would like you to know that I appreciate the personal interest you have taken and the effort you have made on my behalf even though I cannot agree with your opinion. After all, all the outstanding personalities throughout history have been considered odd: Confucius, Jesus Christ, Julius Caesar, Mahomet, Napoleon and even Hitler; all possessed a greater perception of the infinite and a more lucid understanding of the omniscient mind.'

'Posing as an officer' is a favourite cover for post-war crooks. This was one of the things Donald Hume had in common with Neville Heath, together with his ability to fly aircraft and cash false cheques, and a period in Borstal. From his flying club at Elstree he had carried out smuggling missions from time to time. At a time when spivs and barrow boys infested the streets of London and 'wide boys' could make £10 or £12 a week tax free by simply not filling in forms, Donald Hume, who was manager of a small factory for making electric toasters, eked out his legitimate income by selling forged petrol coupons which he obtained from a garage owned by Stanley Setty, formerly Sulman Seti of Baghdad. Mr Setty also had some log books of demolished cars, and Hume occasionally stole cars to fit the log books. Setty paid him £300 a time, then renumbered and resprayed the cars and sold them in London's Warren Street, a used car market.

On 4 October 1949, Hume, rather drunk, returned to his apartment, and found Setty there. They had a row not about business but about Setty's ill treatment of Hume's mongrel dog. Hume stabbed Setty innumerable times with an S.S. dagger, and next day dismembered the body with a hacksaw. He then parcelled up the head and legs, weighted them with lead, and took them to Elstree Airport, where he had hired an Auster light plane, explaining to the authorities that he was going to Southend. Instead he flew over the Channel, dropped his parcels, and was forced by bad weather and shortage of petrol to land at Southend Airport. Next day he called in a painter to remove certain stains on the sitting-room floor and got him to help him carry Setty's torso, wrapped in the underfelt of the carpet, downstairs to his car. Again he hired a plane and dropped his last parcel into the sea; but the lead weights became detached, and the torso, floating, was washed up on to some Essex marshland known as Dengie Flats.

Here it was found by a farmworker named Sidney Tiffin, who, on his day off, was wildfowling, a pastime which, together with eel catching and winkle picking, earned him some extra cash. Mr Tiffin, a widower, was suddenly richer than he had ever been before in his life, for he was able to claim the £1,000 reward offered by the Setty family. Not without difficulty, because the head was missing, and Mr Tiffin had to employ a solicitor to get his money. He had found eight bodies on the marshes over the last few years, and usually all he got was five shillings from the police.

Throughout his trial, Hume stuck to his story that he had merely 'disposed of' the body for three gangsters called Mac, Greenie and The Boy who had both threatened and paid him. He was not to know what the parcels contained. . . . He was acquitted of murder and sentenced to twelve years in prison for being accessory after the fact. Released after eight years, he sold his memoirs, in traditional style, to a Sunday newspaper – with one difference: he gleefully admitted the killing. He lived to shoot a bank teller and a bank manager in England and a bank teller and a taxi driver (fatally) in Zurich, where he was sentenced to life imprisonment.

Haigh had thought that he could not swing for a murder in which there was no body (he forgot the 'sludge'). Absence of corpse was the difficulty in the trial of James Camb, deck steward on the liner *Durban Castle*. On 18 October 1947, as the ship ploughed through the shark-infested South Atlantic on its way from Cape Town to Southampton, an actress known as Gay Gibson, occupying Cabin 126, disappeared. Camb, who was believed to have made use of his opportunities with unaccompanied women passengers on previous voyages, said that he had been making love to her (with her consent) when she had a 'sort of fit'. Panicking, he had pushed her body through the porthole. This, after professing to know nothing about the matter, was his final story. Since he was a deck steward, and not a cabin steward, he had no right to be in a passenger's cabin at all. Two bells, one for a steward, one for a stewardess, had been rung from Cabin 126 at about 3 a.m. A night watchman answered them, and saw Camb at the door of the cabin, who said 'All right'.

If Gay Gibson had died of natural causes, it was argued, then Camb had destroyed the only evidence in his favour. There were scratches on his arms which could have been caused by a woman defending herself. Witnesses were brought from South Africa to testify that Gay Gibson enjoyed normal health and was not promiscuous. The jury, after only forty-five minutes' deliberation, found Camb guilty, but he was not hanged because a Criminal Justice Bill, containing a 'no-hanging' clause, was being debated in Parliament, though it was eventually thrown out.

A year later a Royal Commission on capital punishment was appointed. Public feeling seemed to be turning against the death penalty, yet wasn't strong enough to take a decision. Many lawyers were still for it, including Lord Chief Justice Goddard himself. The Royal Commission took four years to report, during which time convicted murderers went on being hanged. James Camb had been lucky.

What, meanwhile, was happening to big-time organized crime? Towards the end of 1949 it seemed that Paris was becoming the Chicago of Europe. '*La Pègre* [the underworld]', said a Paris reporter of the time, 'is on the up and up. It wears English sportscoats, rides in Lincolns and Buicks, uses American tommy guns, German Lugers and clever intelligence work.' In April 1949 there had been thirty-five armed attacks, rising monthly to sixty-nine in August and seventy-three in September. The Aga Khan and his Begum, driving to the airport, were held up by bandits who robbed them of $750,000 worth of jewellery. 'Were they American gunmen?' the Aga asked the police, who replied with patriotic indignation: 'No. This was conceived, planned and executed wholly by Frenchmen.' The central figure of *La Pègre* at this time was René Girier ('René the Stick') whose car-stealing expert (Jean Debusigne) was a university graduate and whose principal gunman ('Jackie Cruel') was an outstanding watercolour artist. Girier liked to pose as a Robin Hood: 'I use my money to help people around me. . . . Whoever "did" the Begum did no one

any harm.' The Begum, it was generally agreed, had been 'done' by either Roger Senanedj, who always used a tommy gun, or Georges Buisson, known as 'Fatalitas', who used hand grenades and never went anywhere without two bodyguards.

There was another Robin Hoodlum in Los Angeles – Mickey Cohen. He was easily moved by social injustices, such as the case of Mrs Elsie Phillips, a widow who had been taken to court by one Al Pearson, a radio store proprietor notorious for overcharging and faking repairs, and forced to sell up her home. Mickey's henchmen picketed the store and beat up Pearson: all were arrested for assault. From this time on, the Los Angeles police moved in on Cohen and his life became intolerable. This was the man who boasted: 'I'm the best newspaper copy in town. If I spit in the street, it's in the papers.' Mickey, who had been chief operator of the gambling and racewire business along the West Coast, was apt to burst into tears of self-pity whenever anything went wrong. He was determined to accumulate all the trappings of a big-time gangster. His bulletproof Cadillac had a button which switched on a radar screen and searchlights and alerted mastiffs at his $75,000 Brentwood home as he approached it. In daylight the house was a 'must-see' for tourists. He wore cream suits, alligator shoes and $45 hand-painted ties from his own shop on Sunset Strip. He was cut to the quick when Frank Costello, New York's senior racketeer (who is said to have inspired *The Godfather*), called him 'a very little peanut'. He was shockable: 'How *can* things get so tough?' he wailed when Benny the Meatball disappeared into the night with five bullets in him. And when Bugsy Siegel was shot from the garden as he sat on a girl's divan, Mickey Cohen told reporters disgustedly: 'Shooting through a window that way! Why, that could start a *trend*.'

Organized crime had learned to work silently and unseen. Frank Costello, his lawyer biographer George Wolf claimed, 'by 1943 owned New York, appointing judges and district attorneys and even mayors.' He had gambling joints in Florida and Nevada, betting shops in New York and New Jersey; he was always safe in his Long Island country house when the rough stuff was on; he was a lavish contributor to worthy causes, and a vice-chairman of a Salvation Army fund-raising drive. Organized crime had a most curious relationship with the law. It is said that Thomas Dewey had run his campaigns both for Governor of New York and for the White House with underworld money, and that this was why Lucky Luciano had remission of his prison sentence on condition that he went into exile in Italy. Luciano had cast off a good deal of the old Mafia outlook: he admired intelligence, wit and planning, which he found in his old Jewish friend Meyer Lansky. Of Lansky, Costello and Siegel he used to reminisce, in his bored retirement at his Capri hotel as he fought his homesickness for New York, 'We was the best team that ever got put together. . . . We was like the Four Horsemen of Notre Dame.'

For me, the most fascinating crime of the age was the smallest. The most elusive and hunted counterfeiter in the annals of the U.S. Secret Service was known by his file number as 'Old Eight-Eighty'. Who looks closely at a one-dollar bill? A dollar is only a dollar. You pass it on, and if eventually a bank teller notices anything wrong he turns it over to the Secret Service. Most counterfeiters of paper money are skilled engravers, and they reckon to make a lot of money out of – how shall I put it? – prostituting their art. It takes the skill of a lifetime to get those portraits of Washington and Lincoln and other great Americans absolutely right by photo-engraving. Yet Old Eight-Eighty's forgeries, described by the Secret Service as 'photo-etched', were laughably crude. His portrait of Washington looked like a death mask. His numbers, letters and linework were obviously retouched by hand, and he used ordinary cheap notepaper. (They must have *felt* wrong to anyone with any observation at all. Yet some of them turned up as far away as Atlanta and Denver.) Above all he couldn't spell: the name Washington appeared as WAHSINGTON. Yet, from the moment he passed his first dud dollar at a cigar store on Broadway near 102nd Street in November 1938 until his capture in the spring of 1948, he never attempted any higher denomination, and never passed more than fifty in a single month.

Old Eight-Eighty turned out to be a small (5 feet 3 inches) gentle, cheerful, white-haired man of seventy-three named Edwin Mueller who lived in a top tenement flat near Broadway and 96th Street – a few yards away from the various shops where he had passed most of his dollar bills. What people remembered about him, said the cops who arrested him, was his toothless grin: he either didn't have any dentures or didn't bother to put them in. He was a widower and lived alone with his mongrel dog. For most of his life he had been a superintendent of apartment buildings, and had then tried to start a one-man junk business which had failed. His dollar bills were turned out on a hand-operated printing press which he kept in his kitchen next to the sink and never attempted to conceal. He was a dreamer of unrealized ideas, like his invention of a new type of Venetian blind which he could never persuade anyone to manufacture. He did not regard himself as a criminal: he was simply supporting himself and his dog, supplementing his old age pension. It took the collaboration of ten thousand storekeepers all over the West Side of Manhattan, and repeated radio warnings, even to narrow down the area of inquiry.

In the end it was nine West Side boys who found the vital evidence. After a fire in Old Eight-Eighty's apartment, in which his dog had died, they found on a vacant lot, among rusty prams and old motor tyres and miscellaneous junk, two zinc engraving plates and about thirty dollar bills which, with the uncluttered eyesight of youth, they at once identified as 'stage money'. They used them to play poker with until the eldest boy thought they ought to take them to the police. One of the boys had swapped the plates with another boy for a bag of marbles, and the new owner was trying to print more 'stage money' by covering the plates with green paint and turning them upside down on to Kleenex tissues.

'They were only one-dollar bills,' smiled Mr Mueller when questioned by the police. 'I never gave more than one of them to any one person, so nobody ever lost more than the one dollar.' He invented, and for a time stuck to, a story that he had had a confederate, but nobody believed it. He seemed fascinated and amused when the lie detector was used on him.

What to do with him? The judge at his trial wanted to sentence him to nine months in jail, until he was reminded that if he were given 'a year and a day' he could, with remission, be out in four months. However, 'a year and a day' was always accompanied by a fine. Of course, it had to be – one dollar.

Prose and Verse

'Bold, outspoken,' said Cassell's blurb about a best-selling novel of 1941 called *This Above All*, by Eric Knight, better known as the author of *Lassie Come Home*. Better known *now*, because *This Above All*, which seemed socially significant at the time, is now almost forgotten. It was about a class-conscious soldier, Clive, shattered after the evacuation of Dunkirk, who falls in love with a W.A.A.F. Sergeant named Prudence who is his social superior in that, being a General's granddaughter, she believes in the established order to which she belongs. They make love in haystacks and in a hotel room and one of the 'bold' bits is when she suddenly laughs at the sheer difficulty of making love out of doors with most of your clothes on, in particular the obstacle presented by the fearsome knickers worn by women members of the armed forces (they were known as Churchills). In between love-making, soldier and airwoman argue fiercely about the social system, which, it is implied, will be swept away after the War: he attacks, she defends. It is a tender tragedy; for he is killed in an air-raid, leaving her pregnant as London collapses all round her.

Two novelist technicians, very different, were coming to the fore: engineer Nevil Shute, former designer of airships, and Brigadier Nigel Balchin, scientific adviser to the War Office. Each had a fiction formula. Shute, in novels like *Landfall* and *Most Secret*, could wring dramatic tension out of metal fatigue, the male world of engineering, interweaving a love story that never became horizontal. Balchin, his dialogue so brittle that you could almost hear the bombs falling whenever a full stop occurred in *Darkness Falls From the Air*, gave a memorable picture of London blackout life as it was for the kind of people who frequented the Café Royal; and in *The Small Back Room* entered the world of 'boffins', technical advisers to Government and Army, which he knew at first hand (and which would be developed more weightily

by C.P. Snow), in the story of Sammy Rice who, lame in one leg and distrusting his own courage, 'proves' himself by dismantling that beastliest of German weapons, a butterfly bomb.

'Peter has no polish. . . . Life wouldn't be worth a punched denarius. . . .' Well, no doubt the Apostles spoke sometimes in slang, but the dialogue of Lloyd C. Douglas's *The Robe* was something new in Bible stories. *The Robe* shared the 1943 bestseller list with *So Little Time* (John P. Marquand), *A Tree Grows in Brooklyn* (Betty Smith), Ilka Chase's *In Bed We Cry* (described as 'the liveliest agitation of stamens and pistil') and Sholem Asch's *The Apostle*, on the life of St Paul. 'The Robe' is Christ's cloak, and the novel describes the conversion to Christianity, and eventual martyrdom, of the tribune Marcellus Gallio, who carried out the order to crucify Jesus. 'His bodyguard Demetrius,' thought *Time* magazine, 'is rather like Jeeves.' Mr Douglas followed *The Robe* five years later with *The Big Fisherman*.

The Macmillan Company of New York seldom saturated bookstores with as many as 225,000 advance copies of a 971-page novel, but this is what happened in the autumn of 1944. Mrs Robert J. Herwig, wife of an All-American footballer and herself an ex-football writer for the Oakland (California) *Tribune*, was soon to be Mrs Artie Shaw, but was meanwhile writing bawdy Restoration fiction under her maiden name, Kathleen Winsor. She really did write *Forever Amber*, despite a rumour that 'Kathleen Winsor' was the typewriter name of a syndicate of bored and bibulous Hollywood script writers. At sixteen, Amber is the mistress of Lord Bruce Carlton, by whom she is pregnant, but marries the repulsive Luke Channell, who runs off with all her money. Thrown into Newgate Prison for debt, she meets a highwayman named Black Jack Mallard, but their romance is cut short because he has a date with the gallows. She then goes on the stage, marries various other people, one of whom is an earl, which makes her a countess, and this sets her on the right path, when she is widowed, to meet King Charles II, who greets her with 'Od's fish, Ma'am!' Her erotic prose was all her own: 'His shirts . . . still carried the male smell of him' – well, in 1944 that was pretty strong stuff. A.J. Liebling of the *New Yorker* created a special literary classification for the book: it was, he said, 'historico-mammary'.

Forever Amber was banned in Boston on publication, and forbidden throughout the rest of Massachusetts two years later.

As the Allies moved across Europe, an organization called Allied Military Government of Occupied Territory (AMGOT) took over in the wake of the armies. (The joke, at the time, was that it was lucky we didn't have to occupy Turkey, because the two syllables of Am-got in Turkish mean the male and female organs of generation.) AMGOT struggled worthily to create order in defeated countries, and in fiction its work was chronicled by a young *Time-Life* staff man called John Hersey. His novel *A Bell for Adano*, by turns wildly satirical, sentimental and tragic, had as its hero Major Joppolo, an Italian-American from the Bronx, anxious to help the land of his forebears, and as its villain a loud-mouthed general too like Blood-and-Guts Patton for comfort. Hersey, a master of restrained anger, afterwards wrote the short, monumental *Hiroshima*.

After the War, the War books: this is what both readers and writers expected. *Mister Roberts*, Thommas Heggen's novel of life aboard the good ship *Reluctant*, and Calder Willingham's *End as a Man*, about a brutal military academy, showed that something was brewing. Only in 1948 did anything like a serious work of fiction appear that attempted to measure the effect of war on the men who had been in it. Surely there had to be a post-war generation? The spiritual children of Hemingway and Graves and Fitzgerald and Remarque? 'Scarred by war?' Well, if we're that generation we'd better act like it and summon up a few neuroses. If not a lost generation, then a *mislaid* one?

The first attempt to put the *whole* war into a long novel was Irwin Shaw's *The Young Lions*. It shows its characters in peace as well as war, and some of them are Germans. It takes the reader from barrack room to Paris, from New York to concentration camps, from the pre-war ski slopes of Austria, where Sergeant Christian Diestl is an instructor, to the climax in a German forest where he meets, in combat, the two principal American characters Michael Whitacre and Noah Ackerman. Michael is a stage director with a film-star wife; Noah is a poor, shy Jew who endures persecution by fellow-draftees in his Florida barrack room. *The Young Lions* was not the *War and Peace* of World War II, nor has any such book yet appeared; but it was a brave try, and it has endured.

From Britain, no major war novels yet; they would not come until the Fifties, when it would again be shown that British writers almost invariably see war from the officer's viewpoint, as American writers see it from the enlisted man's. For Norman Mailer and his generation of G.I.s in the Pacific, 'the fugging army' was as much their enemy as the Japanese. (Anyone who has served in the ranks knows this feeling: I am thinking of a nineteen-year-old junior officer I knew, just out of school, whose sergeant major used to say to us, in any crisis, 'Look after the kid.') There is no British parallel to the 700-odd pages of *The Naked and the Dead*, a bestselling title if ever there was one. On a drenched, malarious Pacific island a bunch of soldiers go forward on a futile mission from which few return alive. They eat, sleep, daydream, talk about sex. Sergeant Croft thinks about his unfaithful wife. Goldstein, a Jew, is afraid (well, of course he is, but not because he is a Jew). The men despise their officer, Lieutenant Hearn, a college man, a liberal who never had the guts to be a Communist, a weak man in conflict with the sadistic-fascist and near-homosexual General Cummings. Their past lives are filled in by flashbacks headed 'The Time Machine'. The battle for the island is eventually won by accident through the fear and incompetence of a Major Dalleson. The enlisted men are shown as animals, brutalized by war; none of them ever seems to have read a book. If you want to know what American soldiers are like under fire, Mailer will tell you. John Lardner, in the *New Yorker*, did not shrink from comparing him with Tolstoy – '*The Naked and the Dead* is closer to Tolstoy in its sharp colours and orderly plotting than it is to Crane and Remarque, whose stories are . . . formless and impressionistic.'

In Britain, where it was published in 1949, the book was found shocking, chiefly because Mailer printed most of his four-letter words instead of using asterisks.

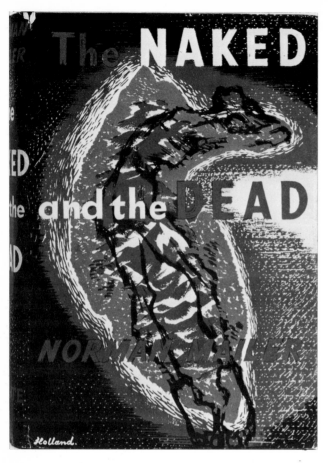

Holland.

tional home of six publishers and the great distributing house of Simpkin Marshall, was obliterated. New books were produced to 'economy standards', which meant bad paper, small print and cheap bindings. After the War there was a curious situation by which *new* publishers could claim paper rations, and the Government didn't seem to know the difference between publishing and journalism, so that journalists came out of the Forces, claimed their small paper rations and sold them to new publishers.

Bibles were in short supply; so were all kinds of school books. The classics were devoured; Tolstoy, Dickens, Trollope, Jane Austen; air-raid shelters were furnished with them; so that for the first time in more than a hundred years books written by candlelight were read by candlelight. Paperback editions of them flourished (but the Penguin bestseller, outstripping all the others by three million copies, was a practical little book called *Aircraft Recognition*). People who had read no history since school now settled down to consolidate their national heritage in Arthur Bryant's *English Saga*, or Trevelyan's cosy *English Social History*, or biographies of Napoleon, because, like Hitler, he had threatened us with extinction. Everybody re-read childhood books, Anstey's *Vice-Versa*, the *Just-So Stories*, *Little Women*, *Just William*, *Diary of a Nobody*. Historical romance, old or new, provided endless escape: Hugh Walpole, whose *The Herries Chronicle*, four books in one 1,500-page volume ('Nearly a million words for 8*s*. 6*d*.!' the author wrote in his journal), had been published in 1939, two years before he died; and Daphne du Maurier, and C.S. Forester's Napoleonic War exploits of Captain Hornblower. The Government became a commercial publisher, printing millions of copies of official reports: *Battle of Britain*, scruffily produced, cost 3*d*. and sold five million. Lord Vansittart's *Black Record*, cataloguing German crimes, was swallowed greedily: Victor Gollancz's reply to it, *Shall Our Children Live or Die?*, was bought by members of the Left Book Club.

James Joyce died of a perforated ulcer in January 1941; ten weeks later Virginia Woolf threw herself into a Sussex stream. Before the decade ended, cerebral thrombosis would strike poor H.L. Mencken, living in the house of his boyhood in Baltimore: now paralysed, teaching himself to speak all over again. He read no more, sitting amid the thousands of books in his library. A lifelong agnostic, he promised his friends

The *Sunday Times* attacked it as 'incredibly beastly . . . no decent man could leave it about the house.'

It is an odd fact that in war, when people are so busy prosecuting hostilities that they should theoretically have no time to read, they somehow find time to read more than they ever read in peace. On both sides of the Atlantic books boomed. At Christmas 1944 a spokesman for Scribner's Manhattan bookshop said: 'At 9 o'clock we just open the doors and jump out of the way.' Despite paper rationing, America was printing 250 million copies a year, many of them paperbacks and reprints for the Forces. In Britain, the War Office was using 25,000 tons of paper a year, which left only 20,000 tons for the entire publishing trade. Five million books were lost in the fire-bomb raid on the City of London, on the last night of 1940, when Paternoster Row, near St Paul's Cathedral, the tradi-

that if there were an after-life, he would apologize to the Apostles at the gates of Heaven: 'Sorry, gentlemen – I was wrong.' H.G. Wells, almost at the end of his tether, had returned to science during the war, working on a thesis ('Personalities of the Mesozoics') for his Master's degree at London University. A flash of the old cocksureness in *All Aboard for Ararat* (1940): Noah is the captain of a new Ark, but God is only a passenger who is allowed to play the harmonium for the hymns. Then, as the split atom takes over all power, *homo* is feared to be no longer *sapiens*, and nature prepares to destroy him, the slow descent to despair and death in the year 1946.

Hemingway's greatest novel, *For Whom the Bell Tolls*, had been about the Spanish Civil War. We read it in our barrack rooms, and 'the earth moved' became a code phrase for making love. World War II gave him no microcosm for a major book, though *Across the River and into the Trees*, about the last three days in the life of an American officer in and around Venice, revealed his final cynicism about the war, which he had reported in several theatres. Graham Greene, sweating in his Secret Service job in West Africa, had followed his great *The Power and the Glory* (published in America as *The Labyrinthine Ways*) with an 'entertainment', *The Ministry of Fear*, and a number of short stories before the West African material was ready to be used. *The Heart of the Matter* (1948) was not immediately recognized as a masterpiece. 'Is he,' asked an American critic, 'expounding a heresy or defending the faith?' 'Not one of his best,' thought George Orwell, who found its construction 'mechanical . . . like an algebraic equation.' The situation of Major Scobie, betrayed by pity but disliked for his uprightness, seemed improbable to Orwell. He even commits adultery out of pity and a sense of duty. 'It is better to be an erring Catholic than a virtuous pagan,' is Orwell's reading of Scobie's predicament. 'This cult of the sanctified sinner seems to me to be frivolous. . . . If he really felt that adultery is mortal sin, he would stop committing it.' There speaks the lapsed Puritan. The suicide of Scobie, and the certainty of his damnation, may seem improbable; but it is not the Catholic doctrine that makes this novel great.

The other uncomfortable convert, Evelyn Waugh, had wicked fun with the evacuees in *Put Out More Flags* (1942); then, for better or worse, *Brideshead Revisited* ('the Sacred and Profane Memories of Captain Charles Ryder') in which he is just getting used to grammar school junior officers whose hair needs cutting; we must wait until the Fifties and even the early Sixties for the definitive statement of Waugh's life, the great trilogy in which the world war often seems merely a background to the class war, told entirely from the officer viewpoint.

John Steinbeck did his share of war reporting, tried a topical theme about occupied Norway in *The Moon Is Down*, and returned triumphantly to Monterey, California, in *Cannery Row* (whose flophouses had been cleaned up, and Doc – Ed Ricketts – had just died, when I made my pilgrimage there in 1951). From John O'Hara, no new novel for eleven years; a fusillade of bitter little short stories, usually about people

Ernest Hemingway

who don't get what they want, or if they do, something goes wrong and there's a fight. . . . *Pipe Night* is distilled O'Hara, and if he had never written any long novels, the stories would survive; however, in 1949 at last *A Rage to Live* appeared. In it he was back in Pennsylvania, writing about Harrisburg and the Susquehanna River under other names, and experimenting with spasms of stage dialogue.

From Elizabeth Bowen, the *Demon Lover* stories, and then, in 1949, the whole atmosphere of wartime Britain in, for her, a very unexpected plot. *The Heat of the Day*, her first novel for ten years, begins in the London blackout of 1942. Everybody is living on some kind of illusion to make life endurable. 'We all lived,' Elizabeth Bowen wrote in another context, 'in a state of lucid abnormality.' Stella Rodney, whose marriage has broken up, has a lover, Captain Kelway, with a conventionally 'fine war record'. But a mysterious stranger, Harrison, who wants to sleep with Stella, persuades her that Kelway is really a Nazi agent; and this is strange, because all three of them are engaged on 'secret work'. But it is true: Kelway *is* a traitor; yet Harrison is somehow worse, because he personifies the new amorality of wartime, the corruption that flourishes in all the rubble of destruction, the deadening of the soul – 'from hesitating to feel came the moment when you no longer could.'

From Arthur Koestler, came *Darkness at Noon*, the first assertion in fiction that behind the façade of Soviet idealism something might be terribly wrong; and in 1945 *The Yogi and The Commissar*, the neat title phrase encapsulating the intellectual dilemma, a rallying point for those for whom the God had failed: sixteen essays, mostly on writing and politics, castigating 'the stupendous . . . ignorance of Soviet reality among the addicts of the Soviet myth.' Then a flare of Zionism, in *Thieves in the Night*, before Koestler settled down to be an international savant domiciled in England.

Four isolated men, each ploughing his own furrow. P.G. Wodehouse, arrested by the Germans at Le Touquet in May 1940, sharing a cell in Loos prison with Mr Cartmell, the Étaples piano tuner, then transferred to other prisons, then quartered in the Adlon Hotel, Berlin: the unfortunate bumbling broadcasts, the attacks by Cassandra of the *Daily Mirror*, by Duff Cooper the Minister of Information ('quis-

ling', 'elderly playboy') by Quintin Hogg ('trading with the enemy' if not treason); defended by A.A. Milne and George Orwell. Imperturbable Wodehouse completed, in these conditions, a novel called *Money in the Bank*, and was allowed to send it to the *Saturday Evening Post*. Somerset Maugham, arrived in America from the South of France, having escaped with five hundred other refugees in a coal-boat, saying 'I am a very old party now', produced *The Razor's Edge*, whose mystical man-of-action hero Larry has something of Christopher Isherwood in him, something perhaps of T.E. Lawrence. Upton Sinclair, the old Muckraker, had been writing a book a year since 1940 about Lanny Budd, a sort of diplomatic James Bond, President Roosevelt's 'special agent No. 103'. In *O Shepherd Speak!* (1949) Lanny, who had, throughout 6,500 pages, interviewed every significant personage of the time on F.D.R.'s behalf, now interviewed God, whom he called 'the Governor', on the future of America; and God replied, 'there will come a man of the people for the people; and the people will know him.' And in the vastness of his stately home, Renishaw, Derbyshire, Sir Osbert Sitwell wrote four of the five volumes of his vast, leisurely autobiography; no men of the people here, except his jokey butler Henry Moat, but the famous, ranging from General Alexander to Massine and Diaghilev.

What's new on the literary scene? Carson McCullers and Truman Capote, Joyce Cary and Eudora Welty, Mary McCarthy and William Sansom (spending his war, like so many British writers, in the Auxiliary Fire Service), Jean Stafford (day dreaming long sentences, labelled 'American Proustism'); a new satirist, Nigel Dennis, hilarious but sympathetic in *Boys and Girls Come Out to Play* (published in America as *A Sea Change*); a new humorist, Stephen Potter, whose Gamesmanship and Lifemanship became a cult in which readers recognized the psychological warfare that we practice in social life; or if they didn't, they were One Down and felt miserably excluded.

To make one's name overnight with a volume of short stories almost never happens. It happened, in 1949, to Angus Wilson, whose *The Wrong Set* made uncomfortable fun of impoverished middle-class people of the kind who are supposed to live in Kensington. Only in the long-established Angela Thirkell do we see the upper and middle-classes in open revolt as their mansions are taken over by the

SOUTH

William Sansom

I'll say
she
does

PETER
CHEYNEY

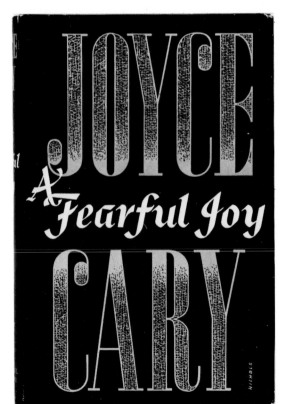

JOYCE

A
Fearful Joy

CARY

NICHOLS

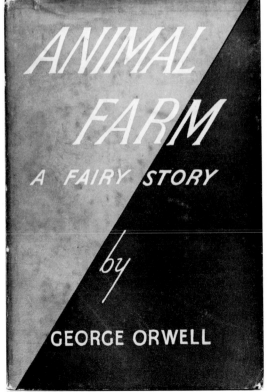

**ANIMAL
FARM**

A FAIRY STORY

by

GEORGE ORWELL

National Coal Board; if only, Mrs Thirkell raged in *Love Among the Ruins*, our rulers were gentlemen who drank and gambled and whored; but then, of course, the rot had really started with the French Revolution; and 'when they've exterminated the middle class, England won't be any better.' Nancy Mitford, slightly Mrs Thirkell's social superior, did not worry about any of this in her similarly-titled *Love in a Cold Climate*. Was it satire or nostalgia for pre-war England? An American critic considered it 'watered Waugh': what is supposed to be so damn funny about the British aristocracy? The barely-disguised Mitford family of the Thirties in *The Pursuit of Love* was now succeeded by the Montdores in earlier days, wonderfully remote from Austerity Britain, Uncle Matthew with his chub-fuddling, the golden-haired Cedric ('Having our lovely cake and eating it, too, *One*'s great aim in life'), the family talking eggy-peggy language and saying 'absolute blissikins' – what froth is here, and how guilty our enjoyment of it.

One more escapist bestseller before the prophecies of doom with which the decade was to end. A little lower down the social scale from Miss Mitford, the Mortmain family are camping out in a ruined Suffolk castle – seventeen-year-old Cassandra, her man-hungry sister Rose, her eccentric father, her ex-model step-mother; enter two prospects of love, wealth and happiness in the shape of two handsome, rich Americans. . . . Dodie Smith, hitherto known as a success-ful cosy-romantic playwright, had written her first novel. She was now living in Pennsylvania, and *I Capture the Castle* had already been chosen by the Literary Guild of America, which in those days meant half a million copies. In London, Heinemann printed fifty-seven thousand copies, and their blurb writer praised Miss Smith's 'knowledge of the mind of a maid'. *The Daily Telegraph* found the novel 'rich in clean sentiment as an English spring is full of blossom', and the *Daily Express*'s Daniel George, who had helped to select it for the Book Society, said it ought to have been called *I Capture the Critics*.

The doom came from George Orwell. V.S. Prit-chett called him 'the conscience of his generation'. He had seldom earned much more than £3 a week, with left-wing journalism and grey books on the social condition of England, and he was comparatively little known until *Animal Farm*, his imperishable allegory on the corruption of Communism, was published in 1946. *Animal Farm*, rejected by many American publishers for fear of disturbing Soviet-American relations, has been called 'as much a landmark as Churchill's Iron Curtain speech.' Like Orwell's next book, *1984*, it was doomed to become a 'set book' for examinations in British schools. It was said just after Orwell's death in 1950 that the pessimism and loss of faith in politics, in socialism as ruined by its prac-titioners, in democracy itself, were attributable to his dying illness, the tuberculosis that he was making worse by living on an island in the Outer Hebrides. Was it a warning, or a despairing recognition of the way man must inevitably go? The brainwashing of Winston Smith, who works in the statistics falsifica-tion department, forbidden to love his Julia, who works in Pornosec; the wonderful diagnosis of the future of language in Newspeak, whose seeds are already seen in totalitarian countries: *crimethink*, *doublethink*, *ownlife*; the concept of perpetual minor warfare; the contempt for the masses, the *proles*, the only people who lead 'normal' lives; the slogans, *War is Peace, Freedom is Slavery*; it *can* happen here, the class war is already a fantasy by which it may soon actually be possible (foreseen long ago by Aldous Huxley) so to condition people that, at the throwing of a switch, Big Brother can be loved, or Emmanuel Goldstein hated. 'What stands between *1984* and *Gulliver's Travels*?' asked Richard Rovere in America; and answered, 'Not much.' Winston Smith, sipping his Victory Gin in the half-ruins of London, learns to love Big Brother. So ends the most haunting novel of my lifetime.

Where can we turn for escape? To the poets? There was no splendid fury, no Sassoons or Owens or Ed-ward Thomases whose 'officer outlook', whose whole mental fabric had been shattered. In World War II, writing poetry was an act of resistance against boredom and mechanization and homesickness, done by soldiers who were seldom more than cor-porals with much 'softness and suffering'. Tam-bimuttu's *Poetry London* collected romantics, and around John Waller in Cairo the Middle East poets gathered, and small anthologies were printed. Small poets squeezing small poems out of themselves. 'Where are the war poets?' editors cried; and some answered, 'in America'. Well, Auden and Isherwood were in America – you wouldn't call them war poets, would you? Auden, teaching English literature at Swarthmore College and Bryn Mawr, for some time lived at Carson McCullers' poets' hostel (known as February House because so many of the lodgers, paying $25 a week, were born under Pisces) in Brooklyn Heights, with Benjamin Britten, Peter Pears, Chester Kallman, and – Gypsy Rose Lee.

For Robert Frost, a new lease of life, as readers turned back with relief to the hard nuts of his pastoralism. For Robinson Jeffers, trouble: when, in 1948, he published *The Double Axe*, Random House found it necessary to add a note saying that they did not agree with his political views. His work was now full of blood, decay and incest, and he was saying that America had been pushed into the war by 'liars', dead soldiers had been betrayed, World War III was coming fast and America would lose it. In St Elizabeth's Hospital, Washington, Ezra Pound, who had broadcast anti-American, anti-semitic propaganda from Italian radio stations and was therefore mad, was writing yet more Cantos, reviewed by a hostile critic who called them 'a chaotic grab-bag in which the reader can find whatever he likes.' He had been arrested in Rapallo and kept in a cage six feet square near Pisa where he was tormented like an animal. In his Washington bedlam Robert Lowell, Marianne Moore, T.S. Eliot came to see him: thus 'America's most illustrious salon was conducted in a madhouse.' In Britain, at the lowest point of the War before Pearl Harbor, people were grateful to Mrs Duer Miller, whose *The White Cliffs* proclaimed her wish to live no longer in a world where England was dead.

After the war, young American poets – Karl Shapiro, Richard Wilbur, Howard Nemerov – tried, in unaggressive ways, to make something of their war experiences; but I choose John Ciardi as a voice of his time – an air gunner in the Pacific, he lost friends by fire and drowning, and with a kind of mild irony felt that the whole experience had been meaningless.

Of Britain's Sidney Keyes, dead at the age of twenty-one 'of unknown causes' after being taken prisoner in North Africa, it was said that he was 'posthumously groomed for martyrdom'. We had all along been seeking a new Rupert Brooke, the untimely death of a golden young man. Was it Keyes?

Was it Henry Reed (*Today We Have the Naming of Parts*)? Nobody fitted. Nobody, not even Brooke, had been killed in action. And when the War was over, Britain's poets seemed to survive by the grace of the B.B.C. William Empson was news editor of the Eastern Service, Roy Campbell was a talks producer, Patric Dickinson, as poetry editor, ran a *Time for Verse* programme every Sunday evening, Louis MacNeice wrote and produced features, and Dylan Thomas – well, you couldn't actually have him on the staff, but he wrote and he read aloud, ah, *how* he read!

Or shall we turn for escape to thrillers? There is not much cosy murder left, though Agatha Christie is still in full flood. Dorothy L. Sayers is translating *The Divine Comedy*: no more Peter Wimsey. Ellery Queen (who now has his own *Mystery Magazine*), Margery Allingham and Ngaio Marsh still provide literate crime, and Simenon (known to a few connoisseurs since before the war) has raised the *roman policier* to the level of art, but there is something much nastier in the woodshed, and war lets it out. In 1940 an advertising man named Gerald Butler published a shocker called *Kiss the Blood Off My Hands* which took James Hadley Chase's *No Orchids for Miss Blandish* a stage further. The new wave loved power and sadism more than it loved sex. Peter Cheyney's Lemmy Caution, hero of books which sold in half-millions in both Britain and America, tortures his victims, and it's O.K. because Lemmy is on the side of law if not of order. Not for nothing had Cheyney been a member of the British Union of Fascists. Mickey Spillane, whose *I, The Jury* appeared in 1947, had a hero named Mike Hammer who loved breaking his victim's fingers, shooting a girl in the stomach and, in one case, burning her alive. It seemed that only women could save the civilized thriller, and they did it with style and wit as a new name, Vera Caspary (*Laura*) appeared in 1943, and another, Patricia Highsmith (*Strangers on a Train*) in 1949. In an age which hanged the Nuremberg war criminals, she seemed to be on the criminal's side, and certainly hated the Mike Hammers and Lemmy Cautions. 'I find the public passion for justice,' she dared to say, 'quite boring and artificial.'

CHAPTER 19

Read All About It

News values in post-war Britain were strange. Thus the sudden availability of bananas to children under fourteen (many of whom had never seen a banana before) in 1945 made the headlines and a Cabinet reshuffle didn't; and readers could be thrown into deeper gloom by 'Dried Egg Shortage Threat' than by any development in the outside world.

One of the few heart-lifting events of the spring of 1949 in Britain was headlined: 'Bigger newspapers again!' This meant six pages instead of four, which was of course a fifty per cent increase, but it looked pretty silly beside the Sunday edition of the *New York Times* which had 168 pages. Any British reporter who learned his trade during paper rationing really knew about 'tight writing', which did his style nothing but good. And how did editors use their two extra pages? The *Daily Express* and the *Daily Mirror* immediately started a circulation war with women's pages and advertising. Other papers used more comic strips, features and fiction. Only the *News Chronicle*, with its old liberal tradition, extended its political and industrial coverage.

Comic strips and cartoons were important. (How important was seen in July 1945, when, during a strike of newspaper deliverers in New York, Mayor La Guardia read the 'funnies' aloud over W.N.Y.C. radio station.) They had been a safety valve all through the war: now they could be used as satire in ways that would not be allowed in words. Strips and cartoons were morale builders, even when they 'knocked'. In World War I there had been the Belgian Louis Raemakers and the British Bruce Bairnsfather, both of them world famous. In World War II there was Bill Mauldin, loved by soldiers, hated by top brass. His infantrymen have seen it all, they're sick of everything, they haven't had a shower or a shave in weeks. An ex-truck driver and sign painter, Mauldin was to be found in the *45th Division News* in Sicily. He graduated to *Stars and Stripes*, the U.S. Army newspaper, which was where General Patton first saw his work and tried to have it banned. Mauldin mocked all official communiqués: 'Fresh, spirited U.S. troops, flushed with victory, are bringing in thousands of hungry, ragged, battle-weary prisoners.' My favourite is his sketch of a chaplain praying in mid-battle – 'for ever and ever, Amen. . . . *Hit the dirt!*'

Gentler was George Baker's 'Sad Sack', the ugly, spindly man who ought not to be in the army at all, always getting less chow than the next guy, always missing out on girls. He flourished in *Yank* magazine.

In Britain (and the Middle East) we had 'The Two Types' by Jon, a send-up of the raffish (and R.A.F.-ish) mustachioed officers to be seen around the safer parts of North Africa; and of course Jane, who, one day in 1943, after several years of nearly losing her pants, appeared starkers in the *Eighth Army News*. A U.S. army paper *Round-up* celebrated this with a leading article beginning: 'Well, sirs, you can go home now . . . Jane peeled a week ago. The British 36th Division immediately gained six miles and the British attacked in the Arakan. Maybe we Americans ought to have Jane too.'

Well, the U.S. Army had 'Male Call', a special 'sharp and lusty' version of Milton Caniff's 'Terry and the Pirates', which now featured a sex symbol called Miss Lace, who never actually stripped, but there were fascinating implications in the way Caniff drew her stocking tops. Even Joe Palooka, hero of Ham Fisher's boxing strip, toughened up for the War, and there was a public outcry when Joe, the clean-fighting American, shot a Nazi *in the back*.

David Langdon, in the R.A.F., had a special Anglo-American 'double-take' type of joke, such as

"LOOK! BRINGING HIS OWN HARNESS!"

David Low cartoon, *Evening Standard*,
21 August 1947

the drawing in which two American and two British sergeants pass each other in the street, each pair muttering: 'They've got their stripes upside down!'

Among political cartoonists David Low was still supreme in Britain; sometimes serious, as after Dunkirk, when he showed a solitary Briton gazing out at the Channel saying: 'Very well, then – alone'; sometimes rejoicing in his new freedom to attack the dictators, especially Hitler, posturing as Lohengrin or a Rhine maiden. Not until the Allied forces opened the concentration camps did any British cartoonist learn to hate. Besides, there was the law of libel: nobody in Britain would have dared to go as far as Herblock, who, in 1946, depicted Richard Nixon as climbing into Washington from a sewer.

By 1949 the London *Daily Mirror* and one or two other papers had a whole page of strips – Batman, Garth, Rip Kirby, and in the *Daily Mail* there was

something entirely new: 'Flook', which from 1949 onwards featured a teddybear-like animal with a magic snout which enabled Flook to change himself into anything he liked. The strip achieved a top drawer audience when it became known that it was often written by Compton Mackenzie. The drawings were by a jazz clarinet player called Wally Fawkes. Another short-lived fantasy animal was invented in 1947 by Al Capp, of 'Li'l Abner' fame. The 'Schmoo' was a superbeast which brought everything to everybody and was happiest when being eaten. A sick society seemed to be confronting itself, and people reacted against Schmoos so that Al Capp felt obliged to kill them all off by 'schmooicide squads'.

'I hate it,' wrote Ernie Pyle. 'I *don't want* to be killed.' But he was, three weeks before VE-Day and five days after Roosevelt died. America's best-loved war correspondent was picked off at the age of

'Rip Kirby', *Daily Mail***, 23 June 1947**

forty-four by a Japanese machine gun on the island of Ie Shima, three miles off Okinawa. This smallish, wiry man had been in the front line in North Africa, Italy and France; a chronicler of pity more than heroics. He earned about $25,000 a year from a column which, syndicated to 122 newspapers, bought him nearly nine million readers. The kind of correspondent who stuck around the bar at Shepheards Hotel or the Ritz was in a minority in World War II. On the British side probably the finest war correspondent on all fronts was Alan Moorehead of the *Daily Express*: he was withdrawn from combat zones only once, when Lord Beaverbrook ordered him from Egypt to the United States to report the American war effort at a time in 1942 when the British weren't yet convinced that it existed. *The Daily Telegraph* even sent its music critic, Richard Capell, to report the War in North Africa. The *New York Times* sent its drama critic, Brooks Atkinson, to Chungking. Francis McCarthy of United Press amd Richard Tregaskis of International News went ashore with the marines at Guadalcanal and had the same dysentery as anyone else. Jack Belden of *Time-Life* shocked millions of Americans in 1944 when, in addition to warning them of 'lying legends' ('falseness is a product of any battle. . . . No one ever knows what happened'), asserted that 'Our men do not believe they are fighting for anything. Not one in a hundred has any deep-seated political belief.'

The war changed some of the press. It didn't change William Randolph Hearst, then in his eighties: his headlines raged between *Stalin's Monstrous Double-Dealing* and *Total War Against Japan NOW*, and there was always space for an article against vivisection. But war did change women's pages. Thus the Chicago *Herald-American* was able to raise its circulation by a feature called War Romance Clinic: 'Shall I have this baby and say nothing to the sailor? He does not know.' – 'My daughter is seventeen and about to have a child . . . the father is a married man in the Army – he took her to a tavern and gave her the first drink she ever had. . . .' Britain, with her four-page newspapers, could not aspire to this. You could, however, start a new magazine if you could show that it was important to the war effort or to harmony among the multi-lingual Allies. Thus a distinguished Frenchman named André Labarthe was encouraged to start a highly successful review called *La France Libre*, and every other foreign minority had its own paper. To explain America to Britain, Allen Lane published a 64-page monthly magazine called *Transatlantic*.

Somehow the glossy social weeklies like the *Tatler* and *Sketch* survived – it was evidently somebody's war work to edit them – and published pictures of débutantes driving ambulances and peeresses wielding fire hoses in their very becoming ATS uniforms which, said the *New Yorker*'s London correspondent, Mollie Panter-Downes, made them look like 'musical comedy Zouaves'. Miss Panter-Downes covered everything from Cabinet meetings to parish magazines, from air-raids to that besetting problem of village stores, 'Will you take the farthing change, ma'am, or a packet of needles?'

The boldest step forward in women's magazines was taken in America, after the War, by the *Ladies Home Journal*. With a circulation of over 4½ million it was now edited by a husband and wife team, Bruce and Beatrice Gould, who had taken the vital decision which nobody in Britain would take for nearly twenty years: that women were the same as men, only different, and that they were interested in the world outside the home. So they printed articles on 'how America lives', alcoholism, V.D., and excerpts from General Stilwell's Diary. To this new outspokenness was added a French influence, one of sheer style. Before the Germans had marched on Paris, Hélène Lazareff, married to a former editor of *Paris-Soir*, had edited *Marie-Claire*, the French *Ladies Home Journal*, which had flourished with 1¼ million copies. She had been a refugee in America during the War, but by Christmas 1945 was back in Paris ready to launch *Elle*. This magazine, begotten in a Europe of exhausted poverty, was sophisticated yet full of money-saving ideas – 'no need to redecorate – a couple of pot plants and a bright cushion will do wonders.' *Elle* showed cleavage and how to make the most of it: the *Elle* model, in almost every issue, was a girl called Nicole de Lamargé. *Elle*, which influenced all women's magazines everywhere, made only one mistake: it said there would never be a topless bikini.

The only British magazines publishing discreet nudes in these years were *Lilliput* and *Men Only*. (Yet *Lilliput* was more famous for Ronald Searle's school-girls at St Trinian's.) In America there was a new breed of pin-up magazine, using drawings as well as photographs (drawings, to soldiers, were more erotic because less realistic), with such titles as *Wink*, *Eyeful* and *Beauty Parade*. Yet it was not these that brought down official disapproval, but the Petty and Varga girls in *Esquire*, a fairly literary magazine, not usually bought by soldiers, which had, however, always published girl pictures of a certain piquancy. In 1944 the U.S. Postmaster General decided that they were obscene and revoked *Esquire*'s 'second-class' mailing privileges'. This, since it would have cost the magazine $500,000 a year to mail it at ordinary rates, was tantamount to banning the pictures altogether. The hearing in the U.S. Court of Appeals in June 1945 was one of the great comic scenes in the history of censorship. Examples of impropriety were quoted from other publications, all of which would have to be refused second-class mailing privileges if the Postmaster General's attitude were upheld – and it was an attitude supported by a panel of five clergymen, a psychiatrist, a 'lady prominent in women's organizations' and an assistant superintendent of schools. H.L. Mencken, a witness for *Esquire*, recalled how he had been persecuted by the Postmaster General when he was editing *The American Mercury*. The judges gently reproved the Postmaster General; but it was too late. For the most indignant sufferers were the G.I.s in the Pacific. Jack Belden of *Time-Life* had been wrong about men not knowing what their war aims were. Three of them wrote to Arnold Gingrich, *Esquire*'s publisher: 'Those pictures are very much on the clean and healthy side and it gives us guys a good idea of what we're fighting for.'

There was no precise American parallel to *Picture Post*, Edward Hulton's crusading weekly magazine which, though its cover at a distance of ten feet was indistinguishable from that of *Life*, had very different contents. Through the War *Picture Post* nagged the Government, mocked the Ministry of Information, campaigned for a post-war programme of social security, and in 1940 even founded its own guerrilla warfare school at Osterley Park from which the Home Guard eventually sprang. Yet America too had a crusader, Ralph Ingersoll, who launched a 'liberal' tabloid, *PM*, in June 1940 with the backing of Marshall Field III of Chicago. Bravely, Ingersoll said he would accept no advertisements, but three years later he was changing his mind, or perhaps Marshall Field, who had started the new *Chicago Sun* in 1941, was changing it for him. The rich man playing with idealistic publishing tends to isolate himself. *PM* could not get advertising from big business because it had always attacked big business. And how was the *Sun* raising its circulation? Crime and divorce. Nevertheless *PM* somehow survived for six years.

There was no idealistic nonsense about the new Los Angeles *Mirror*, launched in 1948, a tabloid so determined to be different that it printed its front page sideways and published advertisements which sometimes looked like call-girl dating.

In Philadelphia, abetted by the Curtis publishing company, an ex-advertising man, Ted Patrick, in 1946 started a luxury magazine called *Holiday*, closely linked to post-war tourism. It dealt, frankly and glamorously, with rich people's holidays – 'even those who can't afford them,' said Patrick, 'like reading about them.' Dare one call it the first of the coffee-table magazines? Weirder was a short-lived magazine called *Flair*, edited by Fleur Cowles. 'Fleur's *Flair*', launched in 1949, had pull-outs, swatches of fabrics somehow bound into it, printed occasional items in invisible ink and was once drenched in scent. Gratifying nearly all senses simultaneously, this publisher's nightmare was difficult to read in comfort, because you needed two hands to hold it and a third hand to pull out the pull-outs. The *New Yorker* spotted this at once and printed a cartoon (was it by Addams or Steig?) of a three-armed lady doing just that.

Another oddity from the Cowles stable, edited by Fleur's husband, Gardner Cowles of *Look*, was the world's *smallest* magazine, *Quick*, also ad-less. It measured 4 × 6 inches, had 65 pages (19 of them illustrated) and was designed for 'reading on a bus or in a beauty parlor.' Summarizing summaries, catering for people who 'haven't time to read *Time*', it lasted about two years.

Perhaps, if magazines were to survive, they would have to do things like this. Already television was threatening the general magazine. In Britain *John Bull*, once Horatio Bottomley's scandal sheet, had been reborn in full colour as the British *Saturday Evening Post*, and flourished for a few years in the apparent belief that the only people left who still read magazines were all in north-west England and semi-literate. As its serial fiction editor I once unwisely billed a new story as 'a sophisticated comedy'. 'You can't say *sophisticated*,' I was reprimanded. 'Up in Oldham sophisticated means *sexy*.' The *Strand* magazine, which had begun in 1891 with Sherlock Holmes, was given a new format (pocket size and a 'modern' cover) and a new young editor, an ex-*Picture Post* reporter named Macdonald Hastings. It came to an end in 1950. As if to keep an old tradition alive at all costs, the *London Mystery Magazine* appeared in 1949, published from Sherlock Holmes's old address, 221B Baker Street, now occupied by the Abbey National Building Society.

In September 1946 the *New Yorker* appeared on bookstalls with a white band around each issue explaining that none of the usual features were present: the entire issue was devoted to John Hersey's 30,000-word report on Hiroshima. This enormous publishing risk was William Shawn's idea, sanctioned by Harold Ross; it was an act of faith with both a moral and a commercial purpose. It was a sell-out. Lee Shubert at once tried to buy the dramatic rights of *Hiroshima* (what for? a musical?) and a radio chain wanted Paul Robeson and Katharine Cornell to read it aloud. The atom bomb had become show business.

Only one British editor dared to do anything like this. Cyril Connolly had edited a literary review called *Horizon* for nearly ten years. It had kept culture alive, seeking out what there was of *avant-garde* all through the War, sweetened and sharpened by Rosamond Lehmann's 'Wonderful Holidays' and G.W. Stonier's 'Shaving Through the Blitz'. Now it complained that there was no 'cultivated well-to-do world bourgeoisie who provided the *avant-garde* artists . . . with the perfect audience.' Soon *Horizon* would die, Connolly claiming that its death betokened a hopelessly ruined society in which 'reality is unendurable', artists would be lonely and despairing – 'closing time in the gardens of the West.' (Gardens, you notice; not streets and people. Ah, well: *floreat Etona*.) In 1948 Connolly, for the first time, took a truly journalistic risk; he devoted a whole issue of *Horizon* to Evelyn Waugh's *The Loved One*, a satire on Forest Lawn Cemetery in California. (*The Loved One*, as I discovered on a visit there two years later, was an understatement.) Waugh, who had been 'caught between laughing and vomiting', had appealed to Connolly's death wish. This issue of *Horizon*, like the *New Yorker*'s Hiroshima issue, was a sell-out.

Where were the new authors? Was there no 'red-brick Lawrence'? Connolly and John Lehmann were asking. Surely they would get out of uniform and lambast the class who had caused the War – for of course they would be left wing. Lehmann had been editing *Penguin New Writing* since 1936, and, like Denys Kilham Roberts's *Penguin Parade*, judiciously mixed new and established writers. Yet the main tide of revolt would not come until the mid-Fifties; and it would come, not from those who had been in the Forces, but from those who had been too young for the War; and they were to be called Angry Young Men.

The British had a special relationship with their favourite columnists, who, because Britain is a small island, were not syndicated; and they looked to them above all for humour. They had no Westbrook Pegler (their law of libel would anyway prevent such a person from flourishing) who could accuse Quentin

Reynolds, veteran correspondent of the London Blitz, North Africa, Italy, Palestine, the Pacific and Moscow, which he had left in a huff as a protest against Soviet censorship, of being a Communist sympathizer and a do-nothing journalist. (But not with impunity, for Reynolds won a mother-and-father of a lawsuit against him.) Nor could Britain boast a counterpart to Drew Pearson, whose 'Washington Merry-Go-Round' caused him to be called a liar by more politicians than any other columnist. (In Britain, the word *liar* is actionable, though you are allowed to say that a man 'shows a reckless disregard for the truth'.) Nor had London any parallel to Billy Rose of the Diamond Horseshoe, who was capable of beginning his diary: 'What I don't know would fill a book and, dear reader, it's going to.'

What Britain had was J.B. Morton, 'Beachcomber' of the *Daily Express*, and Nat Gubbins (whose name really *was* Nathaniel Gubbins) of the *Sunday Express*. Morton, a true anarchist, invented the Ministry of Bubbleblowing, which could be used to defy all wartime bureaucracy and all post-war nationalization. Such as his scheme 'for boiling down Mr Harold Nicolson to make syrup for the nation'; or his criticism of an imaginary plan for 'the zoning of washerwomen', in which something goes wrong and the washerwomen are 'left in heaps all over the country, where they go bad.' Gubbins invented a whole gallery of characters. There were Aunt Maud's letters to her bored nephew on the Home Front, full of news such as the fued between the local Whist Club Committee and the Impoverished Gentlewomen's True Blue Association; Aunt Maud's gardener who reads Karl Marx and says it is no use planting onions 'because the Revolution will be here before they come up'; Uncle Fred and the Ironmonger in the Home Guard; Sally the Cat, the Sweep, Margaret's father who is crazed by the shortage of whisky; letters from a Safe Hotel, and an endless telephone conversation about rationed foods and alcohol, between Gubbins and his own stomach, entitled 'Dialling TUM'.

From the mists of memory comes back an *Evening Standard* readers' letters competition just before VE-Day on 'What shall we do with Hitler?' – 'Tie him to a V-bomb', 'Exhibit him in a cage', 'Appoint him lavatory attendant to the Berchtesgaden Home for Poor Jews'. And three news stories, difficult to check, which circulated during the War: that Hitler had a double, a grocer named Bartholdy from Plauen, Thuringia, and in photographs you could always tell which was which because Bartholdy's ears were bigger; that the Fuehrer had a nephew in the U.S. Navy named William Patrick Hitler; and that an American sailor named Joe Bostock, shipwrecked on an atoll in the Tuamotu Archipelago, 1,000 miles east of Tahiti, in 1933, when discovered in 1945 refused to believe that there had been a second World War, and certainly wasn't going back to America to find out.

Ben Lyon, Bebe Daniels and Vic Oliver in *Hi, Gang!*

CHAPTER 20

Talking to Each Other

'Cherry pie is eaten on George Washington's birthday. . . . Bart's is short for St Bartholomew's Hospital.' If radio had done nothing else in the Forties it had certainly been the principal means by which Britain and America had got to know each other at levels below that of Churchill-Roosevelt-Averell Harriman-Royal Family. The above elementary facts were typical fruits of a B.B.C. programme, which began in 1944 and ran for several years. *Transatlantic Quiz* brought together America's Christopher Morley, Britain's Professor Denis Brogan and various guest pundits to test each other's knowledge of the opposite side of the Atlantic. Despite the omniscience of Brogan, who had written several books on America, the American team usually won by a short head.

Britain had cause to be grateful to her transatlantic friends. Alistair Cooke – well, he wasn't quite American then, and those who had known him at Cambridge marvelled at his 'Bermudan' accent – was the sheet anchor of communication in his 'Letters from America'. Another kind of letter was broadcast by Quentin Reynolds, author of a book called *The Wounded Don't Cry* and narrator of two propaganda films, *London Can Take It* and *Christmas Under Fire*, at the height of the Blitz: it usually began 'Dear Mr Schickelgruber' or 'Dear Doctor Goebbels' and contained such pearls of abuse that the B.B.C. censors covered their ears. Interviewed on a quiz programme about how he maintained the extraordinary timbre of his voice, he said: 'I gargle with gravel!'. One American couple, Ben Lyon and Bebe Daniels, adopted Britain as their country and, joined by Austria's anglicized Vic Oliver, gave a radio show called *Hi, Gang!* of which I can now remember nothing but the catchphrase 'Not you Momma – sit down.' It must have been funny, because I remember laughing at it.

Britain's main channel for talking to America was the B.B.C. North American Service, broadcast from tunnels beneath Peter Robinson's drapery store in Oxford Street. *Radio News Reel* was a bulletin slicked up to American speed. Five days a week there was a serial, *Front Line Family*, recording the adventures of a 'typical family in wartime London' – British radio's very first soap opera. Some of these scripts were heard in Britain as *The Robinson Family*. It featured Father (Yorkshire) who worked in an aircraft factory, Mother (Scottish) who appeared to work at an officers' club, Andy (their son), a fighter pilot, and Kay (daughter in the ATS). It was full of ponderous lines like 'Coo, 'ere comes a blinkin' bomb'; but they seemed to like it in America.

Every week a panel of experts answered American listeners' questions on the War, and there was a radio exchange called *Hello Children* between parents in London and children in the States. Tommy Handley had a half-hour show, Bebe and Ben Lyon interviewed American soldiers in a programme called *Stars and Stripes*, Geraldo's band was relayed from the American Eagle Club. With the assistance of Ed Murrow and Canada's fast-talking Stewart Macpherson (never to be confused with Sandy Macpherson, the B.B.C.'s resident organist), speakers of world importance were persuaded to talk to America, under tub-thumping titles such as *Democracy Marches* and *Britain Speaks*. About 300,000 Americans listened to the direct broadcasts, but nearly all programmes were recorded and re-broadcast from American stations. The B.B.C., with four overseas networks, was broadcasting a total of forty hours a day in forty-six languages. *The Voice of America*, to Europe and Asia (and eventually to Middle East countries), developed more slowly, and by 1949 America was broadcasting in only fourteen languages to Britain's forty-six. As the Berlin Air Lift crisis mounted, the Russians began jamming *The Voice of America* by noises resembling a buzz saw.

By quickly changing the wavelength or getting speakers to raise the pitch of their voices, at the same time speaking more slowly, jamming could be circumvented; and one way or another it was reckoned that up to fifty per cent of American and British Russian-language broadcasts were still getting through.

Radio as a weapon of psychological warfare was so important that propaganda and news became indistinguishable wherever you were in the world. (And yet the great lesson of war was that the tortoise of truth does eventually beat the hare of falsehood.)

You knew that Churchill's orations ('my majethtic thpeecheth') were prepared and rehearsed for hours, were even written out with pauses and stage directions in what looked like free verse; you knew they were meant to fortify our friends and frighten our enemies; and yet, knowing them to be magnificent Old Testament bombast, as if he had consulted Macaulay and Milton and Burke as well as his son Randolph while composing them, you took the conscious decision to believe and draw comfort from them. Most people heard them by radio, when Churchill was tired and had already made the same speech in the House of Commons; but those who heard them in the flesh, seeing his gestures, scowls, tears and mockery, knew themselves to be in the presence almost of a one-man Government, certainly the holder of more power than any Englishman since Cromwell. The blessing was that we had radio to hear them by. As John Gunther once said of Bertrand Russell, 'that guy talks *prose*.'

'Come, then, let us to the task, to the battle and the toil, each to our part, each to our station. . . . There is not a week nor a day nor an hour to be lost.' This, in January 1940, made people say: 'He ought to be Prime Minister!' 'I have nothing to offer but blood, toil, tears and sweat. . . .' Now he *is* Prime Minister. O master of the monosyllable, using polysyllables only for ridicule, that a man can inspire the world with such a statement! Now, thinking of Hitler's speech in which he proposed to settle the fate of Europe for a thousand years, he said, expecting immediate invasion from the air, 'Let us therefore brace ourselves to our duties, and so bear ourselves that, if the British Empire and its Commonwealth last for a thousand years, men will still say: "This was their finest hour."' And so to – 'Never, in the history of human conflict, have so many owed so much to so few'; and 'Some chicken – some neck!'

Churchill truculent, and Churchill tender. Here he is, on 21 July 1945, opening the Winston Club for British Troops in Berlin, after a parade by the 7th Armoured Division, for whom, like a visiting headmaster at prizegiving, he has just asked for a day's holiday. This occasion was not, could not be broadcast: it was too intimate. Suddenly he is in tears: 'I am unable to speak without emotion. Dear Desert Rats, may your glory ever shine. . . . May the memory of this glorious pilgrimage which you have made from Alamein to the Baltic and Berlin never die. May fathers long tell their children the tale. . . .'

Radio was also a dirty-tricks weapon. 'Lord Haw-Haw' (a nickname first applied to the renegade Norman Baillie-Stuart, and later to William Joyce) broadcast from Reichsender Hamburg 'on the 31-metre band'. Joyce had a menacing, hypnotic voice in which an adopted upper-class accent strove to suppress his native Irish-American. This caused him to say 'Jairmany calling,' which gradually became funny. Claiming to reveal 'facts which the British people have a right to know' (such as the 'fact' that H.M.S. *Ark Royal* had been sunk, which she hadn't, or not yet) Haw-Haw succeeded in unsettling many people in Britain during the Phoney War when they were afraid Neville Chamberlain was going to make peace with Hitler. He started a wave of rumours, for example that the town-hall clock at Banstead, Surrey, was ten minutes slow, which seemed to show that Germany had an invincible spy ring in Britain. (Germany in fact had no agents of any consequence in Britain at this time: the rumours were invented and nervously passed round by British civilians, who, if discovered, were technically liable to a £50 fine for spreading 'alarm and despondency'.) The *Daily Mirror* tried to counteract them by a feature called 'Haw-Haw *didn't* say it.'

Haw-Haw, who in his prime had sixteen million listeners, was sometimes quite witty. This graduate of London University (first-class honours in English), who had made a living tutoring children in Latin and French, invented a gallery of imaginary characters such as an elderly clubman called Orpington grumbling about the War, a Jewish banker named Sir Izzy Ungeheimer, and an upper-class twit called Bumbly Mannering. He made a ludicrous mistake when, taking up a British report that 'German bombs were dropped at random', he appeared to think that there really was a town called Random; and he lost all credibility in the end by attacking Churchill as a 'liar' who didn't really believe what he said in his speeches. But he went on all through the War and only went off the air as the 7th Armoured Division entered the suburbs of Bremen. He was hanged – why? For treason, yes; but can you commit treason if you were not born in the country that arraigns you? Or merely if you hold a British passport, acquired by making a false statement? He was born in New York, said he was a British subject, but had meanwhile in 1940 taken German nationality. As if it mattered: we wanted him dead.

One of Joyce's jobs in Germany was to find, from among British prisoners of war, speakers for the 'Concordia Bureau' which ran a 'black radio' station called the 'New British Broadcasting Station', supposed to be operating secretly on British soil, pursued all the time by police. This failed dismally because any British listener could tell at once that the Cockney accents the broadcasters felt it necessary to adopt were faked; and a character calling himself 'Father Donovan' offended Catholics by giving mock sermons which no genuine priest could possibly have delivered. Britain also had a 'black radio' station, run mainly by journalists who today quickly change the subject when it is mentioned. It was called *Soldiers, Radio Calais*, and it worried Dr Goebbels a good deal.

Much cleverer than any of Joyce's propaganda was the broadcasting of John Amery, problem child of Leo Amery, Secretary for India in the British Government. His plan for a 'Legion of St George' of British prisoners who were to fight with the Germans on the Eastern Front to 'save Europe from Bolshevism' was mad, but his approach was dangerous in 1942: 'This conflict between England and Germany is *racial suicide*. . . . Should Soviet Russia ever overcome Germany . . . nothing on this earth would save the Continent from Communism. . . .'

Four years after the end of the War, a Miss Mildred E. Gillers, aged forty-eight, was still being tried in Washington for having been disc jockey, actress and commentator on the German radio from about 1943 onwards. She was American, and was known to G.I.s as Axis Sally or Berlin Bait. Her big role was that of 'Evelyn', mother of an American soldier, in *Vision of Invasion*, a radio soap opera intended to frighten American troops to death just before D-Day. In this she was partnered by a Herr Georg Schnell, who played the father, and who was brought all the way from Germany as witness. Another witness was a Herr Werner Plack, who had been a wine merchant in Hollywood ('Moselles personally selected by Werner Plack') until 1940, when he had suddenly left for Berlin and joined the German Foreign Office (Ribbentrop was a wine merchant too).

There were other Americans broadcasting from Germany: Robert Henry Best, of United Press, jeering at the 'Jew Deal' and shouting 'down with the kikes'; Douglas Chandler, Jane Anderson, Constance Drexel.

Much more insidious an assault on morale is to make hungry, lonely soldiers thousands of miles from home melt within. Seven women, broadcasting to homesick G.I.s in the Pacific, played the part of Tokyo Rose; only one of them was American, Iva Toguri, born in Los Angeles in 1916. After the War she married a Portuguese and so was not subject to United States treason laws; otherwise she might have been America's Haw-Haw. She played records of big bands and sentimental songs, spoke sexily, delicately suggested that girl friends back home were probably tired of waiting. . . . The Armed Forces Radio Service, broadcasting on short waves all over the world, found an answer to her in *G.I. Jill*, a blonde named Martha Wilkerson, who ran a record-request programme and soon built up a formidable fan mail.

Ici Londres. . . . These words introduced the most effective use of radio in psychological warfare coordinated firmly with military operations. The daily B.B.C. broadcast to France, always preceded by the V-sign (three dots and a dash, played menacingly on a drum by James Blades, doyen of percussionists), linking up with Churchill's two-fingered gesture of defiance and eventually with the opening bars of Beethoven's 5th Symphony, gave coded messages to the Resistance. 'Barbara's dog will have puppies' meant that three escaped airmen were due to arrive at the British consulate in Barcelona. 'Romeo kisses Juliet' meant that there would be a parachute landing that night near Chaumont. 'Pierre doesn't like pork' was an order to blow up telegraph cables on a specified road. A certain 'Colonel Britton' (Michel St Denis, the French actor, playwright and director who had escaped at Dunkirk) broadcast news and talks, and so great was the B.B.C.'s reputation for truth and freedom from propaganda (in the sense of optimistic lies) that French patriots trusted every word and implicitly obeyed its instructions. (French radio could not be trusted because the Germans had a clever trick of playing back Churchill's and De Gaulle's speeches, edited so that they appeared defeatist.) There were warnings against a premature uprising as the Allies approached Paris, and an 'information service for saboteurs'. In French homes ears were pressed to illegal radio sets, and the news that Paris was about to be liberated was heard a day before it happened, on 23 June 1944, when the bells of Westminster Abbey rang and were faintly heard all over France.

At home, listening was very different. An American child of three was considered definitely retarded if it could not sing 'Rinso White, Rinso White, happy little washday song!' The singing commercial had come to stay. 'Mooo-to-Yooo!' crooned Borden's Milk; and if you were around at the time, you might also recall *Pillsbury's Pancake Serenade*, a calypso called *Chiquita Banana*, and the standard Pepsi-Cola jingle which, since a nickel actually bought something in those days, ended 'trickle-trickle-trickle, nickel-nickel-nickel.' It may have been in a determined attempt to bring a fresh mind to this kind of thing that the *New York Herald Tribune* in 1946 appointed its new radio critic, John Crosby, because he hadn't got a radio.

The live promotion of commercial products produced a reaction in the shape of Arthur Godfrey. 'The makers have paid me to tell you that these razor blades are the sharpest in the world. Well, I don't know — they look just like any other razor blades to me. . . .' It

Rosalyn Silber, Gertrude Berg and James R. Waters in *The Goldbergs*

Arthur Godfrey

was as if the buying public actually preferred to be *sold* something rather than go out and use their own judgment. For Godfrey was *not* the originator of the unscripted 'knocking commercial': several years before, Joe Gentile and Ralph Binge, on Station CKLW (Detroit-Windsor), had found that no fewer than forty sponsors were willing to pay to have their goods insulted.

If, as a child, you sang the Rinso song, you probably also listened to *Gang Busters* and *Lone Ranger*. The serial and the soap opera almost held American domestic life together, for the wonderful thing about radio is that you can listen to it while moving around the house doing chores. There was a sharp break with the past in February 1943 when, after fifteen years, *Amos 'n' Andy* went off the air. Five nights a week was too much, explained their sponsors the Campbell Soup Company; besides, with war priorities, there was a national shortage of cans. Never mind – *The Goldbergs*

(Proctor & Gamble) were still around, with Molly saying 'Enter, whoever' whenever there was a knock at the door, until 1945; and in 1948 they transferred without a hitch to television. The narrative flow was occasionally interrupted with 'a special announcement' which, like as not, turned out to be 'Send a box top and twenty-five cents for a gorgeous lovebird brooch.' *Duffy's Tavern* always began with a telephone call taken by Archie the manager to establish the scene and the central personality. Characters wandered in and out, and one who almost became the anchor man of the show was Raffles the mynah-bird who laughed, whistled, shouted 'Quiet!' and 'Hello darling!' and sang 'The Star-Spangled Banner', all in the American idea of an Oxford accent. So popular was Raffles that Elsa Maxwell gave a party for him, and there was talk of his starring in a film with Dorothy Lamour.

Cole Porter was hopelessly addicted to N.B.C.'s *Stella Dallas*. Stella always had problems, among them her daughter Lolly-Baby and a society woman who was always referred to as 'the mad Ada Dexter'. If Porter was away from home, his wife Linda was deputed to tell him what happened to Stella in the missed instalment, if necessary telephoning coast to coast. Guests, even Lady Mendl and Orson Welles, neither of them accustomed to silence, were forbidden to speak while *Stella* was on.

There were, in several soap operas, characters who specialized in folksy philosophy about life and how to deal with its problems, and one of them was the hero of *Life Can Be Beautiful* (the show was known in the radio business as 'Elsie Beebe' – LCBB, get it?) who was confined to a wheel chair long before Chief Ironside. Papa David was also the only Jewish character in any soap opera after 1945: sponsors were nervous about 'upsetting either Jews or anti-Semites'. In all these shows sexual morality was strict (one heroine with many suitors used to make this clear with the line 'After all, I have never been in your arms'), and any reference to cigarettes (pipes were okay) or alcohol brought in hundreds of protesting letters. Perhaps this is the moment to record that the first Alcoholics Anonymous broadcast was in March 1945 from Station WWJ, Detroit.

James Thurber, in a masterly survey of radio soap opera, observed how frequently characters lost the use of their legs or suffered from amnesia, in order to

Tommy Handley with Diana Morrison in *ITMA*

satisfy the demands of plot, so that they couldn't get to a telephone or send for the police. In a show called *Young Dr Malone*, young Dr Malone was tried for murder while confined to a wheel chair. In the old days, you had measured the success of a show by sales of merchandise; now, in the late Forties, 'audience measurement' was becoming more precise. The Hooper organization had 1,500 women in thirty-six large cities telephoning cross sections of the public

asking them what they were listening to at a given moment; the more scientific A.C. Nielsen Company took in rural districts as well and saved a lot of telephoning by attaching audimeters to people's sets.

Hardy old programmes like *Fibber McGee and Molly* (Jim and Marion Jordan) were caught up in wartime propaganda about gasoline rationing and war bonds: the McGees had their own 'Wistful Vista Bond Rally'. On Sunday afternoons N.B.C.'s *The Army Hour* gave firsthand stories of fighting in all theatres of war, which was good for home front morale. A new type of programme arrived with *The American Woman's Jury*, in which attorneys debated listeners' problems: it was sponsored by Lewis-Howe, makers of an indigestion remedy called Tums. Ed Wynn ('So-o-o-o?') returned to radio after seven years in 1944 – as King Bubbles of Happy Island, promoting Borden's homogenized milk. In 1947 Ruth Etting came back too: the voice, so famous fifteen years before, had to be reintroduced to the younger generation. There had been a mystery about her luckless life, now explained: she had divorced her Chicago gangster husband, Moe Snyder, known as 'the Gimp', who had then been jailed for a year, during which time Miss Etting had married her pianist, Myrl Alderman. Coming out of jail, Moe went straight to her Hollywood home and shot Myrl.

A development of the post-war years was the jackpot quiz, or giveaway show, especially *Stop the Music*. You guessed, if you did not know, the name of a tune and suddenly you were showered with more goods than the average apartment could possibly hold. Thus, one evening in 1949, an elderly Negro couple, Mr and Mrs Hubert of Philadelphia, were the astonished recipients of $35,000 worth of prizes, including clothes, savings bonds, a year's supply of various luxuries, free hairdressing for five years, furniture, a TV set, a $2,700 car, two motorcycles, a spinet, two Great Dane puppies, a trip to Paris and Monte Carlo and a custom-built kitchen.

One of the things Lord Haw-Haw knew, though they had never been published, was the B.B.C.'s evacuation plans when war was declared and all B.B.C. programmes were merged. The B.B.C. Orchestra went to Bristol, which eventually had some of the worst air-raids. Worcestershire suddenly became full of Londoners as the Air Ministry occupied a workhouse at Worcester. The Ministry of Information took over the Abbey Hotel, Malvern, and the B.B.C. Drama Department found themselves in the fruit-rich vale of Evesham, at a village called Wood Norton, which was at once rechristened Hogsnorton after the imaginary milieu of a comedian named Gillie Potter. Hogsnorton was for some time deeply suspicious: it had never before seen so many men with beards on bicycles, all looking like spies. B.B.C. Variety went first to Bristol, then to Bangor in North Wales where hardly anyone spoke English;

and from here, in the church hall, ITMA was broadcast for four years.

The words 'That Man' had always meant Hitler before, in 1939, *It's That Man Again* (ITMA) came on the air and ran for ten years. Forever after, it meant Tommy Handley, and a weird gallery of characters, each with a catchphrase that, if repeated often enough, somehow became funny. Why on earth should 'Good morning, *nice* day' be funny? or 'After you, Cecil?' or 'Ain't it a shame?' Colonel Chinstrap, Mrs Mopp the charlady, Ali Oop, Bigga Banga, Vodkin the Russian inventor, Fusspot the civil servant, Sophie Tuckshop, Poppy Poopah, Pansy Cowe-Parsley . . . each introduced or got rid of by a radio version of what film-makers call 'jump-cutting', with no explanation at all but the opening and shutting of a door. One phrase, T.T.F.N. – ('ta-ta for now'), became part of Auxiliary Fire Service telephone code: my sister-in-law, manning a switchboard during the Blitz, once received a message: FAMPITTFN, which being interpreted means 'False Alarm Malicious Police Informed Message Ends'. The ITMA scripts, criticized by an M.P. as 'nothing but a welter of bad puns', depended entirely on speed. It was the aim of Ted Kavanagh, who wrote about fifteen hundred scripts, to get a hundred gags into eighteen and a half minutes of a half-hour show, the remaining eleven and a half minutes being taken up with songs, music and announcements.

The show, which had an unprecedented audience figure of fifteen million, ended only with the death from a heart attack of Tommy Handley in January 1949. He was fifty-five. It is difficult to convey the place this North Country man occupied in the nation's affections. He had somehow kept people's spirits up in a way complementary to the speeches of Churchill and Roosevelt. He was the first comedian ever to be given a memorial service in St Paul's Cathedral.

War almost succeeded in abolishing anonymity at the B.B.C. For security reasons, we were at last told the names of announcers – Alvar Lidell, Freddy Grisewood, Bruce Belfrage (who once read the News to an audible background of bombs), John Snagge (well, one knew his voice as the annual commentator on the University Boat Race, but in war he and Stuart Hibbert were reserved for very momentous announcements such as Dunkirk and D-Day). They were never allowed to show any emotion: Britain had no 'voice of doom' like Gabriel Heatter in America, or Hilmar Robert Baukage, who once introduced, with his usual breathless 'Baukage talking – ', an eight-hour report on the Pearl Harbor attack. The B.B.C. gambit would have been an unruffled: 'Here is the News, and this is Frank Phillips reading it.' Emotion was the privilege of war correspondents like Frank Gillard, Richard Dimbleby and Wynford Vaughan Thomas; though Dimbleby was once reprimanded for 'excessive optimism', and Charles Gardner, the air correspondent, for an exciting description, during the Battle of Britain, of a Spitfire-Messerschmitt dog fight over the Channel: 'too racy – like the Grand National or a Cup Final.'

The Radio Doctor, Charles Hill

In the War's darkest days the Yorkshire *basso profundo* of J.B. Priestley went reassuringly out on the air in the famous *Postscripts*. This was the war of the Common Man, he said; and if there was a little too much Us-and-Them antagonism to please the authorities, he said the right things about shortages, such as his triumphant claim to have made a razor blade last a month.

One heartening feature of early wartime radio in Britain was the playing, before the News on Sunday evenings, of *all* the Allied national anthems, some of which, such as the unpompous mazurka-like Polish anthem, were almost unknown. This went on until Russia entered the War, when the B.B.C. was suddenly faced with a problem: should the *Internationale* be played as well? For one thing, it was so *long*. . . . No, it was not a *national* anthem, in fact it was an incitement to general revolution. The *Internationale* was not played.

It was in the War, too, that keep-fit morning exercises were first broadcast; and the voice of the Radio Doctor, Charles (now Lord) Hill, then Secretary of the British Medical Association, bumbled every morning at breakfast time about constipation and prunes, and on one appetite-killing occasion about worms: 'Do you ever notice,' the voice began without warning just after the News, 'your children scratching their bottoms?'

The nation's insatiable appetite for information was stimulated rather than satisfied by *The Brains Trust* (1941-8) in which a panel of experts – Julian Huxley the scientist, C.E.M. Joad the philosopher, Commander A.B. Campbell (and sometimes another Commander, Rupert Gould) with guests such as Anna Neagle and Barbara Ward, and an advertising man, Donald McCullough, as Question Master – answered listeners' questions. Soon this show too had a catchphrase, Joad's 'It depends what you mean by . . .', and much of its fun lay in what the experts *didn't* know, such as exactly how flies can land upside down on a ceiling. For about six weeks the embattled British became a nation of fly watchers. They weren't too certain about the Seven Wonders of the World, either. Occasionally, they all collapsed into giggles (Joad had an unmistakably squeaky hee-hee) on a question such as 'Do engineers make good husbands?' Joad, a ribald man, sometimes offended listeners, as with a bogus saying of Confucius: 'What economy is it

The Brains Trust, 1941

to go to bed to save candles if the result be twins?'
Commander Campbell was famous for his tall stories:
'When I was in Patagonia I met a man who was
allergic to marmalade.' McCullough was replaced by
Gilbert Harding, an old B.B.C. hand who, when not
completely sober, was apt to be aggressive, rude and
terribly sorry afterwards.

Intuition was the secret of the fun of *Twenty Questions*, a 'panel game' in which Anona Winn, hitherto
known on radio as a singer, displayed almost tele-
pathic powers as she leapt straight to the solutions of
questions asked, in a sepulchral voice, by Noël
Coward's accompanist, Norman Hackforth. The pro-

gramme and Miss Winn are with us yet.

Some wartime entertainment was endearingly
awful; yet played back today it has moist-eyed nos-
talgia-value. Jack Warner (catchphrases: 'Little gel'
and 'Mind my bike!') in *Garrison Theatre*, with his
imaginary brother Sid 'somewhere in France', and
Joan Winters as the programme-seller (at the height of
shortages she intoned cheerfully: '*No* programmes, *no*
chocolates, *no* cigarettes'). A show called *Happidrome*
with Harry Korris as 'Mr Lovejoy', assisted by 'En-
och' and 'Ramsbottom'. Robb Wilton as Mr Muddle-
combe, J.P. ('The day war broke out, my missus
said to me: "You've got to stop it"'). A strange

LONDON PALLADIUM

"Garrison Theatre"
...ve-ree good Sir!
Jack Warner

6ᴰ

experiment, never repeated, by which the B.B.C. made Wilfred Pickles, a Yorkshire actor, read the News, which ended 'Good neet, everybody, good neet.' Pickles afterwards had his own show, *Have a Go*, which toured the country making ordinary people sing, recite and play instruments for money prizes.

Serious drama began with adaptations of classic novels, often by H. Oldfield Box, and in *Saturday Night Theatre* reached a climax with Dorothy L. Sayers' *The Man Born to be King* (1945), a down-to-earth life of Christ, which, since Christ had never been portrayed in a radio play before, caused a great outcry from Mr H.H. ('Misery') Martin of the Lord's Day Observ-

ance Society, who not only thought it 'blasphemous' but took advertising space to say how dangerous it was to 'provoke the Almighty at a time of national need.'

A more officer-class show was *Much Binding in the Marsh*, which began during the war as a burlesque of life on an R.A.F. station – the three main personalities, Kenneth Horne, Richard ('Stinker') Murdoch and Sam Costa were all in the Air Force. When peace came, *Much Binding* became a country club (just as Eric Barker's *H.M.S. Waterlogged* became *Waterlogged Spa*). These two programmes were George VI's favourite listening, and he never failed to be convulsed by Sam Costa's 'Was there something, Sir?' and Jon Pertwee's Devonshire postman ('What does it matter so long as you tear 'em up?').

The post-war reorganization of the B.B.C. into Home, Light and Third Programmes showed that broadcasting was attempting to cater for audience segments as well as masses of people. The 'Third' was the only programme of its kind in the world. With total lack of 'presentation' and, at first, few concessions to humour (Stephen Potter and Joyce Grenfell in the *How?* series was one of them), it seemed at times to be hurling dutiful chunks of culture into space, anything from Indian music to scientific disquisitions which only specialists could understand, too often delivered by people with thick Central European accents. No matter: it was bravely done to broadcast Sartre's *Huis Clos* which had been banned from the theatre, and five hours of *Hamlet* 'in its eternity'.

Signs of a breakaway from the wartime variety formula came in 1949 with *Take It From Here*, written by two enormously tall members of the Kavanagh script organization, Frank Muir and Denis Norden. True, Jimmy Edwards was still basically the mustachioed R.A.F. officer; but here was a higher level of wit and satire, and a new use of visual gags somehow conveyed by sound (such as Dick Bentley, the Australian comedian who played the gormless 'Ron' in the Glum Family sketches, getting his head stuck in the park railings). Joy Nichols, another Australian, as Ron's suffering fiancee, 'Eth', and Jimmy Edwards as Pa Glum are among the few creations of those years that revive well today. This was Southern England humour, that frequently made fun of the grim North ('Ee, there's trouble at t'mill!'), and invariably burlesqued a current film. Script writing, which ten years

Wilfred Pickles in *Have A Go*

Jimmy Edwards, Joy Nichols and Dick Bentley in *Take It From Here*, **1949**

before had earned around a guinea a minute, was now well paid, and Norden and Muir were reputed to take home £100 a week each.

Britain now had two radio serials. *Mrs Dale's Diary* was the adventures of a doctor's wife; but *Dick Barton, Special Agent* was a return to boyhood pulp fiction, inspired by the new Head of the Light Programme, Norman Collins, who with unprecedented speed was to become, in 1949, Head of Television. Promoted by the Director General, Sir William Haley, he was known as 'Haley's Comet'. *Dick Barton*, with Snowy White, Jock and other henchmen, was dedicated to the destruction of villains with foreign names, includ-

ing one who roamed the Atlantic in a self-propelled iceberg. Introduced by a galloping signature tune, he was the most exciting thing that had ever happened on radio, representing the military virtues which had been lost since the war. Reporting the show for a magazine, I was allowed to see Barton's huge fan mail, and my enduring memory is of a letter from a girl of eight, the daughter of a Derbyshire publican. It began: 'Dear Dick, when I hear your lovely voice, I sweat. . . .'

The Archers, which began in May 1949, was meant to be a 'farming Dick Barton'. But waiting for a cow to calve, or to know who is going to win the biggest-

NEB cartoon, *Daily Mail*, **22 December 1947**

" The trouble I've had to get panto tickets—and now you want to stay at home and hear Dick Barton."—*by NEB.*

marrow prize at the Ambridge village fête, didn't have quite the same tension. Yet the programme is still with us, the all-time long-distance runner.

Disc jockeys, not yet so called in Britain, began to multiply. One of them, specializing in Jazz, was the Marquis of Donegall. Linking soldiers in Occupied Germany with their families at home was *Family Favourites*, a record-request programme introduced by Jean Metcalfe in London and Cliff Michelmore in Hamburg (they eventually married each other). A cosy little programme, dependent as much on the personality of the presenter as on the records played, was *Housewives' Choice*, introduced by David Jacobs, Sam Costa, Sam Heppner, 'Mrs Elrick's wee son George' and others. These years too, first heard the voice of Mrs Thomas's son Dylan, and that we ever heard it at all stands to the credit of a brilliant producer, Douglas Cleverdon.

In Britain television, which started again in June 1946, was having a struggle. All other media cried it down: it was anti-social, the programmes were terrible, the screen was too small (just under 9 inches high), the novelty was bound to wear off, it was a time-waster because you couldn't do anything else while you were watching it. Only one journalist, Caroline Lejeune the *Observer* film critic, dared to say that it had a potentially more exciting future than the cinema. Did it really matter if TV *did* kill the talkies? Look what was happening in America, where 16,500 people had TV in 1947, 189,000 in 1948, one million in 1949, and, it seemed probable, four times as many in 1950. Of course, they were financing it by advertising, selling about $400 million of air time a year. In 1948 Americans were asked: 'Would you rather listen to your favourite radio programme, or look at *any* television programme?' An overwhelming majority said *any* TV programme (or *video* as many then called it).

Film companies for a long time refused to let their pictures be shown on TV. Sadler's Wells and Covent Garden withheld their ballets; no first-class sporting event was televised because of fears that this would reduce the 'gate'. You can't have a Cup Final in the studio, but you can send to Paris for Roland Petit's ballet company, which B.B.C. television (then centred at Alexandra Palace, a converted exhibition hall in North London) did. Another trouble about television was that you had to be given something to look at all the time: must concerts be seen as well as heard?

A *New Yorker* drawing showed a couple in front of a TV set listening to a symphony: one of them says 'It's even better if you shut your eyes.'

For culture America had *Omnibus*, sponsored by the Alcoa Aluminum company; and Ed Murrow's *Hear It Now* became *See It Now* on TV, produced by Fred Friendly.

In America they had no doubt at all where television was leading. They had shown champion wrestling on *video* and it sent hundreds of new enthusiasts to Madison Square Garden a week later to see the real thing. As early as 1945, by coaxial cable, the Army and Navy football game had been shown on several Eastern stations, and in 1948 New York, Washington and Boston were linked, to be joined the following year by Chicago and St Louis. The world was being made safe for the 1948 Presidential Election, Hopalong Cassidy and Milton Berle. Hopalong, linked to a promotion selling cowboy outfits to children, went round the world. Television might be killing films, but it was saving the lives of vaudeville and music-hall performers. Berle had tried radio and movies, and had flopped. He couldn't be tied by a script, and it was unkindly said of him that he used too many old comedians' routines – he was 'the thief of Bad-gags'. Television changed a lot of that: 'anything for a laugh', as he impersonated Carmen Miranda, singing 'The Lady in the tutti-frutti hat', Li'l Abner and – you never knew what next. His guest stars were made to do undignified things. For him, Lauritz Melchior blacked his face; for him, Gracie Fields came on in a swimsuit. They called him 'Mr Television', for he was what the mountains had brought forth; and he was sponsored by Texaco automotive products.

Nobody in British television was ever paid anything like Mr Berle's reputed $6,500 a week, and very few earned more than this amount per annum. When B.B.C. Television started up again in 1946, there were just about a hundred thousand sets in the London area. There couldn't be more sets yet because the materials they were made of were all 'in short supply', but you could, for vanity's sake, put one of the H-shaped aerials on your roof until you could buy a set.

It was known that, in a static kind of way, a spectacular outside event could be covered – the Victory Parade in June had demonstrated this. It was still fashionable to sneer at the new medium, just as the upper crust for years had deprecated 'that dreadful wireless': not until the great achievement of televising the Coronation in 1953 would they suddenly be converted. (Television cameras, for technical as much as any other reasons, were not allowed inside Westminster Abbey for the wedding of Princess Elizabeth and Prince Philip.)

In the immediate post-war years brains and improvisation had to make do for money. From Alexandra Palace (known as Ally-Pally) came pleasant, amateurish shows which it was somehow patriotic to support. Those of us who were learning to write for television discovered that the cameras (there were never more than four in a studio) had stiff necks, they couldn't pan or track quickly, there were no 'zooms'. Some of them were on 'dollies' which meant that they could be wheeled about. Actors still had to be heavily made up (though they no longer had to have their noses painted blue, as in pre-war days); the heat of the arc-lights was so great that rivers of sweat washed away the make-up; and there was a phenomenon called 'strobe' which meant that you could only wear clothes of certain patterns and colours or you might make viewers crosseyed. Most stage actors hated television, it made them nervous having no audience but a lot of technicians, forgetting which camera was on them; many 'dried', and one or two actually fainted.

The announcing and compering pre-war team of Joan Gilbert and Leslie Mitchell were joined by an actor named MacDonald Hobley, an announcer named Sylvia Peters (whom even people's mothers liked because she was 'so *natural*') and an aristocratic lady, Mary Malcolm, who in private life was Lady Bartlett. There were variety shows, ballet (Fonteyn was not too proud to dance at Ally-Pally), and sudden visual victories which made one see the full possibilities of television, such as David Low showing us how he drew his cartoons, and a plump, bearded Philip Harben demonstrating elementary cooking ('don't forget to fill the kettle before boiling it') and on one memorable occasion burning sausages to cinders as he talked on and on. Even the non-cooperation of British show business had its unexpected advantages: since foreign artists were more than willing to appear on British television, a whole show, *Café Continentale*, was built around them: its signing-on and off tune was a chorus from *The Merry Widow*.

An entirely native production was *Muffin the Mule*. The B.B.C. had always provided excellent children's programmes, and *Muffin*'s values were sound. Muffin, a puppet accompanied by other animals, first appeared in 1947. He was the invention of, and was animated by, John Mills's older sister Annette. Muffin took his place, with Mr Toad, among the gallery of English fictional characters who, pompous by nature, do not see when they are being deflated. Muffin lived in a world of grandiose ideas going wrong. *Our* world, in fact. And his New Year's resolution for 1949, at the height of the Berlin Air Lift, was a voice crying in the wilderness: 'Be Kind to Humans'.

Very few people, anywhere, were being kind to humans. If the Thirties had been the Decade of Escape, then for sure the Forties had been the Decade of No Escape. We were about to enter a new decade in which those of us who were under forty felt an irrational optimism, stopped grumbling, learned to live with insecurity and to 'love the Bomb'.

One young man in the world stood apart. In 1949 Garry Davis, son of a bandleader and an ex-bomber pilot, camped out on the doorstep of the United Nations and then held meetings in Paris at which he said the world would never be any better until nationhood was abolished. Russia and America were both to blame, all great powers were aggressive; the first step to peace was the abolition of passports, and to make his point he publicly tore up his own American passport. President Auriol courteously invited him to stay in France as long as he liked without a passport. André Gide and Albert Camus were among several writers who declared their support of Davis's ideals. Davis received hundreds of letters from people who wrote things like 'You must be Christ returned.'

Davis then wandered through France calling upon towns and villages to vote for world citizenship. One village that responded was Trouillas, in the foothills of the Pyrenees, 17 miles from Perpignan. From my office at the magazine I was then working on in London I telephoned the Mayor, M. Gaston Méric: could I come and interview him? 'No. The press always make fun of us. Come and stay if you like, but no interview.' I took a chance and went, taking with me the art editor, an outstanding illustrator named Edgar Ainsworth. Trouillas turned out to be a community of eleven hundred souls which made nothing but wine and espadrilles. We reached it by the twice-daily bus from Perpignan. The driver, a gnarled old Spaniard named Joseph Fabrégas, knew why we had come. He was a refugee from the Spanish Civil War, like many people in Trouillas, and he was the leader of the local Garry Davis movement.

Nobody spoke to us for several days, and when they did, it was in Catalan, not French. Ainsworth set up his easel and painted. People came to watch. Then farm workers returning from the fields silently dropped gifts of fruit in his hat. We were accepted. We called on the Mayor, a knotty, nut-brown peasant with shrewd humour in his eyes. I was not surprised to learn that he had been a link in Escape Line Comet, which had smuggled hundreds of escaped British and American airmen out of Occupied France into Spain, guiding them over the Pyrenees. (So I stumbled on a second story.) Méric showed me a document of which I have, to this day, the only carbon copy: 'We declare the commune of Trouillas world territory. . . .' Garry Davis had moved on into, as it turned out, oblivion. 'After Gandhi was killed, we turned to Garry Davis,' Méric said. 'Maybe he's a nut, but he's what we need. Well, Governments are not good, are they?'

We stayed a fortnight, helped with the wine harvest, drank far too much. In the Decade of No Escape, we had, for two weeks, escaped.

I had a friend in Fleet Street who specialized in 'back page stories', tiny events and insanities which, flung together, produced a distorting mirror of a day, a year, a decade. Let us try it with the Forties.

January 1940. In the days when British censorship was so complete that you had to read American and Swiss newspapers to find out what was happening, *Life* magazine confirmed that nothing was happening. 'War does not interest the English,' its London correspondent reported irritably. 'They talk too much.' A feature in the same issue: 'Old Art of Rug Hooking Revived by Party-Loving Southern Women.' It had all been started by Mrs Harry King, of Beebe, Arkansas. Now whatever happened to her? Or to the baby boy advertising toilet paper under the slogan, 'I'm on a sit-down strike till Mom gets Delsey? He must be rising forty now.

June 1946. I am just out of uniform. In the Strand I meet a friend whom I haven't seen for eight years. I shoot out my right hand to grasp his: I encounter nothing, his right arm has been shot off. I meet another man who greets me: I don't recognize his face, only his voice: he has a new nose, chin, left ear, eyelids, lips, given him after twenty-six operations by Archibald McIndoe the plastic surgeon; his plane was brewed up. It's difficult to tell, but I think he is smiling.

Was there really a song called 'God Bless You, Mr Chamberlain'? A rumour in 1948 that Noël Coward was going to marry Princess Marina, widowed when her husband's plane crashed six years before? A man accused of selling rhubarb without a licence: he only had a licence for vegetables, and rhubarb was, in law, a fruit? . . . What did the Duke of Windsor and Leopold of Belgium talk about when the two exiles played golf together on the Riviera?

There was a time when El Qantara transit station on the Suez Canal had ten lavatories – for Officers (European, Asiatic, Coloured); Warrant Officers and Sergeants (European, Asiatic, Coloured); Other Ranks/Enlisted Men (European, Asiatic, Coloured); and Women's Services (ATS, WACs, WRNS, etc., apparently of any colour, race or creed). Americans, you observe, are Europeans; otherwise, all in order?

No: the planners, who had obviously never served in India, forgot that Hindus and Muslims never used the same loos.

'I believe America to be the hope of the world and I wish my children to grow up in a land of liberal thought.' Who said it? Bertrand Russell, at U.C.L.A., California. Almost immediately he was invited to lecture on philosophy at City College, Manhattan, only to find himself up against Episcopal Bishop Manning, who pronounced the thrice-divorced agnostic 'morally unfit to teach'.

What keeps people going in times of great adversity? Faith, hope, courage, oh yes; but also tobacco, drink, betting and colour. Churchill knew this. Almost the only colour Britain had was flowers, and most cut flowers came from the Scilly Isles. In the autumn of 1942, as the battles for Alamein and Stalingrad and Guadalcanal were being fought, the transport authorities suddenly cancelled the flower trains which, miraculously, still ran to London from Cornwall. In revolt, the flower growers boarded ordinary passenger trains, filling the corridors with baskets of flowers, standing all the way if necessary, and took them to market. When spring came again, Churchill personally ordered the flower trains to be reinstated. This was the same instinct for public morale that made him order the Rock of Gibraltar to be restocked with apes, for there was a legend that if ever the apes left the Rock, the Rock would cease to be British. So, to this day, there is an Officer-in-charge-of-Apes (usually a Major of the Royal Artillery).

All things matter. One of T.S. Eliot's contributions to the Forties was *Notes Towards a Definition of Culture*. Culture, he said, includes 'dog races, boiled cabbage . . . and the music of Elgar'. Keep the regional, keep the conflict of ideas: international unity of culture would kill culture altogether. For him, the Dark Ages were round the corner. Are we in them now? Will someone in A.D. 2008 write a nostalgic book about the Seventies? Probably, if the editors of *Esquire* magazine are any guide. In October 1971 they turned back to their scandalous youth, complete with a pull-out Petty pin-up, and these words: 'Welcome back to the 40s: the last time America was happy.'

☆ ILLUSTRATION ACKNOWLEDGMENTS ☆

Associated Newspapers Group Ltd: 21 (*above*)

B.B.C. Copyright Photograph: 206, 212, 214, 215, 217 (*both*)

Courtesy Beaverbrook Newspapers: 201

Bell, Book and Radmall: 194, 197 (three)

The Bettmann Archive Inc.: 8, 34, 72, 82, 95, 96, 147, 210

British Lion: 108–9

Camera Press Ltd: 177

Courtesy William Collins Sons & Co. Ltd: 164 (*below*), caricature illustration from *Pont*, by Bernard Hollowood, 1969

Covent Garden Archives, the Royal Opera House: 85, 86

Daily Mail, London: 12, 202, 218

Photograph by Dominic: 86

EMI Film Distributors Ltd: 117

The Hamlyn Group: 173

Courtesy the Harvard Theatre Collection, photograph by Angus McBean: 85

John Hadfield Collection: 37 (*below*), Fox Photos Ltd

The Imperial War Museum: endpapers, frontispiece, 13, 19, 20, 21 (*below*), 22, 23, 25, 33, 37 (*above*), 38, 39, 43, 45, 88, 89, 167, 169, 174–5, 175

Keystone Press Agency Ltd: 18, 26–7

The Raymond Mander and Joe Mitchenson Theatre Collection: 76 (*left*), 79 (*both*), 80, 108–9, 149, 150, 151, 152, 153, 154, 157, 158, 159, 160 (*both*), 161, 216

From the MGM release *Mrs Miniver* © 1942 Loew's Incorporated. Copyright renewed 1969 by Metro-Goldwyn-Mayer Inc: 104; from the MGM release *National Velvet* © 1944 Loew's Incorporated. Copyright renewed 1971 by Metro-Goldwyn-Mayer Inc: 99

The National Film Archives: 78, 97 (*above right*), 99, 104, 106, 107, 110 (*both*), 110–11, 112, 113, 114–15, 116, 117, 119

The National Motor Museum, Beaulieu, Brockenhurst, Hampshire: 138 (*both*), 139

The Radio Times Hulton Picture Library: 6, 10, 15, 17, 24, 46–7, 51, 54, 56, 58, 60, 61, 67, 90, 91 (*above*), 92 (*both*), 93 (*below right*), 94 (*both*), 97 (*below left*), 101, 121 (*both*), 125, 126, 127, 128–9, 130, 133, 141, 162, 186, 188, 195

Reproduced by kind permission of the Rank Organisation: 106, 107, 113, 119

Samuel Goldwyn Productions: 116

Mr and Mrs A.G. Sanders: 197 (*above right*)

The Tate Gallery, London: reverse of frontispiece, 164 (*above*), 166, 168, 171

United Press International, Inc.: 35, 40, 41, 42, 48, 65, 74–5, 76 (*right*), 77 (*both*), 84, 93 (*above left*), 98, 102, 122–3, 128, 211

Walt Disney Productions: 110 (*below*)

Collection Mrs Agnes Whitaker: 14, 36, 91 (*below*), 172

✪ INDEX ✪

Page numbers given in *italics* indicate illustrations

Acheson, Dean, 69, 148
Adenauer, Konrad, 134
advertising, 176, 210
Agar, Herbert, 62, 64
Air Raids (Battle of Britain, the Blitz), *11*, *12*, *23*, 48–9, *50*, 63, 132; news reports of, 11–12; way-of-life during, 22–5; on Café de Paris, 44, 73; on Buckingham Palace, 52; and theatre, 151, 155; *see also* bombs
air travel, 140–4
Alamein, (El), Battle of, 29, 46, 136; film on, 106
alcoholic beverages, 38, 41, 81
Aldeburgh Festival, 55
Alexander, A.V., 147
Ambrose, 73
America, *see* United States
American Legion, 145
American Veterans Committee, 145
Amery, John, 209
Anderson, Lale, 81
Andrews Sisters, 81
Animal Farm (Orwell), 60, *197*
Antheil, George, 87
Anzio, Battle of, 30
Appiah, Joe, 70
Apple Sauce, 73
Arab nations, 131–2
architecture, 173, *175*
Ardennes offensive (Battle of the Bulge), 33–4, 148
Armstrong, Louis, 82
Armstrong-Jones, Antony, 56
Arnhem, Battle of, 33
Arnold-Foster, Mark, 28
Arsenic and Old Lace (Kesselring), 159
art and artists, 165–77 *passim*
Asch, Sholem, 192
Ashton, Frederick, 86
athletics, 130
Attlee, Clement, 41, 53, 58, *65*, 66, 147
atom bomb, 64, 66, 144, 146–7, 180, 205, 220–1
Atomic Energy Commission, 146
Atomic Weapons Research Establishment, 147
ATS (Auxiliary Territorial Service), 43, 52, 107
Attenborough, Richard, 109

Auden, W.H., 197
'Austerity', 69, 185
automobiles, 137, 138, *138*, *139*

Babington-Smith, Constance, 32
Bacall, Lauren, 115
Bacon, Francis, 170
Baker, Bonnie, 73
Baker, George, 200
Balchin, Nigel, 192
Balcon, Michael, 117
ballet, 86–7, 219–20; choreography, 156
Barber, Chris, 83
Barbirolli, Sir John, 85
Barnes, Dr (Bishop of Birmingham), 179
Barnet, Charlie, 75
Barrault, Jean Louis, 118
Barton, Bruce, 139
baseball, 122
Basie, Count, 73
Bataan, 112
Bax, Sir Arnold, 87
'Beachcomber', *see* Morton, J.B.
Beaton, Cecil, 56, *175*, 177
Beaufort, Duke of, 57
Beaverbrook, Lord, 36, 61, *61*, 202
Beck, Martha, 186–7
Beebe, Lucius, 43
Beecham, Sir Thomas, 85
Behrman, S.N., 12
Beinum, Van, 85
Belden, Jack, 202, 203
Benson, Ivy, 73
Bentley, Elizabeth, 144–5
Bergman, Ingrid, 93, 115, 118
Berle, Milton, 219
Berlin: capture of, 34–5; Airlift, 132–4, *133*, 207, 220
Berlin, Irving, 41, 43, 81, 112, 155, 156
Bernadotte, Count (of Sweden), 132
Bernhard, Prince, 50
Bernstein, Leonard, 85
Best Years of Our Lives, The, 115, *116*
Bevan, Aneurin, 61
Bevin, Ernest, 69, 133, 147, 185; Bevin Boys, 70; and Israel, 132
Bicycle Thieves, 118
Big Sleep, The, 115
Bing, Rudolf, 87

Black, George, 151
blackouts, 14, 27, 36, 177
Blankers-Koen, Fanny, 130, *130*
Bliss, Arthur, 86
Blithe Spirit (Coward), 159, *159*
Blitz, the, *see* Air Raids
Bogart, Humphrey, 105, 115
Bohr, Niels, 184
bombs, 22; unexploded, 12, *21*; incendiary, 12; land mines, 12–13; shelters from, 22–3, *23*; bomb-boasting, 25; buzz-bomb (VI), 32, *33*, 49, 180; Katyusha (Russian) 113; *see also* atom bomb
Bong, Major Richard, 48
Bonhoeffer, Dietrich, 179
Borah, William E., 13
Borden, Lizzie, 187
Borge, Victor, 43
Bowen, Elizabeth, 196
Bowlly, Al, 76
boxing, 127
Bradley, General Omar, 30, 32
Brando, Marlon, 163
Brandt, Bill, 177
Brecht, Bertolt, 81, 162
Brick, Charity, *18*
Brief Encounter, 118
Britain, Battle of, *see* Air Raids
Britten, Benjamin, 55, 86, 199
British Broadcasting Corporation (B.B.C.), 11, 16, 23, 78, 81; Symphony, 85; soap operas, 153, 211, 218; light entertainment, 207–8, 212–13; quiz and panel games, 214–16; reorganized 216; *see also* propaganda, radio
Brook, Peter, 86
Brooke, Rupert, 48–9, 199
Brooke-Popham, Air Chief Marshal, 29
Browder, Earl, 144
Brown, Joe E., 156, 161
Brown, Les ('Band of Renown'), 75
Browne, Sam, 76
Buckingham Palace, 12, 35, 51; bombed, 52; wedding reception at, 53
Bulge, Battle of the, *see* Ardennes offensive
bull-fighting, 128
Bunche, Ralph, 132
Burma, 105; World War II in, 29

227

Burns, Tito, 83
Butler, Nicholas Murray, 146

Café de Paris, 44, 73
Cagney, James, 105
Campaign for Nuclear Disarmament, 147
Campbell, Judy, 79
capital punishment, 190
Capote, Truman, 196
Capp, Al, 201
Carousel, 156
Carter, Ernestine, 100
cartoons, *see* comic strips; wartime, 21
Casablanca, 115, *114–15*
Casson, Lewis, 155, 161
C.E.M.A. (Council for the Encouragement
    of Music and the Arts), 155
censorship: newspaper, 22, 25; of songs, 79;
    in films, 116–17, 118; of radio, 207
Chamberlain, Neville, 14, 22, 208
Chambers, Whittaker, 147–8
Chapman, Eddie, 49
Chaplin, Charles, 118–19
Charles, Prince, 55–6, *56*
Chase, Ilka, 192
Chase, James Hadley, 199
Chennault, Colonel Clair, 135
Chiang Kai-shek, 28, 29, 135
China: World War II in, 29, 70, 71; goes
    Communist, 132, 135, 146
Choltitz, General von, 33
Christie, Agatha, 199
Chuikov, General, 31
Churchill, Winston, 27, 35, 52, 65, *92*, 92,
    176, 180, 221; and Home Guard, 22; and
    Singapore, 29; at Yalta, *34*, 34; after the
    war, *60*, 61–2, 68; and Truman, 64;
    Speeches, 208, 210
C.I.A. (Central Intelligence Agency), 146
Ciardi, John, 199
cinema, *see* film industry
Citizen Kane, 109, *110–11*
Civil Aviation Act, 142
Clark, Sir Kenneth, 165
Clark, General Mark, 30
Clark, Tom C., 145
Clarke, T.E.B., 117
Clay, General Lucius, 133
Clifford, Clark, 134
Clift, Montgomery, 97, 161
clothing, *see* fashion, rationing
Cochran, Charles B., 156, 159
Cocktail Party, The (Eliot), 161–2
Cocteau, Jean, 118
Cohen, Mickey, 190
Colby, Anita, 98
Cold War, 66
Cole, Nat King, 76, *78*
Coleman, Blanche, 73
comic strips, cartoons, 27, *164*, 200–1, *202*
Como, Perry, 76
Compton, Denis, 124
computer technology, 184
concentration camps, 62, 186

Condon, Eddie, 82
Connolly, Cyril, 165, 205
Cook, Thomas (holidays), 140
Cooke, Alistair, 135, 207
Cooper, Gary, 145
Coral Sea, Battle of the, 29
Costello, Frank, 190
Cotten, Joseph, 118–19
Cotton, Billy, 73
Coudenhove-Kalergi, Count, 18
'Countess Mara' ties, 103
Covent Garden, 86–7, 219
Coward, Noël, 78, *108*, 108–9, 118, 159,
    215, 221
Cowles, Fleur and Gardner, 205
Crawford, Joan, 116
Crawford, Marion (Crawfie), 52
Crazy Gang, 151
cricket, 124
crime and criminals, 44, 185–91 *passim*
Cripps, Sir Stafford, 69, 81, 137, 175, 185
Crosby, Bing, 75, 81, 109, *110*
Culbertson, Ely, 18
Cunningham, John 'Cat's Eyes', 36–7, 142
Currie, Lauchlan, 144

D-Day, *see* France, invasion of
Dali, Salvador, 86
Dalton, Dr Hugh, 69, 91, 117, 175, 185
Damone, Vic, 76
dancing, in wartime, 25
Daniels, Bebe, *see* Lyons, Bebe
Dare, Zena and Phyllis, 154
Darkness at Noon (Koestler), 196
Davies, Joseph E., 113
Davis, Garry, 220–1
Davis, Miles, 83
Davison, Wild Bill, 82
Day, Doris, 75
Death of a Salesman (Miller), 163
debutantes, 98
Deep Blue Sea, The (Rattigan), 63, 163
de Havilland, Sir Geoffrey, 142
de Havilland, Olivia, 116
de Mille, Agnes, 156
demobilization, 60–1, 62
Dempsey, General, 32
Dennis, Denny, 76
Dennis, Nigel, 196
Desert Victory, 106
desertion and deserters, 66
De Sica, Vittorio, 117, 118
Dessés, Jean, 55
devaluation of currency, 69, 117
Dewey, Tom, 134–5, 190
Dickens, Charles, 118
Dickson, Lovat, 49
Dies Committee, 105
Dietrich, Marlene, 43
Di Maggio, Joe, 122, *122*
Dimbleby, Richard, 214
Dior, Christian, 55, 98, 100
Disney, Walt, 109, *110*
Displaced Persons, *see* refugees

Divine, Father, 180
Doenitz, Admiral Karl, 34
Dolgun, Alexander, 81
Donat, Robert, 105, 112
Donovan, General 'Wild Bill', 146
Dors, Diana, *96*, 97, 117
Dorsey, Tommy and Jimmy, 73, 75
Douglas, Lloyd C., 192
Douglas, Sharman, 53, 55, 98
Douglas-Home, William, 161
drugs, 83, 182
Du Bois, Dr W.E.B., 70
du Maurier, Daphne, 194
Dulles, Allen, 146
Dunkirk, evacuation of, 18, *18*, 28, 46
Durbin, Deanna, 109

Eagle Squadron, 46
Ebert, Carl, 86
Eckstine, Billy, 76
Ede, Chuter, 55
Edinburgh, Prince Philip, Duke of, 52–3,
    101; wedding of, 53–5
Edrich, Bill, 124
education, wartime, 16–17; university, 146
Edwards, Jimmy, 103, *215*
Eisenhower, General D.D., 32–5, 48, 62,
    134, 146
Eliot, T.S., 161–2, 199, 222
Elizabeth, Princess (later Elizabeth II), 57,
    100, *101*; during wartime, 51–2; wedding
    of, 53–4; birth of children, 55
Elizabeth, Queen, 12, 35, 50–2, *51*, 128
Ellington, Duke, 73, 76, 82
Enfants du Paradis, Les, 118
E.N.S.A. (Entertainments National Service
    Association), 153
Epstein, Jacob, 165
Erhardt, Ludwig, 134
Ernst, Max, 166, 169
espionage: German, 18, 22; British, 49,
    145, 146; Russian, 144–6; American,
    144–5, 146–7
evacuation, *14*, 16–17, *17*, 57; of pets, 16
Evans, Geraint, 87
Existentialism, 179

Fairbanks, Douglas (Sr), 14
Falkenburg, Bob, 98, 126
Falkenburg, Jinx, 98, 126
Falling through Space (Hillary), 48
Farjeon, Herbert, 151
fashion: wartime, 39, 88–100 *passim*, *91*, *92*,
    93, *94*; New Look, 53; designers, 55;
    men's, 100–1, 103
Fath, Jacques, 100
Faye, Gloria, 73
Fergusson, Bernard, 29
Fernandez, Raymond, 186
Ferrier, Kathleen, 86
Field, Sid, 159
Fields, Gracie, 73, 81, 140, 219
film industry (cinema), 105–19 *passim*
Finland; invasion of, 13, 28

Fisher, Eddie, 76
Fitzgerald, Ella, 75
Fitzgerald, F. Scott, 105
Flagstad, Kirsten, 87
Flynn, Errol, 105, 115
Fonteyn, Margot, 86, 220
food and drink, *see* rationing
football, 120–2
Forester, C.S., 194
Forever Amber (Winsor), 192
For Whom the Bell Tolls, 93, 195
Foss, Captain, Joe, 48
Franklin, Sidney, 128
France; fall of, 14, 28, 50; Free-French, 25,
    33, 44; D-Day invasion, 31–4, 49; films
    from, 118; radio in, 209–10
Freedom at Midnight, 58
Freeman, Bud, 82
Fresnay, Pierre, 118
Freyberg, General, 30
Frost, Robert, 199
Fry, C.B., 124
Fry, Christopher, 161
Fuchs, Dr Klaus, 144
Fürtwangler, Wilhelm, 85

Gable, Clark, 115, *138*
Gabreski, Francis, 48
Gail, Zoë, 81, *81*
Gandhi, Mahatma, 58–9
Gang Busters, 13, 211
Gardner, Ava, 97, *97*
Garland, Judy, 75
Garson, Greer, 93, 105
gas and gas masks, 14
Gehlen, Lieutenant-General Reinhard, 146
George VI, King, 12, 35, 132; during
    wartime, 50–2, *51*; and racing, 128
Germany: during World War II, 28–35,
    57, 62; 'pastoralization' proposed, 65;
    under occupation, 70–1, 132–4, 193
'G.I. Brides', 62
Gielgud, John, 112, 154
Gillespie, Dizzy, 82, *82*
Gingold, Hermione, *152*, 153
Girier, René, 190
Girls of Slender Means, The (Spark), 68
Girodias, Maurice, 170
Glass Menagerie, The (Williams), 163
Glyndebourne Festival, 86–7
Goddard, Paulette, 93
Godfrey, Arthur, 210, 212
Godse, Nathuram, 59
Goebbels, Josef, 31, 78, 81
Goering, Herman, 70, 81
Gold, Harry (Heinrich Golodnitsky), 144
golf, 120
Golos, Jacob, 144
Gone With the Wind, 105
Goodman, Benny, 73, 83, 156
Gould, Bruce and Beatrice, 203
Grable, Betty, 94, *95*, 97, 109
Grace, W.G., 124
Graf Spee, 14

Graham, Dr Billy, 180
Granger, Stewart, 115
Grant, Rupert, 83
Great Britain: German invasion plans,
    11–12; relations with U.S.A., 46–7, 131,
    185, 207; demobilization in, 60–1, 62
Greece, Communism in, 68
Green, Rev. Bryan, 180
Greene, Graham, 118, 159, 195
Groundnuts Scheme (Overseas Food
    Corporation), 69–70
Guadalcanal, 30
Gubbins, Nat, 205
Guétary, Georges, 159
Guggenheim, Peggy, 166–9, 173
Guinness, Alec, 118, 155
Gumpert, Dr Martin, 182–3

Haakon, King (of Norway), 50
Haigh, John George, 187, *188*, 188–9
Hamm. Jeffrey, 132
Hammerstein II, Oscar, 156
Hammond, Walter, 124
Handley, Tommy, 207, *212*, 213
Harewood, Lord, 55
Hart, Lorenz, 155
Harvey, 159, 161
Haskins, Minnie, 50
Haw Haw, Lord *see* Joyce, William
Hay, Will, 105
Hayworth, Rita, 98, *98*
Health Service and medicine, 181–4
Hearst, William Randolph, 202
Heath, Neville, 187, 189
Heath, Ted (bandleader), 73
Helpmann, Robert, 86, *86*, 118
Hemingway, Ernest, 32, 128, 193, 195, *195*
Henke, Pfc Milburn, 44
Henry IV (play), 155
Henry V (film), 112, *113*
Herbert, A.P., 156
Herblock, 201
Herman, Woody, 73, 81
Hersey, John, 64, 193, 205
Hill, Dr Charles (Radio Doctor), 36, 176,
    183, *214*
Hillary, Richard, 48–9
Hindu religion, 58–9
Hiroshima, 30, 35, 62, 64, 71, 134
Hiroshima (Hersey), 193, 205
Hirschmann, Ira A., 83
Hiss, Alger, *147*, 147–8
Hitchcock, Alfred, 109
Hitler, Adolf, 57, 142, 179, 205; strategy of,
    11–12, 28; and Russia, 31; orders Paris
    destroyed, 33; suicide of, 34
Hobbs, Jack, 124
Hocking, William Ernest, 178
Hogan, Ben, 120
Hokinson, Helen, 14, 27
Hollywood, witch hunt in, 105, 145–6; *see
    also* film industry
Home Guard, *21*, 22, 203

Homma, General, 29
Hoover, Herbert, 13
Hope, Bob, 73, 109, *110*
Hopkins, Harry, 62
Horizon Holidays, 140
Horne, Lena, 75, *77*
horse-racing, 128–9
housing shortages, 63
Howard, Leslie, 52, 106, *106*
Hughes, Howard, 113, 142
Hulton, Edward, 203
Hume, Donald, 187, 189
Huston, John, 49, 115
Huxley, Julian, 178, 184, 214
Hylton, Jack, 137

India, independence for, 58–9
Ingersoll, Ralph, 203
Ingham's Holidays, 140
internment, 22, 27
Intrator, Max, 185
In Which We Serve, *108*, 108–9
Ironside, Janey, 100
Israel, 131–2
Issigonis, Alec, 139
Italy: World War II in, 30–1; films in,
    117, 118
ITMA (It's That Man Again), 213
Ives, Burl, 83
Iwo Jima, 30

Jamaica Inn, 105
James, Harry, 81
Japan, 62; war objectives, 27–8, 30; defeat,
    35, 64–5, 70; rehabilitation of, 71
Jeffers, Robinson, 199
Jenkins, Alan, 50, 136–7
Jews: refugees, 63, 66; in Israel, 131–2; in
    the army, 178
Jinnah (Muslim Leader), 58–9
John, Augustus, 165
Johns, Glynis, 97
Johnson, Bunk, 82
Jolson, Al, 13
Jones, Spike, 81
journalism, 200–5; newspaper, 200–2;
    magazine, 202–3, 205
Joyce, James, 194
Joyce, William (Lord Haw Haw), 186,
    208–9, 213

Kaiser, Henry, 41, 113
Karajan, Herbert von, 85
Karas, Anton, 87
Kaye, Danny, 55, 103, 162, *162*
Kazan, Elia, 163
Keeler, Ruby, 13
Kent, Duke of, 52, 57
Kenton, Stan, 82
Kelland, Clarence Budington, 18
Kennan, George, C., 66
Kenyatta, Jomo, 70
Kesselring, Field Marshal, 30–1
Kesselring, Joseph, 159

Keyes, Sidney, 199
Keynes, Maynard, 68
Khama, Seretse, 70
Khomich, 121–2
Kilroy, Francis J., 46
Kinsey Report, 156, 184
Knight, Eric, 192
Koestler, Arthur, 48, 131, 196
Korda, Alexander, 105, 118
Korean War, 135
Koussevitzky, Serge, 85, 86
Kramer, Jack, 125–6
Krupa, Gene, 83
Kubelik, Rafael, 85

Laine, Frankie, 76
Lake, Veronica, 93
Lamour, Dorothy, 93, 109, *110*, 211
Langford, Francis, 73
Last Enemy, The (Hillary), 48, 49
Last Tycoon, The (Fitzgerald), 105
Laughton, Charles, 105, 162
Laver, James, 100
Lawrence, Gertrude, 43
Lawrence, T.E., 48, 137, 196
Lawton, Tommy, 121–2, *121*
Leadbelly, 83
Leahy, Admiral, 64
Lean, David, 118
Leclerc, General, 33
Lee, Peggy, 75, *76*
Lehár, Franz, 87
Leigh, Vivien, 112, *112*, 118, 163
Lelong, Lucien, 98, 100
Leningrad, 31, 178
Lerner, Alan J., 156
Lewis, C.S., 179
Liberty ships, 41, *41*, 43
Lifeboat, 109
Life magazine, 14, 98
'Lili Marlene', 81
Linklater, Eric, 48
Linden Tree, The (Priestley), *160*, 161
literature, 192–9; classics, 194; fiction,
   192–4, 195–6; history, 194; poetry,
   197–9; thrillers, 199
Litvak, Anatole, 116
Lockwood, Margaret, 97, 115
Loesser, Frank, 79
Loewe, Frederick, 156
Lomax, John and Alan, 83
Lone Ranger, 13, 211
Long, Huey, 148
Lord, Leonard, 139
Loss, Joe, 73
Louis, Joe, 112, 127, *127*
Low, David, 201, *201*, 220
Lowell, Robert, 199
Lunceford, Jimmy, 81
Lynn, Vera, 73, *76*, 79
Lyon, Ben and Bebe, *206*, 207
Lysenko, Trofim, 184
Lyttelton, Humphrey, 83

MacArthur, General Douglas, 29, 71
McCarthy, Joseph, 145, 148
McCarthy, Mary, 196
McCullers, Carson, 196, 197
McNarney, General, 71
MacNeice, Louis, 199
Mailer, Norman, 193–4
Maltese Falcon, The, 115
Man is Obsolete (Cousins), 180
Man Who Came To Dinner, The, 151
Mao Tse-tung, 135
Margaret Rose, Princess, 55, *55*, 98, 100,
   140
Marianas, invasion of, 30
Marina, Princess, 57, 221
Maritain, Jacques, 178
Marquand, John P., 192
Marshall, General, 135
Marshall Plan, 68–9
Marten, C.H.K., 52
Martin, Glenn L., 141
Martin, Kingsley, 25
Martin, Mary, *154*, 159
Marx, Groucho, 41
Mary, Queen, 53, 56–7
Maschwitz, Eric, 79
Masefield, John, 50
Maskelyne, Jasper, 165
Mason, Herbert, *12*, 13
Mason, James, 115, *116*
Matthews, Stanley, 121–2, *121*
Maugham, Somerset *169*, 196
Mauldin, Bill, 200
Maxwell, Elsa, 98
Maxwell-Fyfe, Sir David, 70
medicine and health, 181–4
Meegeren, Hans van, 177
Melachrino, George, 73
Melville, Alan, 151
Menjou, Adolph, 145
Mencken, H.L., 194, 203
Menotti, Gian Carlo, 87
Merman, Ethel, 43, 156, 173
Metcalfe, 'Fruity', 57
Metropolitan Opera, 87
Michael (of Kent), Prince, 57
Midway, Battle of, 28, 29–30
Milestone, Lewis, 109
Milland, Ray, 118
Miller, Arthur, 163
Miller, Glenn, 73, *73*, 75, 85
Miller, Jonathan, 17
Mission to Moscow (Davies), 113
Mrs Miniver, 93, *104*, 105, 112
Mitford, Nancy, 197
Mix, Tom, 14
model girls (mannequins), 98
Molyneux, 55
Monk, Thelonius, 83
Montagu, Judy, 55
Montagu, William Pepperell,
   178
Monte Cassino, Battle of, 30
Montgomery, Field Marshal, Bernard, 29,
   30, 71, 81, 146–7, 165, 176; and D-Day,
   31–2, 33–5
Montgomery, Robert, 145
Moore, Henry, 165, 170, 177
Moore, Marianne, 199
Moorehead, Alan, 30, 140, 165, 202
moral beliefs, 178–80, 211
Morgenthau, Henry (Jr), 65
Morley, Robert, 151
Morrison, Herbert, 147
Morton, J.B. ('Beachcomber'), 205
Moscow: Germans attack, 31
Moses 'Grandma', 173
Mosley, Sir Oswald, 63, 69, 132
Mountbatten, Edwina, Countess, *58*, 58–9
Mountbatten, Louis, Earl (of Burma),
   57–8, *58*, 59, 108, 180
Mueller, Edwin, 191
Muir, Frank, 216, 218
Mulberry Ports, 32, 180
Munch, Charles, 85
Munich Agreement, 14–15
Murphy, Audie, *48*, 48–9
Murrow, Ed., 11, 12, 207, 219
music: calypso, 83; classical, 84–5; jazz, 73,
   82–3, 219; opera, *85*, 86–7; popular, 73–81
Muslim religion, 58–9, 83
Mussolini, Benito, 30, 87

NAAFI, 43
Nagasaki, 35, 64, 71
Naked and the Dead, The (Mailer), 193–4, *194*
National Service conscripts, 70–1
Nationalization: of coal, 67; of air
   transport, 142; of steel, 132; of sugar,
National Velvet, 97, *99*
Neel, Edric, 63
Nehru, Jawaharal, 58–9
New Faces, 79
New Look, 53, 100, *101*
Nimitz, Admiral, 30
1984 (Nineteen eighty-four, Orwell), 60, 66,
   131, 197
Niven, David, 107, 115
Nixon, Richard, M., 147–8, 201
Nkrumah, Kwame, 70
Norden, Dennis, 216, 218
Normandy invasion, *see* France, D-Day
   invasion
North Africa: World War II in, 29, 52
Norway: an ally, 50; occupied, 28
Notes towards a Definition of Culture (Eliot),
   222
Novello, Ivor, 79, 137, 153–4, 159
Now Barabbas . . . (Douglas-Home), 161
Nuremberg trials, 65, 70, 199

Oakes, Harry, 57–8
Oberon, Merle, 105
Oberammergau Passion Play, 179
Obolensky, Lance Corporal Prince
   Nicholas, 137
O'Hara, John, 195–6
Okinawa, 30

Oklahoma!, 155–6, *157*, 159
Old Vic Company, 154–5
Oliver, Vic, 207
Olivier, Laurence, 112, *112*, *113*, 118, 148, *150*, 154–5, 162
Olympic Games, 120, 130
On The Town (Bernstein), 85
Oppenheimer, Robert J., 144, 180
Orwell, George, 60, 66, 195–6, 197
Ory, Kid, 82
Overseas Food Corporation, *see* Groundnuts Scheme

Pacific, war in the, 27–9, 30, 47
Paige, Satchel, 124
Pakistan, 58–9
Pan-African Conference, 70
Panter-Downes, Mollie, 92, 202
Paris, 57; liberation of, 32–3
Parker, Charlie, 82
Patrick, Ted, 203
Patton, General George, 30, 32–3, 178, 200
Paulus, General Von, 31
Pearl Harbor, 18, 27, 27–8, 29, 46, 64
Pearson, Drew, 205
Peenemünde, 32, 146, 180
Pegler, Westbrook, 205
Pelletier, Vincent, 11
Persia (Iran), war in, 28
Peters, Dr Bernard, 144
Peterson, Oscar, 83
Petiot, Dr Marcel, 186
Philip, Prince, *see* Edinburgh, Duke of
Philippines, Battles for, 29–30
Phoney War, 13, 17, 28, 51, 57
photography, 176–7
Piaf, Edith, 87
Picasso, Pablo, 170
Pickles, Wilfred, 216, *217*
Piggott, Lester, 129
Piper, John, 86, 165
Plummer, Sir Leslie, 70
Poland and Poles; invasion of, 13, 28; as allies, 44; in U.S.A., 64
Pollock, Jackson, 166, 169
Pons, Lily, 32
Porter, Cole, 81, 156, 173, 211
Potsdam Conference, *65*, 66
Potter, Stephen, 196, 216
Pound, Ezra, 199
PQ.17, 28–9
Present Laughter (Coward), 159
Priestley, J.B., 11, 18, 86, *160*, 161, 214
propaganda: allied, 42, 112, 177, 210; German, 208–9; radio, 207–8, 211–12
psychiatry: during wartime, 49, 182; on film, 116

Queen, Ellery, 199
Quisling, Vidkun, 87

race relations, 57–8, 70, 124
radar, 16, 37, 134
Radio: during World War II, 11–12, 23, 78, 207–8, 209–13, *210*, *214*; in U.S.A. 13, 18, 79; news broadcasts, 213–15. *See also* B.B.C. propaganda
Radio Doctor, *see* Hill, Dr Charles
R.A.F. (Royal Air Force), 22, 32, 36, 49, 50, 63; Eagle Squadron, 46
railways, 140–1
Rainbow Corner (Lyons), 6, 46, *46–7*, 75
Randolph, Nancy, 53
Rank, J. Arthur, 97, 117
Rankl, Karl, 86
rationing and shortages, *endpapers*, 36, *37*, *38*, 60–1, 146, 200; batteries, 16; in Britain, 36–8, 68, 100; in the U.S.A. 39–41, 68, 92; of alcohol, 38, 41, 81; of clothes, 39, 88, 91–2; of petrol, 136–8; post-war, 69
Rattigan, Terence, 63, 162–3
Ray, Johnny, 76
Rayburn, Sam, 64
Read, Dr Grantly, Dick, 182
Reagan, Ronald, 112, 145
record companies, 83
Red Badge of Courage, The (film), 49
Reed, Carol, 117, 118
Reed, Henry, 199
refugees (Displaced Persons), 66
religious beliefs, 178–80
Remington, William, 144, 145
Richards, Gordon, 129, *129*
Richardson, Sir Ralph, 105, *149*, 154–5, 161
Rickenbacker, Eddie, 48
Ritchie, Captain L.A., 52
Robinson, Sugar Ray, 127, *128*
Roc, Patricia, 97, *97*, 115
Rodgers, Richard, 155
Rogers, Roy, 81
Rogers, Will, 81
Roller Derby, 127
Rommel, Erwin, 28–9, 81
Roosevelt, Eleanor, 46, 52, 64
Roosevelt, F.D., 14, 27, 62, 65, 132; and Churchill, 46; and Pearl Harbor, 27; at Yalta, 34, *34*, 148; death of, 47–8, 64
Ross, Alan, 25
Rossellini, Roberto, 117, 118
Rouault, Georges, 170
Rouff, Maggy, 98
Rous, Sir Stanley, 121
Russell, Bertrand, 221
Russell, Jane, 113
Russia, and atomic power, 146; art, in, 165; during World War II, 28, 31, 34–5; films about, 113; Nazi-Soviet peace pact, 13, 64; post-war policies, 62, 65–6, 68, 131; Science in, 184
Ruth, Babe, 122
Rutherford, Margaret, 159, *159*

Sabata, Victor de, 85
Sadler's Wells, 86; *see also* ballet, opera
St Exupéry, Antoine de, 49
St Paul's Cathedral, *12*, 13, *175*, 177, 194
Salzburg Festival, 87

Sandburg, Carl, 155
Sargent, Malcolm, 85
Sartre, Jean Paul, 179, 216
Saturday Evening Post, 18, 69
Sayers, Dorothy L., 216
Scala, La (Milan), 87
Schiaparelli, 98
Schulberg, Budd, 105
Schultz, Norbert, 81
science and technology, 180–1
Scofield, Paul, 163
Scott, Ronnie, 83
Screwtape Letters (Lewis), 179
Searle, Ronald, 203
Selznick, David O., 118
Sevareid, Eric, 11
Seven Lively Arts, The, 156
sex, 183–4, 211; and crime, 18,
Shapiro, Karl, 199
Shaw, George Bernard, 118, 163
Shearer, Moira, 86, 118
Sheean, Vincent, 11
Sheen, Fulton J., 13, 145, 178–9
Shelton, Anne, 75
Shephard, Firth, 151
Sherwood, Robert E., 151
Shore, Dinah, 75
Shostakovich, Dmitry, 85
Shute, Nevil, 192
Sibelius, 87
Sillitoe, Alan, 17
Silvermaster, Nathan, 144
Sinatra, Frank, *75*, 75–6, 103
Sinclair, Upton, 196
Singapore, capture of, 27, 29
Sitwell, Sir Osbert, 196
Skin of Our Teeth, The (Wilder), 161, *161*
Skolsky, Sidney, 81
slang: 185; clang-, 55; during wartime, 46
Slater, Montagu, 86
Smith, Betty, 192
Smith, Dodie, 197
Smith, Kate, 81
Smuts, General, 53
Snake Pit, The, 116
Snead, Sam, 120
Snow, C.P., 192
South Africa: apartheid in, 70; Jenkins in, 136; royal tour to, 53
South Pacific, *154*, 156
space travel, 180–1
Spanish Civil War, 22, 195
Spark, Muriel, 68
Spellman, Cardinal, 179
Spence, Basil, 165
Spencer, Stanley, 165, *167*
Sperry, William Learoyd, 178
spies, *see* espionage
sport: athletics, 130; baseball, 122; boxing, 127; bull-fighting, 128; cricket, 124; football, 120–1; golf, 120; horse-racing, 128–9; televised, 219; tennis, 124–6
'squatting', 63
Stafford, Jo, 75–6, *77*

Stalin, Joseph, 13, 31, *65*, 66, 133; at Yalta, *34*, 34
Stanley, Sidney, 185, *186*
Steinbeck, John, 195
Stengel, Casey, 124
Stewart, James, 115
Stiebel, Victor, 100
Stilwell, General Joe, 29, 135, 203
Stimson, Henry L., 64
stirrup-pump, 25, *25*
Stokowski, Leopold, 85, 87
Stone, Lew, 73
Stotesbury, Mrs E.T., 42
Strachey, John, 69
Strauss, Richard, 86
Stravinsky, Igor, 156
Streetcar Named Desire, A (Williams), 163
Strike a New Note, 80, 161
Stroheim, Erich von, 105
Suffolk, Jack Howard, 20th Earl of, 49
Sutherland, Graham, 165, *169*

Target for Tonight, 105
Taylor, A.J.P., 30, 32, 48
Taylor, Elizabeth, 97, *99*
Taylor, John, 101, 103
Taylor, Robert, 112, 145
Teddy Boys, 103
teenager, cult of the, 100
television, 219–20
Temple, Shirley, 13
tennis, 124–6
Ternent, Billy, 73
theatre, 151–63 *passim*; classics, 154–5; comedy, 156, 159; contemporary drama, 162–3; musical shows, 153, 155–6, 159; revue, 151–3, 156, 159
Thieves in the Night (Koestler), 131, 196
Third Man, The, 87, 118–19
This Happy Breed (Coward), 159
Thomas, Dylan, 199, 219
Thomas, J. Parnell, 145
Thorndike, Sybil, 155, 161
Thurber, James, 212
Thurmond, Strom, 134
Tibbetts, Colonel, 35
Time magazine, 13, 32, 43, 98, 113, 131, 147–8
Tizard, Henry, 147
Todd, Mike, 155
'Tokyo Rose', 209
Topolski, Feliks, 165
Toscanini, 85, 87
transport: air, 140, 141–4, *141*; automobile, 137–40; railway, 140–1; sea, 140; *see also* travel
Trapp Family Singers, 87
travel: during wartime, 136–7; holiday, 140–1, 143 (air); *see also* transport

Trevelyan, J.M., 194
Truman, Harry, 62, 145, 146; becomes President, 64, *65*, 66, 68; foreign policy of, 68–9, 133–4; re-elected, 135
Tucker, Orrin, 73
Turner, Lana, 97, 105
Tynan, Kenneth, 162

U.F.O.s (Unidentified Flying Objects), 181
Un-American Activities, House Committee on, 145, 186
underground stations, 43; as bomb shelters, 22–3, *25*
unemployment, 67
United Kingdom, *see* Great Britain
United Nations Organization, 64–5, 148; and Israel, 131–2; buildings for, 173; subsidiaries of (UNICEF, WHO, etc.), 66
United States, demobilization in, 60–1, 62–3; during 1940, 13–14; evacuation to, 17; loans to U.K., 68; race relations in, 70; refugees reach, 66; relations with British, 46–7, 131, 185, 207; war with Japan, 27–30; wartime conditions in, 39–41; women's services in, 43
U.S.O. (United Services Organization), 43
Ustinov, Peter, 118
'Utility', *91*, 92, 101, *173*, 175

Vandenberg, Arthur, 64
van der Post, Laurens, 62
Vaughan Williams, Ralph, 85
VE-Day, 35
VJ-Day, celebrations, *8*, 20, *35*
venereal disease, 178, 181, 203
Voice of America, 207
von Braun, Wernher, 180
V-Weapons, 32, *33*, 49, 180

WAAF (Women's Auxiliary Air Force), *39*, 43
Wagner, Richard, 87
Wainwright, General, 29
Walk in the Sun, A, 109
Wallace, Henry, 134
Wallis, Barnes, 180
Walpole, Hugh, 194
Walter, Bruno, 85, 86
Walton, William, 115
war correspondents, 201–2, 214
Warner, Jack, 215
Waugh, Evelyn, 195, 205
Wavell, Field Marshal Lord, 58
weather: droughts, 68; floods, 68; freezing, 53, 66–7, *67*
Webb, George, 83
Welles, Orson, 118–19, 211
Wells, H.G., 181, 195

Welty, Eudora, 196
West, Rebecca, 131
White, Josh, 83
'White Christmas', 81
Whitman, Mrs Malcolm D., *see* 'Countess Mara'
Wiley, Senator, 62
Wilder, Thornton, 161
Wilhelmina, Queen (of Holland), 50
Williams, Emlyn, 163
Williams, Tennessee, 163
Wilson, Angus, 196
Wilson, Harold, 103, 117, 85
Wilson, Scottie, 171
Winchell, Walter, 14
Windsor, Duke and Duchess of, 51, 221; during wartime, 57–8
Wingate Expedition, 29
Winnick, Maurice, 73
Winslow Boy, The (Rattigan), 162–3
Winsor, Kathleen, 192
Wodehouse, P.G., 70, 196
women: and fashion, 91–103 *passim*; in films, 116; in sport, 120–30 *passim*; magazines for, 202–3; military services of, 43; wartime role of, 36–8, *38*, *39*, *41*, 41, 107, 202–3
Women's Land Army, 38, *38*, 93, 105
Wood Henry, 85
Woodcock, Bruce, 127
Woolf, Virginia, 194
Woolton, Fred Marquis, Baron, 18, 36–7
Woolwich Arsenal, 11–12
World War I, lessons of, 17–18; music of, 78
World War II, aims of 17–18; early stages, 11–25; lessons of, 70; shooting war, 27–35 *passim*; *see also* Pacific, war in; Italy; Russian front, etc.
Wright, Cobina, 53
Wright, Frank Lloyd, 173
WRNS (Wrens), 43
WVS (Women's Voluntary Service), 23, 38, *88*

Yalta conference, 1945, 34, *34*, 62, 64–5, 148
Yamamoto, Admiral, 30
Yeager, Chuck, 142
Yogi and the Commissar, The (Koestler), 48, 196
You Are Younger Than You Think, (Gumpert), 183

Zaharias, Mildred Didrikson, 120
Zatopek, Emil, 130
Zhukov, Marshal, 34
Zoot Suits, *102*, 103

TRAVEL IN
COMFORT
LMS
Look ahead
SAVE
for
VICTORY
& YOUR FUTURE
POST OFFICE SAVINGS BANK
CREAMOLA
CREAMOLA
Poppy